Twentieth-century Jewellery

On the first day God turned himself into a zephyr and created air,
wind and clouds while on the second day he created Earth and,
turning himself into a gnome, hid gold and precious stones
there with divine malice, in order to drive us mad.

Gio Ponti, 1957

To Carlo and Angelica, my joys

Alba Cappellieri

Twentieth-century Jewellery

*From Art Nouveau
to Contemporary Design
in Europe
and the United States*

SKIRA

Cover
Van Cleef & Arpels
Necklace, 1937
Gold and diamonds
Van Cleef & Arpels Collection

Editor
Valerio Terraroli

Design
Marcello Francone

Editorial Coordination
Emma Cavazzini

Copy Editor
Timothy Stroud

Layout
Antonio Carminati

Translations
Judith Mundell

Iconographical Research
Paola Lamanna
Federica Borrelli

First published in Italy in 2010
by Skira Editore S.p.A.
Palazzo Casati Stampa
via Torino 61
20123 Milano
Italy
www.skira.net

© 2010 Skira editore, Milano
© Getulio Alviani, Arman,
Giacomo Balla, Gijs Bakker,
Harry Bertoia, Onno
Boekhoudt, Georges Braque,
Pol Bury, Giuseppe Capogrossi,
César, Sonia Delaunay, Max
Ernst, Georges Fouquet, Otto
Künzli, René Lalique, Meret
Oppenheim, Ruudt Peters,
Jesus Raphael Soto, Peter
Skubic, Yves Tanguy, Line
Vautrin, Tone Vigeland,
Philippe Wolfers by SIAE 2010
© Calder Foundation,
New York, by SIAE 2010
© Fondazione Lucio Fontana,
Milano, by SIAE 2010
© Salvador Dalí, Fundació
Gala-Salvador Dalí, by SIAE
2010

Printed and bound in Italy.
First edition

ISBN: 978-88-6130-532-8

Distributed in North America
by Rizzoli International
Publications, Inc., 300 Park
Avenue South, New York, NY
10010, USA.
Distributed elsewhere in the
world by Thames and Hudson
Ltd., 181A High Holborn,
London WC1V 7QX, United
Kingdom

Contents

6   Foreword

9   Twentieth-century Jewellery

59   Works

231   Glossary

239   Bibliography

245   Index of Artists, Designers
and Manufactures

248   Photographic Credits

The history of twentieth-century jewellery. Yes, but which history? That of the artists? The designers? The international *maisons*? The ideas or the products? The jeweller's craft or the goldsmith's art? And which jewel? *Pièce unique* or *prêt-à-porter*? Precious or *couture*?

There is no history of jewellery. There are histories of jewellery. Above all in an unstable and volatile century such as the twentieth with its jagged and disputed boundaries. "Nobody can write the history of the twentieth century like that of any other era", wrote Eric Hobsbawm in the introduction to his *Age of Extremes: The Short Twentieth Century*.[1] Jewellery does not escape such a laborious and problematic division into periods. Indeed, the twentieth was the most eventful century for a sector which had, over time, valiantly resisted change. Of all the objects that accompany our lives and adorn our bodies the jewel is the most static. Production techniques and materials have not changed from those used in the past, and neither have formal references or typologies. The acceleration of the "short century" has, all of a sudden, assailed the jeweller's art with innovations in technology, materials and sociology, which have radically altered its meaning as well as its form, transforming its aesthetics as well as its significance.

Traditionally a jewel indicated an object made of metals and precious gems and this material preciousness has represented an inviolable and unquestionable line of demarcation in history. The same cannot be said of the contemporary age, where the status of the jewel, to echo Walter Benjamin, has lost its "aura", whilst its status of being not quite an accessory requires terminological acrobatics.

One cannot arrive at an understanding of twentieth-century jewellery without considering its offshoots in art and fashion, decisive not just due to their continuous stylistic references but, above all, because they are bearers of two new figures: the *bijoutier-artiste* and the *bijoutier-couturier*. The twentieth century com-bined art and costume jewellery with traditional *haute* jewellery and the former are responsible for the majority of technological, formal and semantic innovations in the jeweller's repertoire. It must be pointed out that art and costume jewellery were not established in the second half of the twentieth century, as we are generally led to believe, but at its dawn, beginning with the Universal Exposition of 1900 that provided palpable evidence of the new values of jewellery. Those of its design first and foremost, and therein lies its *Art Nouveau* soul but also its ability to transform the meaning of the jewel from investment to ornament, creating a jewel-system that is something very different from the jewel-product. In the twentieth century we saw the shift from jewel-product to jewel-system, which this book has chosen to examine, exploring the complementary nature of its components: design, production, distribution, advertising, training and promotion. The coexistence of each piece of the mosaic is reflected in the next and completes the puzzle. This is demonstrated by French jewellery. If, as they say, "Paris is not a city but a monopoly", this is due to its systemic vision of bringing together artists and jewellers, magazines and universal exhibitions, schools and *boutiques*, tradition and progress.

When, in 1900, Théophile Gautier wrote "Art was represented alongside industry, white statues rose next to black machinery. Paintings and jewels appeared among rich oriental fabrics",[2] he was warning us about the proximity of art and industry that would shortly come to represent the hermeneutic *ring* of the jewel but also its driving force. Granted that I am fascinated by neither industrialisation *tout court* nor *revenge avant-garde*, I feel it is likewise undeniable that the intervention of designer or design engineer can extend equally efficiently from the collector's piece typical of art to industrial production typical of design. In both cases it is a *plus*, not a *minus*, as some schools of thought would tend to have us believe. Gjis Bakker is an excel-

[1] E. Hobsbawm, *Age of Extremes: The Short Twentieth Century 1914–1991* (London: Abacus, 1995).
[2] Quoted in G. Metken, *Fest des Fortschritts*, in *Weltausstellungen im 19. Jahrhundert*, exhibition catalogue (Munich, 1973).

lent example. What changes is the design method articulated by the rules imposed by manufacturing, which become design themes for the designer. On the contrary, these constraints do not undermine the work of the artist, who has the faculty to choose the design limits he prefers, whether they regard materials, technology, form or time. Moreover, the designer has to make sure his jewels can be worn, whilst the artist creating body sculptures can choose to ignore this. What matters is the ability of the object to crystallise and testify to the *Zeitgeist*, or the spirit of the times. As Jean Fouquet wrote in 1931, "a truly social art falling in line with progress can integrate present-day industrial forms and technologies which are struggling against classicism and tradition".[3] A struggle not so much against the classical or against serial production as against the values of tradition, which, in the case of jewellery, cannot simply be expressed by those of its materials. In the past as in the present.

Whether we like it or not, twentieth-century jewellery is based on the coexistence of miscellaneous values, where the preciousness of metals and gems is no longer a necessary and sufficient condition to establish the value of an object and define the difference between what is and what is not a jewel other than on a purely lexical level. In the post-materialist contemporary age the value of the material has been placed on a par with the value of the design and this is why we will find traditional jewellery, experimental jewellery and *couture* jewellery and their creators given equal treatment. Nevertheless, the usual monistic[4] concept of a joint history – in terms of typologies, styles, monographs – has been replaced by a pluralistic vision that highlights jewellery's link with the context, ideas, fashions and protagonists of its age, since, as Ferrarotti observes, objects "do not naturally emerge from nothing and do not develop in social, political, artistic and economic voids. Neither are they simply dead mirrors, inert specular reflections of the reality which lives and moves around

them. Instead, they witness, represent, bring back to life and, in any case, provide relief for the fundamental, harmonious, contradictory and conflicting characteristics of the environment from which they emerge".[5]

Our chosen methodological approach is the "cultural reduction" theorised by Renato De Fusco, which makes complex things simple by means of seeking invariants in paradigmatic contexts, styles and works, or rather the models and not the replicas. Aware – to echo Ernesto Rogers – that history is a fluid process of *continuity* and of *crises*, then "one might say that there is always either continuity or crisis depending on whether one wants to stress permanencies or emergencies".[6] In twentieth-century jewellery continuity – understood as a variation in tradition – is represented by *mode blanche*, natural *imagerie* or geometry, all underlying themes that sinuously weave together different periods and eventually return, whilst crisis – the revolution of the *new* – is manifested in the altered meanings and in the transitions between jewellery, technology and the arts: design, architecture and fashion but also cinema and photography.

Each chapter refers to a style, considered as the continuing presence of similar features in different works since, "while there is no doubt that style belongs to history-reality it also certainly represents a tool of historiography".[7] In this sense the alternation of stylistic periods – from Art Nouveau to Minimalism – is marked by events that are fundamental to the growth of society, such as the World Wars, the Wall Street Crash of 1929, the economic boom following the Second World War, student revolts and the "Reaganomic hedonism" that embraces the aporia of the present day.

Time present and time past
Are both perhaps present in future time,
And time future contained in time past.
If all time is eternally present
All time is unredeemable.[8]

[3] J. Fouquet, "Bijoux et orfèvriere", in *Art International d'aujourd'hui*, 16 (Paris: Charles Moreau, 1931). Quoted in M. Gabardi, "L'arte come gioiello", in *L'arte del gioiello e il gioiello d'artista dal '900 ad oggi*, exhibition catalogue, Florence, Museo degli Argenti, March–June 2001 (Prato: Giunti, 2001), p. 154.
[4] This observation was codified by T. Maldonado: "Arte e Industria", in *Avanguardia e razionalità* (Turin: Einaudi, 1974), p. 144.
[5] F. Ferrarotti, *Libri, lettori e società* (Naples, 1998), pp. 62–63.
[6] E. N. Rogers, "Continuità o crisi?", in *Casabella Continuità* 215 (1957). Quoted in R. de Fusco, *Mille anni di architettura in Europa* (Rome: Laterza, 1993), p. 135.
[7] R. De Fusco, *Made in Italy: Storia del Design Italiano* (Rome: Laterza, 2007), p. vii.
[8] T. S. Eliot, *Four Quartets* (New York: Harcourt, Brace & Company, 1943).

LE MAGASIN DE BOUCHERON
A L'EXPOSITION UNIVERSELLE
DE 1900

BOUCHERON
JOAILLIER
26, PLACE VENDÔME
LONDON   PARIS   NEW·YORK

Twentieth-century Jewellery

The Boucheron stand
at the Exposition Universelle,
Paris, 1900

I. 1900-1918: Art Nouveau and *mode blanche*

"The chrysalis matures for a whole century until it finally opens and the butterfly emerges in all its splendour: the floral style, Art Nouveau, with the ephemeral life of butterflies".[1] The twentieth century began in that atmosphere of "happiness and wellbeing" that only extended periods of peace and stability can generate. Bourgeois material culture thus had a chance to emerge and became the expression of the new age. Exclusive luxury, the prerogative of the elite, was joined by the moderate luxury of the bourgeoisie, who bought their status symbols cheaply. With regard to this it is interesting to note that, in his important essay *Luxus und Kapitalismus* of 1919, Werner Sombart opposed Max Weber's Calvinist asceticism, vigorously upholding the theory that it was luxury goods and sophisticated and superfluous consumption that had determined the growth of capitalism. Hume, Defoe, de Mandeville and Voltaire are the theoretical sources of Sombart, who laments the lack of heed paid to luxury in nineteenth-century studies on capitalism. "Luxury", asserts the German sociologist, "has gradually encouraged the development of the system of credit and debt and, more in general, stimulated exchange processes between different social classes and groups that are not merely economic, thus accelerating, expanding and, in some sense, freeing taste dynamics from being constricted in stable and closed social hierarchies and inducing the need for continuous and increasingly rapid updates of lifestyle".[2] Thus was Art Nouveau born: embracing the new century and greater freedom, "...the face of a woman unashamedly sensual, framed by recklessly untamed hair, became a symbol of Art Nouveau jewellery, and is its most widely recognised motif".[3]

After the fragmentation of nineteenth-century historicist eclecticism and with the temporal advantage of the turn of the century, Art Nouveau represented the latest great international style[4] to affect almost every European country and the United States. It took on different names in different local contexts: Modern Style in Great Britain, Liberty in Italy, Catalan Modernism in Spain, Jugendstil in Germany and Sezessionstil in Austria. Yet, the underlying theme that fluidly linked them to one another began with a concord of forms and principles. As evidence of its "modernity" the international nature of the movement was in keeping with the logic of the capitalist establishment of the period, based, in other words, on the liberalisation of economic, cultural and social exchanges.

The epicentre of Art Nouveau was Belgium where architects-artists Victor Horta and Henry van de Velde, at the Tassel House in Brussels (1893), which belonged to Horta, and the Bloemenwerf House in Uccle (1896), which belonged to Van de Velde, established the formal and semantic rules of the new expression: organic and twisting "whiplash" lines, concave-convex forms, phytomorphic references, fluid volumes, spatial penetration, visible metallic elements and vast glass surfaces. "The line transmits the strength and energy of what has traced it", said Henry van de Velde, thus establishing a connection between the geometrical lines that shaped the space or objects and the dynamographic movement of natural elements such as wind, water and fire. In particular Van de Velde was a firm advocate of what Richard Wagner had defined as *Gesamtkunstwerk* or the total work of art, where the project embraced architecture, furnishings, clothes[5] and accessories to equal effect, and where artists produced a painting, building, sculpture, piece of furniture, item of clothing or fabric with the same degree of involvement, to the point that the Secessions, and especially the Viennese Secession, aspired to transform society by eliminating any hierarchy between the arts. Van de Velde and the Art Nouveau movement were revolutionary in considering fashion to be an extension of the iconography of interiors, where furnishings "inhabited" the home just as clothes "inhabit" the body, according to the dictates of a total look much explored in that period. Their clothes were

---

[1] M. Praz, *Bellezza e Bizzarria* (Milan: Mondadori, 2002), pp. 1051–52.
[2] *Werner Sombart, dal lusso al capitalismo*, edited by R. Sassatelli (Rome: Armando Editore, 2003), p. 10.
[3] V. Becker, "Il nuovo secolo e l'Art Nouveau", in *I gioielli della fantasia*, edited by D. Farneti Cera (Milan: Idea Books, 1991), p. 17.
[4] Cf. P. Greenhalgh, *Art Nouveau 1890–1914* (London: V&A Publications, 2002); G. Fahr-Becker, *L'Art nouveau* (Cologne: Könemann, 1999); K.-J. Sembach, *L'Art Nouveau. L'utopie de la réconciliation* (Cologne: Taschen, 2000).
[5] In *Nowhere* William Morris emphasised that women's clothes should be consonant with the new aesthetics.

designed to be placed against the new domestic backdrops and represented the formative incipit of the education of taste to which artists aspired. The graceful forms of the buildings of Victor Horta, Henry van de Velde, Hector Guimard and Antoni Gaudí were reflected in their interiors and furnishings but also in the pleats of Mariano Fortuny's gowns or Paul Poiret's long, thin silhouettes.[6] Van de Velde had intrinsically linked the so-called higher arts to the lower arts,[7] encouraging those shifts of context that represent one of the most significant contributions of Art Nouveau. The real, ideological rather than typological, constant was instead represented by production, be it industrial or craft, depending on whether the artist identified the contemporary age with the culture of the machine, as was the case of the Deutscher Werkbund and Bauhaus or, on the contrary, with artistic craftwork, according to the model conceived by the Arts and Crafts movement and the Wiener Werkstätte.[8]

"It is incontestable that for some years now … numerous attempts have been made to revive the ancient formulas our predecessors used and abused. The precious metal industries were among the first to associate themselves with the efforts of the new generations of artists in order to break away from tradition and free themselves from the tyranny of conventional styles."[9]

In 1895 Henry van de Velde[10] designed the interiors and a series of objects for Siegfried "Samuel" Bing's Parisian gallery L'Art Nouveau, in which René Lalique, the undisputed protagonist of Art Nouveau jewellery, also played a part. This partnership afforded an opportunity to diffuse Art Nouveau in France[11] where it became, as Vivienne Becker observes, "an emphatically French obsession reaching its peaks of maximum purity".[12] Samuel Bing was a collector of mainly Japanese art, or Japonisme, which provided Art Nouveau with numerous formal ideas, purifying its forms of eclectic superfluity. Bing's gallery rapidly became a reference point for major international artists. It was here that jewellers Émile Gallé, René Lalique, Georges Fouquet, the Vever brothers, graphic artist Alphonse Mucha, *couturiers* Jean-Philippe Worth and Paul Poiret, textile producer Mariano Fortuny and furniture-maker Louis Majorelle sketched out the definitive features of the Parisian *Belle Époque*, simultaneously producing clothes, fabrics, posters, furnishings and jewellery. Bing's gallery was followed by German art critic Julius-Meier Graefe's La Maison Moderne, which gave an enormous boost to jewellery production by commissioning unique pieces from designers such as Paul Follot, Maurice Dufrêne, Theodore Lambert and René Lalique. But it was only in 1895, when decorative arts were admitted for the first time to the prestigious Salon de la Société des Artistes Français, that Lalique exhibited his jewellery under his own name.

From this moment on jewellery was acknowledged to be "the most intense expression"[13] of Art Nouveau while the best designers of the age turned themselves into brands, producing and marketing their work through the distribution and advertising channels normally used by the large *haute* jewellery *maisons*, where, however, the name of the designer never appeared. Art met commerce. An artist-businessman model was derived in which the limits imposed by production and the need to interact empathetically with the consumer became elements of the design, in accordance with the *Einfühlung* principle then theorised by Robert Vischer.

France became the country of reference for Art Nouveau as it was there that artistic crafts flourished, experimenting with new techniques and bold juxtapositions of materials in more elegant and precious objects that reached and were embraced by new consumers. The jewel represented one of the most accomplished symbols of modernity due to its ability to combine art and technology, culture and progress, elitism and democracy, as well as its potential applications in other product categories. This, for instance, is the case of furnishings, where we find furniture decorated with semiprecious stones, enamelling, gilding and silver engravings. The jeweller's materials and techniques infiltrated fields that were usually far removed from those traditional ones, demonstrating how extremely versatile the new style was.

"Woman rules our domestic arts. When they aren't for her, it is by her that they are inspired, prettified by her body, illuminated by her smile. She is a human being who is half flower or half animal, with spread wings, leafy tresses, limbs stretching into branches."[14]

The most powerful and evocative image in Art Nouveau jewellery was the female body with her long flowing locks of hair that represented the serpentine lines of the "coup de fouet", introducing the dynamism that Hector Guimard had imprinted on his subway stations and the softness of the Knossos silk of artist Mariano Fortuny into French jewellery. Recurring themes included nature and its metamorphosis. "Jewellers and designers are signally inspired by a few highly allusive images: the languid lily, the blooming and almost wilting rose, the iris with its undulating petals like blades, the swollen umbellifers, the humble thistle, the poppies with their soft, dark petals, the fragile and transparent sycamore seeds, the granulated hardness of the fir cone. The hothouse orchid, a frequent symbol of this age of decadence and aestheticism, was drawn with extraordinary realism

6 "After a trip to Vienna to visit the Wiener Werkstätte, Poiret returned to Paris where he founded the Martine atelier, dedicated to interior design. Here, working with famous artists such as Raoul Dufy, he designed furnishing fabrics, wallpaper, furniture and objects for the home with extraordinarily decorative patterns. His entrepreneurial vision came to the fore in 1911 when a desire to venture into the field of perfumes and cosmetics prompted him to generate his 'Rosine' range, characterised by sophisticated scents and rare bottles made of silver or crystal, some of which were designed by Lalique. In 1913, when Erté joined the atelier staff, Poiret went to the United States, where he signed agreements and licences for selling his own label of models and accessories, including bags, gloves and stockings, on a vast scale." Cf. A. Fiorentini, ad vocem "Poiret", in *Dizionario della Moda 2004*, edited by G. Vergani (Milan: Baldini Castoldi Dalai editore, 2003), p. 965. For a bibliography of Poiret cf. P. Poiret, *King of Fashion: The Autobiography of Paul Poiret* (Philadelphia, Pennsylvania: B. Lippincott Company, 1931); A. MacKrell, *Paul Poiret* (Teaneck, New Jersey: Holmes & Meier Publishers, 1990); Y. Deslandres, *Paul Poiret* (London: Thames and Hudson, 1987); H. Koda, A. Bolton and N. J. Troy, *Paul Poiret* (New York: Metropolitan Museum of Art Publication, 2007).

7 It is indeed no accident that during the fourth lecture of the seminar on applied arts and decoration held at the New University of Brussels in 1894, Henry Van de Velde exhibited a dress he had designed for his wife Maria Sèthe. The dress was loose-fitting, embellished with fabric patterned with large flowers, whose snaking folds concealed a small bag made of the same material. Brussels, Bibliothèque Royale, Fonds Van de Velde FSX 43; in F. Dierkens-Aubry and J. Vandenbreeden, *Art Nouveau in Belgium* (Paris: Duculot, 1991), p. 191.

8 The Wiener Werkstätte grew in Vienna between 1903 and 1932. The Secession's idea of bringing art to the people was accomplished in 1903 with the foundation of the Wiener Werkstätte, Viennese crafts workshops. The aim was to create tasteful pieces, veritable design objects, for the middle class.

The project was directed by Koloman Moser and Josef Hoffmann, members of the Secession who, having also become teachers at the Kunstgewerbeschule (school of decorative arts), established a system of exchanges between the school and the workshops. The workshops used the most diverse materials (ceramics, fabric, metal, paper, glass) to produce original and innovative results. The movement also ventured into interior design, furnishing a number of stores and dwellings such as the Fledermaus cabaret in the heart of Vienna, designed entirely by artists from the workshops and inspired by an idea of Hoffman's. In the twenty years he worked at the Wiener Werkstätte he succeeded in attracting hundreds of artists of the calibre of Gustav Klimt and Oskar Kokoschka, and in producing all kinds of things from stamps to wallpaper, cutlery, lamps, furniture, clothes, jewellery and buildings, and thus imposing his unique style on the whole world.

[9] H. Vever, "Boucles de ceinture", in *Art et Décoration*, January–June 1898, p. 156.

[10] Cf. *Henry Van de Velde* (Milan: Rizzoli, 1989).

[11] Van de Velde also introduced Art Nouveau to Germany, teaching first at the Darmstadt artists' colony and then in Weimar, at that academic institution which would subsequently become the Bauhaus. The versatile nature of his work led him to produce a series of designs, many of which were of furnishings and collectibles.

[12] Becker 1991, p. 20.

[13] V. Becker, *Art Nouveau Jewelry* (London: Thames and Hudson, 1985), p. 8.

[14] L. Riotor, "Les bijoutiers modernes à l'Exposition: Lalique, Colonna, Marcel Bing", in *L'Art Décoratif*, August 1890, p. 173; quoted from *L'arte del gioiello e il gioiello d'artista dal '900 ad oggi*, exhibition catalogue, Florence, Museo degli Argenti, 10 March – 10 June 2001 (Florence: Giunti, 2001). Cf. also G. Hughes, *International Exhibition of Modern Jewellery, 1890–1961* (London: Worshipful Company of Goldsmiths, 1961); and R. Turner, *Jewelry in Europe and America. New Times, New Thinking* (London: Thames and Hudson, 1996).

[15] K. Snowman, *The Master Jewelers* (London: Thames and Hudson, 1990).

in order to highlight its almost sinister eroticism, an incarnation of the mysteries of nature."[15]

The Art Nouveau movement was purified of bucolic lyricism and romantic affectations. René Lalique and the French jewellers were entomologists and architects of plant structures. It is worth remembering that in 1902 Alphonse Mucha, Sarah Bernhardt's graphic artist, published his *Documents Décoratifs*, which illustrated metallic objects inspired by pictures of plants. Artists were more fascinated by the constructive aspects of plant and animal life than the sentimental ones: the ribbing of branches, the shapes of leaves, the whorls of buds, the graffiti of barks. They preferred decay to the vibrancy of flowers in bloom, and the melancholy of withered petals, drooping irises or poppies, fragile roses at the mercy of the first gust of wind. Lalique used his liquefied gold, brightened by enamels, to render the organic life dynamic and to freeze the drama of transience: dried and shrivelled autumn leaves, ruffled water, twisted shoots, budding twigs, wrinkled and knotty roots. Between 1891 and 1894 he worked with Sarah Bernhardt on stage jewellery for the play *Théodora*. His friendship with the renowned actress and his familiarity with theatre environments encouraged his tendency for the dramatic and freed him from inhibitions regarding costs, sizes and materials. It was almost certainly Bernhardt who introduced Lalique to Calouste Gulbenkian, a collector of Turkish origin who was the first to sense Lalique's talent. In 1895 Gulbenkian commissioned Lalique to make one hundred and forty five jewels and *objets d'art* which, produced between 1895 and 1910, form an extraordinary collection of Art Nouveau jewellery. The Gulbenkian jewels reproduce the entire collection of Lalique's ornaments: flowers, vegetables and, as Kenneth Snowman has noted, "…reptiles, fish and sea creatures recall the continuous swaying movements of water and suggest prehistoric life, the repulsive elegance of strange animals that dwell at the bottom of the ocean. Insects like grasshoppers look shimmering and translucent, hovering mayflies become magical and ethereal, beetles are black and menacing. Lalique made much use of bats, while his bird motifs range from the proud peacock, the gliding swan (symbol of pride and metamorphosis), and cockerel (symbol of France and dawn), through owls and plump doves, to vultures and terrifying eagles in shadowy silhouette".[16] On the other hand, we know that Lalique's vision of nature was influenced by symbolist poetics. "His art depicted what the poet Mallarmé referred to as a 'veiled essence of reality', with a highly disciplined emotional intensity that became achingly lifelike, compelling and often uncomfortably decadent."[17]

The materials and techniques were no less innovative. The colourful harmonies of Art Nouveau jewellery contained the warm shades of gold and the pastel colours of enamels, opals, glass and gems, these too subsequently enamelled with transparent dyes which made the colours sparkle. There was an extraordinary variety of materials and techniques. Gems, semiprecious stones and stones of little value, metals, materials of animal origin (such as horn[18] or tortoiseshell) were used as well as all the most elaborate and ingenious enamelling techniques,[19] such as transparent, opalescent, *champlevé*, *cloisonné* and *plique-à-jour* – a technique brought back into fashion by Lalique and André Fernand Thesmar and which distinguishes the majority of jewellery of the period. At the turn of the century Lalique had already experimented with horn, a highly versatile material widely used in the seventeenth and eighteenth centuries in the production of combs and small personal luxury accessories, and first used in jewellery in the 1890s, influenced by Japonisme. In 1897, when Lalique proposed an entire collection of horn combs, enamelled and studded with semiprecious stones, this material became a popular innovative feature of Art Nouveau jewellery. Lucien Gaillard too, profoundly influenced by Japanese art, specialised in the creation of horn jewellery, engraved or treated with a special, silvery patina that gave it an almost organic skin, while Fouquet put the finishing touch to his pendants with baroque pearls in the Renaissance fashion and Vever revealed a particular liking for ivory.

The choice of not necessarily lofty materials of little economic value is Art Nouveau's most innovative contribution to the culture of jewellery design. Indeed, for the first time ever, the value of jewellery did not come from the materials but from the design. Jewellers felt they were designers even before they were technicians or merchants and this was clearly a novelty. The preciousness of gems and metals responded to an elitist and distinctive concept of art that had nothing in common with Art Nouveau, whose egalitarian principles, as has been observed, "are to be traced to William Morris's Arts and Crafts movement, which aimed at the ennoblement of crafts and redeemed humble manual work, giving it dignity. But this concept gradually came into conflict with Modernism's general trend of spreading and increasing production, a spread which benefited both the desire to fashion the whole of society with beauty and to provide market incentives. Modernists increasingly underlined the importance of the design, or the formal idea, reserving the possibility of replica, albeit controlled, for its execution. This laid the foundations of design".[20]

Nevertheless, the jewel confirmed its close ties with fashion, representing the ultimate accessory of female attire. As Georg Simmel acutely emphasised in 1911, luxury, through fashion, became an occasion for distinction within the system of encoded values of the community,[21] finding its most complete expression in jewellery. For this reason, every type of jewellery was rendered in the new style: diadems and combs, necklaces, rings, brooches and hairpins, even belt buckles. Only earrings were excluded as ear piercing was considered uncouth. Earrings generally consisted of small clusters or solitaires. As for clothing, Art Nouveau jewellery had a functional as well as an ornamental role, shown by pins on corsets or hats, belt buckles or hairpins. In c. 1910 Paul Poiret and Mariano Fortuny launched a soft line of clothing, accompanied with asymmetrical accessories such as the *lavallière*, a long necklace with diamonds suspended from it. Long strings of pearls or amber beads, *collier de chien*, pendants held by velvet ribbons, *aigrettes* and tiaras, usually detachable so they could be used as brooches on less official occasions, were also very popular.

The official consecration of Art Nouveau jewellery took place at the great Universal Exposition in Paris in 1900 where the stylistic motifs of the new style acquired cosmopolitan connotations, its geographical variants emphasised by delegations from different countries. Art Nouveau found the universal expositions to be an extremely efficient means of distributing and advertising its products. Art and technology met in crowded pavilions and the wealthy bourgeoisie flocked to admire the aesthetic of the machine in the wonders of Art Nouveau. The displays at the Grand Palais and the rooms of the Viennese Secession, curated by Austrian architects Josef Hoffmann and Josef Maria Olbrich, Samuel Bing's Maison de l'Art Nouveau, René Dulong and Gustave Serrurier-Bovy's Pavillon Bleu restaurant, Loïe Fuller's theatre – designed by Henry Sauvage and decorated with Pierre Roche's sculptures – systematically integrated the arts. Samuel Bing's pavilion was an emblematic example. The six rooms were laid out like a private home complete with all the trappings: William Morris furniture, Emile Gallé and Louis Tiffany glass, Bigot ceramics, René Lalique jewellery, Auguste Rodin sculptures, Walter Crane wallpaper, paintings by Beardsley, Bonnard, Pissarro, Sérusier, Signac, Toulouse-Lautrec, Vuillard. This layout tended to deliver the objects from a partial and fragmentary reading and accurately narrated the period context. It was here that the public were able to admire the masterpieces of the new international *bijoutiers* and perceive the similarities and differences between various countries.

Bing's La Maison Art Nouveau was the result of the industrious project which Samuel Bing had begun in 1895 by opening the Galerie de l'Art Nouveau, whose purpose was to spread the important contribution made by the decorative arts and the freshness of Art Nouveau to everyday objects too. In jewellery Bing sought the feminine grace and the dynamic and fluid lines of architecture, interiors and objects. One of the artists who worked for him was Edward Colonna[22] who, interested in and knowledgeable about the aspirations of the new style, was particularly fond of plant forms interpreted starkly in the Japanese manner. The jewellery Bing exhibited included *collier de chien* with elongated pearls in which the rhythmical spirals of the design were illuminated by the enamel and the glow of the baroque pearl, mother-of-pearl or *cabochon* emeralds. Critics who visited the pavilion declared that Colonna's work denoted a discreet charm, a somewhat belittling description for such modern and unique designs. The severity of the judgement was probably dictated by the understatedness of his works, not terribly glitzy but in perfect tune with the dictates of the new aesthetics and its values. The small brooches, curvaceous pendants and soft undulating ribbons woven with gold constituted an extremely abstract and sensual interpretation of nature and its movement. Colonna also made furniture, porcelain, fabrics, items of silverware and other objects for Bing which were showcased for the occasion. His son Marcel also worked on the production of Bing's jewellery. His designs were exhibited in his father's pavilion. Marcel's interpretation of the female figure was highly peculiar with its thin and graceful silhouette and unusual facial features – long, straight and somewhat pointed – perhaps inspired by the perfectly oval face and the ribbons of ballerina Cléo de Mérode.

"René Lalique was the undisputed protagonist of Esplanade des Invalides, where his jewellery was exhibited, and was awarded a Grand Prix and the rosette of the Légion d'Honneur. He also exhibited furniture, objects and interior decorations, but it was his jewellery that stirred the curiosity and admiration of visitors. Lalique diffused the taste for these milky and cerulean, fresh, opaline and rainbow-hued harmonies dominated by blues, greens and whites, which brought back into vogue corresponding materials that had once been disdained … a whole motley rabble of semiprecious stones or gems which he puts on the same plane as the most precious *joaillerie*, rubies, emeralds, diamonds. The deeply coloured sapphire, the opal and the moonstone introduce blue and milky notes. The emerald, the chrysoprase, jade are chosen for their green shades."[23]

[16] Ibid.

[17] Becker 1985; taken up again in Snowman 1990, p. 137.

[18] Horn is an extremely difficult material to work with. While we have no information about the techniques used by René Lalique, a record survives of the procedures adopted by Elizabeth Bonté. Bull's horn was cut into circular sections and heated and flattened to form plaques, on which a template was traced which was then cut by a saw. The next stage consisted of soaking the horn in hydrogen peroxide for a day, so as to give it its typical translucent appearance. At this point the edges of the piece were smoothed and polished and then, while it was still ductile, the horn was dipped into various chemical baths to give it its typical beige or pearly patina. The other colours or patinas were applied with special dyes. In the final stage of the process, the horn was again polished and every detail (such as the veining on insects' wings) added with pen and ink.

[19] Cf. L. Darty, *The Art of Enameling: Techniques, Projects, Inspiration* (London: Lark Books, 2006).

[20] R. Bossaglia, "L'Art Nouveau e le Arti Applicate", in *L'arte del gioiello e il gioiello d'artista* (Florence) 2001, p. 42.

[21] G. Simmel, "Zur Psychologie der Mode", in *Die Zeit. Wiener Wochenschrift für Politik, Volkswirtschaft, Wissenschaft und Kunst*, 54, vol. V, 1895. The philosopher observes that "fashion means, on the one hand, the cohesion of those who find themselves belonging to the same social rank and the unity of any social circle characterised by it, and, on the other, the closure of this group towards inferior social ranks and their characterisation through the fact of not belonging to it".

[22] Colonna was German but, thanks to his partnership with Samuel Bing, he is considered to be a French Art Nouveau jewellery designer. After studying architecture in Brussels, he left Europe to settle in New York, where he made a successful career working for Tiffany.

[23] L. Bénédite, "Le bijoux à l'Exposition Universelle", in *Art et Décoration*, vol. VIII, 1900, pp. 65–67.

"Crowds flocked to Lalique's showcase at the Exposition to press their noses against the window and gaze in amazement at the fantastic creatures and dream objects that were causing such a stir in Paris and all around the world. His display was eerie, erotic and eye-catching. Black velvet bats swooped against a grey gauze star-studded night sky. Below this a semi-circular grille was formed by five patinated bronze figures, a tribute to femininity and perhaps at the same time to the American dancer Loïe Fuller, who also had a triumph at the Exposition Universelle. With her free-form serpentine dances, in which she seemed to change into one of Lalique's winged jewels, a strange, hybrid creature with floating incandescent wings, she personified both the swirling Art Nouveau line and the theme of metamorphosis."[24]

The central, most exceptional piece was the grid of wrought iron formed of a series of voluptuous women-butterflies in glazed bronze, naked and coupled in languid poses with spread wings. It was a woman-allegory, half woman and half animal, mysterious and disturbing, endowed with an alarming sensuality and an intense appeal. The jewellery was exhibited in frosted glass display cases where it was placed on extremely elegant white moiré silk. Henri Vever in his *La bijouterie française au XIXᵉ siècle* wrote that the works of Lalique at the exposition consisted of about twenty horn combs with enamelling, chrysoprase, amethysts, opals and moonstones, necklaces, diadems, glittering enamels depicting entwined snakes from whose mouths cascaded baroque pearls: "I felt a shiver", he said, "everywhere a profusion of gems, harmoniously arranged and cut with perfect taste: bracelets, *plaques de cou*, a thousand different objects. Faced with these wonderful things I almost felt as though I were dreaming … a cockerel with an enormous yellow brilliant in his beak; a gigantic dragonfly with the body of a woman and diaphanous wings; rural scenes in enamel sparkling with brilliants; ornaments resembling fir cones".[25] In the wake of this success there were so many orders it proved impossible to fill them all.

Other French *bijoutiers* who exhibited in Paris in 1900 included Vever, Fouquet, Grasset, Feuillatre, Gaillard, Tèterger and the works of designers Paul Follot, Maurice Dufrêne and Victor Prouvé. Critic Léonce Bénédite wrote that "at the Universal Exposition Lalique in one way and Vever in another are enough to represent every aspect of the art of jewellery",[26] a forthright opinion but not lacking in truth. While Lalique drew attention with his disturbing creatures, the work of brothers Paul and Henri Vever stood out due to the delicacy of the line and the elegance of the form, but above all due to their ability to wed the tradition of the jewel and its most precious gems with the new stimuli of Art Nouveau. The works shown at the Universal Exposition were evidence of a familiar and reassuring creative vigour, not just due to their number but also their quality: "Contrary to the norm, the glass display cases do not contain just a few important pieces created for the competition, which stand out from the flow of pieces produced daily. There are innumerable interesting themes in which the artist has insisted on expressing his personality. Every piece is evidence of research and has its own special charm."[27]

The Vever firm indulged in the use of traditional precious stones and typologies, especially diadems. Numerous diadems were shown at the exposition, some extraordinarily original with special features. One was made of fern leaves, studded with irregular diamonds, which encircled the temples and then curved upwards to culminate in a large yellow diamond. Another had bands of diamonds topped by a peacock tail with eyes made of opals and feathers made of diamonds. One model was made of moonstones, diamonds and opals. The hairpins were signally interesting, combining diamonds and enamel with horn, tortoiseshell and ivory, producing the floral motifs then in vogue. Another had five teeth made of pale tortoiseshell, while the upper part was decorated with mistletoe leaves in green enamel, dotted with pearls. In yet another, two cyclamen leaves made of ivory encrusted with opal were topped with transparent enamel flowers lightly veined with gold. The softness of the human figure emerged in an ivory embrace while the animal kingdom was represented by the hairpin with a horn owl with eyes of emerald and decorations of gold and transparent enamel. Metal jewellery included articles in embossed gold and enamel. There were pendants with Roty and Bottée medallions and brooches and buckles in which flowers and women played a decorative role in keeping with the current taste. The objects designed by Henri Vever were juxtaposed with approximately twenty pieces produced in partnership with Eugène Grasset, an elegant illustrator of *affiches*, in whose works there were echoes of Japonisme, as shown by *Naiade*, a hairpin depicting a swimmer surrounded by waves. Moreover, Vever commissioned Grasset to produce a design destined to be made by Tourette in *cloisonné* enamel on gold mounted on the setting. The work was a triumph, although the most important piece of all was *Sylvia*, a pendant with a winged creature, half woman and half butterfly, made of gold, agate, rubies, enamel and diamonds, whose slender silhouette and combination of colours beautifully conveyed the aspirations of Art Nouveau.

[24] Snowman 1990, p. 126.
[25] H. Vever, *La bijouterie française au XIXᵉ siècle*, 3 vols. (Paris, 1906–1908), III, pp. 652–89.
[26] Bénédite 1990, p. 40.
[27] Ibid.

The Fouquet maison also received an award in Paris in 1900, as did Falize, which was awarded two Grand Prix, and Lucien Gaillard, who drew the attention of critics with the expressive strength of his butterflies, the result of extensive studies of glazing techniques.

In order to mount the most spectacular display of the Universal Exposition, Georges Fouquet, Alphonse's son, turned to Bohemian artist Alphonse Mucha to involve designer Charles Desrosiers. The working partnership with Mucha was probably supported by Sarah Bernhardt at the time Fouquet was creating the famous *Serpent* bracelet for her. The pieces Georges made from Mucha's designs represented an innovation in his style. They were highly glitzy, theatrical objects – jewellery for the shoulders and chest, head ornaments with draped chains and enamelled plaques with a Byzantine flavour – completely different from the naturalistic jewellery that dominated the scene. Not many examples from the collection have survived. Those which stand out are the *Fuchsia* necklace, dating from 1905, an elegant and delicate cascade of flowers on a mosaic of opals, pearls and diamonds, where the three-dimensional effect is highlighted by translucent opalescent enamel with inclusions of *plique-à-jour* silver leaf and opal *cabochon*, and the spectacular brooch dating from 1900 in gold and olive-green *plique-à-jour* and white *champlevé* enamel, in which nine baroque pearls are mounted on loose bezels, creating an interesting kinetic effect. Then there are the horn hairpins, which demonstrate Fouquet's ability to use assorted materials, producing excellent results. Critics' opinions of the work of the *maison* were divided. They either admired the baroque opulence of goddesses with naked arms and chests or were scandalised.

Of all the large international jewellery *maisons* Boucheron was especially celebrated at the Paris Exposition where Frédéric received the gold medal, the Grand Prix and a special mention by "Revue de la Bijouterie" in its section dedicated to the exposition. The *maison* in Place Vendôme managed to convey the new themes of Art Nouveau with the quality and elegance that distinguished their jewels from the mid-nineteenth century onwards.[28] The wealth of the plant and animal world materialised in the precious jewels of Boucheron, including a magnificent gold pendant made in 1900 called *The Three Daughters of Eve*, which reproduced a group of three children's heads. In a spirit of innovation Boucheron started to use ivory in his figurative jewellery. One piece showed a graceful young oriental girl in the act of emerging from the sea while a black woman holds her robe out to her. Other themes include Eros and a

druid. At the exposition of 1900 the firm also exhibited a variety of precious objects: mirrors, scent bottles, *lorgnettes* and buckles. A decisive contribution to Boucheron's success came from Jules Debut, who designed some pieces of jewellery for Sarah Bernhardt, and Lucien Hirtz, a famous designer who kept the link between the *maison* and the early twentieth-century artistic avant-garde fertile and vital. They designed brooches and buckles made of finely engraved gold, depicting heads and bodies grappling with snakes, wild beasts and fish that snap at or fight over spectacular semi-precious gems.

In Belgium Van de Velde devoted himself to designing jewellery characterised by his typical undulating and sinuous lines whilst the jewellery scene was dominated by Philippe Wolfers, who commissioned Victor Horta to design for his company. Horta provided him with the inspiration for his asymmetrical jewels with stylised floral motifs, insects and human figures. He designed bronzes, furniture, lamps, glass vases and, above all, jewellery decorated with gems and enamel. Only a part of his work has been preserved as, unlike other Art Nouveau jewellers, he used many precious stones that, once they had gone out of fashion, were dismantled and recycled. Wolfers was one of the first to use ivory from the Belgian Congo, indulging the taste for the exotic that was typical of Art Nouveau. Like Wolfers, Paul Dubois too used "national" materials, such as metal and ivory, whilst Leopold van Strydonck preferred the colour contrasts of oxidations.

The Paris exposition also confirmed the United States' success in Art Nouveau jewellery. The cult of progress was expressed by both the skyscrapers of Louis Sullivan and the Chicago School and by the objects of Tiffany, the only American company that, at the beginning of the century, was able to keep pace with European fashions. On that occasion the *maison*, under the guidance of Paulding Farnham – who had become chief designer of both the jewellery and the silverware divisions – received six gold medals, the Grand Prix for jewellery and silverware, two silver medals and one bronze. All the objects exhibited were recognised as being highly representative of the American style whilst *La Revue de la Bijouterie* confirmed that Tiffany had its own special sparkle. The American jewel was born. One of the most spectacular pieces was *Iris*, a brooch made with one hundred and thirty-nine sapphires from Montana where the harmony of the colour palette, the proportions of the composition, the constructive boldness – it measured 22.86 cm – made it one of the finest examples of Tiffany

[28] On the story of Boucheron, cf. Snowman 1990, pp. 77–92 and relative bibliography.

14

workmanship. The analogies between the works of the American firm and that of Alphonse Mucha, who enjoyed a large following in the United States, are interesting. These include Byzantine opulence and eccentric naturalism but also the multidisciplinary approach, which led Tiffany to excel in glass as well as in jewellery.

The Paris exhibition was visited by jewellers from all over the world and companies like the Unger Brothers and William Kerr of Newark began, after 1900, to mass-produce Art Nouveau pieces in silver lamina, whilst the work of more important European jewellery artists influenced the contemporary production of Marcus & Co., one of the most prestigious American jewellers.

The same degree of success was enjoyed by Russia, which in Paris featured the works of renowned court jeweller Carl Fabergé, who exhibited a diadem of brilliants, his *bibelots* and the famous "imperial eggs", famous for being presented as gifts to the czars every year. On this occasion the jeweller was proclaimed "maître" and awarded the Légion d'Honneur. Less significant was the contribution from northern European countries, whose production had been anticipated by Bing's exhibition in 1895. The works shown in Paris were "traditional in design and only hinted at the beginning of an artistic revolution"[29] that was to reach its peak at the end of the 1920s in the works of Georg Jensen. Jensen opened his shop in Copenhagen in 1904 and was influenced by the works of the British Arts and Crafts movement.

In Spain the new wave penetrated and adapted to the local historicist tradition in a highly unusual way. The undisputed master of the new style was Antoni Gaudí, who hybridised the motifs of Art Nouveau with the eclectic local culture in order to create a one-of-a-kind architecture concentrating on the imaginary dimension of the design. In jewellery the most interesting contribution came from Luis Masriera – already a pupil of famous enameller Lossier in Geneva – who, after seeing the work of Lalique in Paris, returned to Barcelona, melted down all his work and closed the shop for six months, only to reappear with a production in line with the French models which "were immediately successful and sold out in a single week".[30]

Artistic production in Great Britain was shaped by the influence of William Morris and the Arts and Crafts movement[31] and their rejection of the industrialisation of art in favour of fine craftsmanship. Morris not only wanted to produce something beautiful but, above all, detested modern civilisation. This became an out-and-out rejection of the serial component and machine aesthetics. The major exponents of British jewellery were John Paul Cooper, Henry Wilson, Charles Robert Ashbee and Archibald Knox, whose works crystallised the aporia of the Arts and Crafts movement and were distinguished by strong geometrical shapes, intended to simplify the sinuous dynamism of Art Nouveau. Ashbee and Wilson's jewellery pursued the chromatic harmony of the gems, selected for their clear contrasts and as translucent as the sophisticated French enamels. Ashbee preferred garnets and amethysts for their strong, deep colours, and one of his favourite motifs was the peacock, which symbolised the proud and decadent beauty of nature and the luxurious line of Art Nouveau. He made his first brooch in the shape of a peacock for his wife in 1900. From that moment on peacocks in various forms and shapes were among the most popular jewels, to the point of being immediately ascribable to the Guild of Handicraft. Ashbee's works began with his total rejection of the machine (in 1908 he wrote "We are here to bring you back again to the realities of life, to the use of the hand and the brain, of which your Industrial machinery has deprived over half your population"[32]) although they aimed to spread art to an increasingly vast public. This purpose was instead achieved by the works of Archibald Knox for Liberty, thanks precisely to industry. Indeed, notwithstanding their understandable ideological aspirations, the handmade jewellery of Ashbee had the disadvantage of being significantly more costly than Liberty's industrial jewels of equivalent quality. The bourgeoisie wanted striking, well-made and fashionable objects and accessories whose affordability depended in large part on industrialisation. Arthur Lasenby Liberty, Samuel Bing's London counterpart, understood this and made it the key to his success. With the help of Archibald Knox, Liberty & Co. indeed proposed affordable and fashionable jewels combining the curlicues of Art Nouveau with the colours of the Celtic style revived in Garment of Ornament by Owen Jones in 1856, meeting with an international success that eclipsed that of Ashbee's Guild of Handicraft. Knox's famous Celtic interlaced pattern, often made of openwork silver mottled with faded blue and peacock green enamel, was combined with the equally famous whiplash line with its small tail curled back on itself. Triangles, squares, roses and stylised heart-shaped leaves were essential elements of Knox's iconography and were instrumental to Liberty's success. Equally, Fordham's shop entrusted the design of its jewellery to Cooper, who adopted unusual materials such as coconut shells, oyster shells and even sharkskin (shagreen), which he then combined with more traditional materials, such as gold, silver, copper and semiprecious

[29] Becker 1985, p. 200.
[30] Ibid., p. 212.
[31] On Arts and Crafts cf. P. Todd, *The Arts & Crafts Companion* (London: Bulfinch, 2004); B. Mayer, *In the Arts and Crafts Style* (London: Chronicle Books, 1992); *Christopher Dresser e le Arts & Crafts 1834–1904*, exhibition catalogue, Milan, 2001–2002 (Milan: Skira, 2001).
[32] C. R. Ashbee, *Craftsmanship in Competitive Industry* (London, 1908), p. 110.

stones, in order to create outlandish, multifarious pieces. His notoriety began in 1899 when he exhibited his first metal artefacts accompanied by four pieces made of sharkskin at the Arts and Crafts Exhibition in London. Between 1899 and 1915 Cooper sold more than two hundred and seventy-five works from the Fordham shop, with whom he had signed a sales agreement on the occasion of the London exhibition.

Thus, although they had been strict advocates of crafts, the artists of the Arts and Crafts movement began to collaborate with industry, recognising the value of design as a fundamental premise of mass production. It was the first step towards a renewal of the applied arts and the growth of industrial design in a contemporary sense.

No less interesting in Great Britain was the contribution of Charles Rennie Mackintosh, founder of the Glasgow School of Art, which provided training for the most important Scottish artists of the age and where a veritable Glasgow style was developed that flourished, above all, in the field of interior decoration. However, there was no lack of good jewellery, including the works of Jessie Marion King and Phoebe Anna Traquair, whilst the most original contribution came from the group known as "The Four", formed by Mackintosh with James Herbert MacNair and their respective consorts, sisters Margaret and Frances MacDonald. The latter pair in particular succeeded in creating a highly original and evocative graphic style that was applied to various spheres. It consisted of painstakingly decorated floating and ethereal figures placed on statues, wrought metal objects and embroidery and mosaics, accompanied by plain surfaces so the juxtaposition of "sophisticated" and "simple" could be better appreciated. The works of Mackintosh – from the School of Art to Hill House – ranged from architecture to furnishings and to the decorative arts, showing a predilection for geometrical and abstract shapes unlike the voluptuous arabesques of Art Nouveau. The same approach also connoted Viennese production thanks to the exchanges between the two countries. Indeed, after taking part in the Paris Exposition Universelle, Mackintosh was invited by artists of the Viennese Secession to take part in their eighth exhibition, inaugurated in November 1900. The Four enjoyed phenomenal success and the firm friendship established between Mackintosh and Josef Hoffmann determined, de facto, an osmotic exchange between the two countries.

Austrian jewellery at the turn of the century was instead represented by the production of Wiener Werkstätte, the Viennese art workshops founded in 1903 by architect Josef Hoffmann, artist Koloman Moser and banker Fritz Warndorfer, with the aim of making a profit for their members through the design, production and sale of artistic craft items. The aim was to create tasteful objects destined for the international bourgeoisie, following an agenda which once again raised themes already explored by the Arts and Crafts movement. However, Hoffmann, despite sharing Morris's ideas, did not believe that artists should be "society's saviours", a task he willingly delegated to political organs. Moreover, he was aware of the difficulty of succeeding in producing high-quality craft objects whilst keeping their prices affordable to everyone. Such pragmatism can be deduced from his programme where he says: "The work of the craftsman should be evaluated in the same way as that of the painter and sculptor. We cannot and nor do we intend to compete with low-cost production. This operates to the detriment of the workers and we feel it is our utmost duty to restore to them the joy of work and an existence worthy of a man", and further still: "We want to establish a close relationship between the public, the designer and the craftsman, producing simple, quality objects for domestic use. Our point of departure is the object, our first condition is functionality, our strength lies in the harmony of proportions and the excellent quality of the workmanship".[33]

Wiener Werkstätte designed furnishings, fabrics, ceramics, bookbinding, graphics and jewellery for a rich, sophisticated and cosmopolitan customer base, working on the principle that quality can only be achieved if each piece is designed, supervised and personally seen to by the designer. In the exciting atmosphere of turn of the century Vienna, one of the first European metropolises with its two million inhabitants, a unique convergence of the arts took place whose greatness was fully expressed in the workshops.

Moser and Hoffmann's jewellery constituted a perfect synthesis of the style of Wiener Werkstätte: "We love silver and gold for their special light", it says in their manifesto, "but, from the artistic point of view, we think copper is just as valuable as precious metal. We have to admit that, for us, a silver jewel may be as valuable as a jewel made of gold or precious stones".[34] This is also seen in the fabric ornaments made by Max Snischek and Anna Schmedes. Making the preciousness of the materials secondary to the quality of the design was something that was reflected in the principles of Art Nouveau and in Lalique's work in particular. However, the Wiener Werkstätte differed in its preference for two-dimensionality, its work on surfaces and its choice of geometrical patterns, which brought the workshops' production closer to the Glasgow school than to the French school. The characteristic elegance of Moser's

[33] These two short paragraphs extracted from *Arbeitsprogramm* define in crystal clear fashion the goals pursued during the period of activity of the Viennese workshops. From K. Moser's and J. Hoffmann's Wiener Werkstätte programme, published in Vienna in 1905, p. 15; quoted in R. De Fusco, *Storia del design* (Rome–Bari: Laterza, 1985), p. 121.
[34] From K. Moser's and J. Hoffmann's Wiener Werkstätte programme, quoted in *L'arte del gioiello e il gioiello d'artista* (Florence) 2001, p. 56.

works transpires from the delicate spiral motifs and lizard tails found in various of his pieces, whilst Hoffmann made great use of squares. In the early stages Hoffmann's jewels were delineated by grids, squares and a stark linearity. He often combined decorative filigree motifs with semiprecious coloured *cabochon* stones arranged in Cartesian geometrical shapes. After 1908 the architect preferred to devote himself to more convoluted compositions made mellower with flowers and leaves. The influence the works of Hoffmann and Moser had on each other was considerable and can be seen in the necklaces and tiaras created in c. 1920. The work of Czescha was very different from the output of these two artists. His style was distinguished by a fixed geometrical framework around which he created different modules, producing long necklaces, belt buckles, brooches and bracelets. He leaned towards the rich legacy of English folk jewellery and a symbolic representation of flora and fauna.

As Elisabeth Schmuttermeier[35] observed, the geometrical precision of the workshops was replaced after 1906 by the adoption of vibrant and richly decorated forms. To the even greater delight of their customers a decidedly more opulent style was chosen. Lance-shaped and heart-shaped leaves became the favourite motifs after 1910. Stones were used more and more infrequently until they disappeared altogether with the newer jewels distinguished solely by the working of single metals. Stylised motifs were reintroduced thanks to the influence of Dagobert Peche who, after 1915, became a permanent partner of Wiener Werkstätte. Peche made an important contribution to Austrian jewellery. The asymmetrical forms and voids in his jewels very often included figures of animals or lance-shaped leaves. His brooches and necklaces were almost always made from mother-of-pearl and ivory combined with gold.

"German *Jugendstil* aims at increasing abstraction and deformation of patterns derived from nature, seeking to achieve a metamorphosis that might result in the creation of an indefinable, organic and elementary mixture of forms."[36]

The German pavilion at the Paris Exposition was pervaded by Jugendstil influences, of pure Belgian derivation. Starting in 1901 Van de Velde himself had taught in Darmstadt. Here he had come into contact with Peter Behrens, whose partnership with EG (Allgemeine Elektrictäts-Gessellschaft) indelibly scored the relationship between design and industry. Jewellery was unaffected by the winds of change, which instead swept through architecture, art and design. Jewellery production was still deeply rooted in nineteenth-century historicism and therefore designers who adopted the new language of Art Nouveau were relatively few in number. These included Robert Koch, Hugo Schaper, Georg Kleeman and Karl Roth Müller of Munich, who showed opulent jewels, influenced by natural forms, flowers and birds – above all the enamelled peacock – containing dreamlike symbolism, and Wilhelm Lucas von Cranach, probably the most original German jeweller, whose works, made in Berlin by Louis Werner, included curious, fierce and menacing creatures and plants. Cranach's most famous jewel had a central nucleus of baroque pearls surrounded by enamelled wings in deep colours. The industrial districts of jewellery were clearly defined: Berlin for classical production, characterised by floral and ribbon motifs, with Louis Werner and J. H. Werner as its main producers, and Pforzheim for experimentation and more innovative jewellery. The most interesting companies were Zerrenner and Louis Fiessler, Gebruder Falck and, above all, Theodor Fahrner, who involved numerous designers, in particular from the Darmstadt school, in the making of its jewels. Like Liberty, Fahrner had a better and earlier understanding of the close link between jewellery and fashion than the others and proposed economical objects made of silver in elegant forms, in line with the fashions of the day.

Many of these producers exhibited at the Paris exposition but were slammed by the French critics, who, with their usual patriotic fervour, accused the Germans of copying French designs. In reality, after an initial period of effective exchange German jewellery kept its distance from French jewellery, preferring a geometricised style to the intricacy of Art Nouveau. As Vivienne Becker observes, "The abstract style grew from a reaction to the floral and figurative styles of French Art Nouveau.... This counter-movement represented a radical change in jewelry design and marked the turning point in the development of Art Nouveau … in Germany. The new German abstract jewels rejected ornamental and symbolic imagery and concentrated on line and form and increasing abstraction of shapes".[37]

Italy took part in the 1900 Exposition with the works of Neapolitan Vincenzo Miranda, who exhibited a gold buckle in the Art Nouveau style decorated with floral motifs, and Giacinto Melillo, who won an award for his filigree creations. Moreover, the works of Giovanni Ascione and Morabito, with their Pompeii inspired coral jewellery, drew attention: Bacchante, rams, vine shoots, small amphorae, laid out in high relief and in-the-round compositions, with naturalistic themes such as "bouquets of leaves and flowers", *en papille*, demonstrating elegance and technical skill. At the beginning

[35] E. Schmuttermeier in *L'arte del gioiello e il gioiello d'artista* (Florence) 2001, p. 134. Also K. Moser and J. Hoffmann in *L'arte del gioiello e il gioiello d'artista* (Florence) 2001, pp. 130–45.
[36] Quoted from Becker 1985, p. 106.
[37] Ibid., p. 108.

of the century Italian jewellery continued to favour nineteenth-century style and its neo-renaissance, neo-baroque and neo-rococo motifs, distinguishing itself by the absence of any cultural programme of innovation. The first to raise the question of the design of the object of use with reference to the new means of industrial production and the demands of a rapidly expanding bourgeois market were intellectuals of the likes of Camillo Boito, Alfredo Melani, Vittorio Pica and Enrico Thovez. The presence of informed companies and jewellery designers oriented towards change (as well as the names mentioned above there were the works of Musy, Giuseppe Gillio, Casa Calderoni, Cusi, Villa, Melchiorre & Co., Gaetano Jacoangeli, Giorgio Ceraioli) did nothing to halt the observation that "Italy does not boast such a bountiful yield of new jewellery as France, Germany, Belgium, England, Austria. If, however, it were able to combine its efforts, which are preparing to triumph definitively in archaic jewellery, the future of Italian jewellery would be safer".[38]

After Paris the International Exposition of Decorative Arts in Turin[39] of 1902 and the International Exposition of Sempione in Milan of 1906 proved to be the most interesting in terms of the evolution of the jewel.[40] It was with the Turin Fair that Italy succeeded in joining the international debate, sharing the need for a more "democratic" art and an artistic product that might reach a wider sector of the public. Moreover, there was a creeping awareness of the problems generated by industrialisation, the links between art and industry, mass production and craft production, and the nature of the markets they addressed. An interesting novelty that emerged from the Turin debate was the exhortation to Italian manufacturers to abandon the eclectic and worn-out nineteenth-century formulas in favour of modernist ones. At the Exposition of Sempione in Milan in 1906,[41] sixty-one Italian jewellery firms were united for the first time in a single pavilion, a sign of their growing awareness of belonging to a category. However, the greatest difficulty lay in the attempt to standardise taste throughout the whole of Italy, which struggled against deep-rooted cultural provincialisms. Indeed, with the "French jewellery" formula, experts wished to show what was new and fashionable, in contrast with traditional models.

The Paris Exposition divided opinions, though local critics did not fail to express their "glowing" admiration. With regard to this Charles Saunier wrote: "the Exposition of 1900 will number amongst the most magnificent exhibitions dedicated to the French jewel. Our *bijoutiers* and *joailliers* emerge victorious from stiff competition and their creations once more reveal both perfect taste and unequivocal technical skill". Although this opinion was not unanimously shared, the influence of French jewellery was unquestioned, above all in terms of its influence on Italian jewellery. French jewellery was a reassuring source of inspiration, due to its "trendy" Art Nouveau models as well as the ones in the more traditional Garland or Edwardian style. This trend, which owed its name to Edward VII and his wife Alexandra – sovereigns of Great Britain from 1901 to 1910 – affected the production of collector's pieces or limited series of *haute* jewellery, that is to say jewellery in which the symbolical value of status was still measured in terms of grams, carats and rarity. The Edwardian style was just as important worldwide as Art Nouveau, insofar as it was pursued by large jewellery firms, whose consolidated *allure* proved familiar and reassuring for the international aristocracy. Edwardian style countered Art Nouveau's confusion of colours by choosing stark white for the most sophisticated pieces of jewellery, with the variations in hue of pearls and diamonds. The latter were by then easier to come by thanks to the discovery of numerous deposits in South Africa, which had led to a significant drop in the price of the stones. The settings were made of white gold and, later, platinum, metals which exalted the diaphanous luminosity of these extraordinary jewels. The greatest interpreter of this style was the Parisian jeweller Cartier who, inspired by the jewels of the period of Louis XVI and Marie Antoinette, proposed garlands, laurel leaves, bows, tassels, spider-web motifs, lattices and laces. This created an elegant and simple style with sinuous yet controlled forms, made dazzling with the lavish inclusion of diamonds. Sometimes coloured stones, especially peridots, believed to be Edward VII's favourite, or amethysts, were added. After 1910 a sober and linear arrangement of stones became popular. Its pioneers were Garrard, Van Cleef & Arpels, Fabergé, Tiffany and Buccellati, as well as Cartier and Boucheron, who laid down the rules of the trend which would soon oust the "brief but intense" season of Art Nouveau and establish the dictates of a new extraordinary style: Deco.

II. 1919–29 Art Deco: white, black and *Tutti frutti*

Eric Hobsbawn's book *Short Century* opened with the First World War, an event that marked the beginning of "an Age of Catastrophe for this society. For forty years it stumbled from one calamity to another. There were times when even intelligent conservatives would not take bets on its survival".[42]

[38] A. Melani, "Gioielli di Vincenzo Miranda", in *Ars et Labor* 2, February 1911, p. 89.
[39] Cf. M. G. Imarisio and D. Surace, *Torino. Tra liberty e floreale* (Turin: Testo & Immagine, 2003).
[40] Cf. L. Aimone and C. Olmo, *Le esposizioni universali: 1851–1900: il progresso in scena* (Turin: Allemandi, 1990; D. Alcouffe, *Le arti decorative alle grandi esposizioni universali, 1851–1900*) (Milan: Idea Books, 1988).
[41] *Il Liberty a Milano*, edited by R. Bossaglia and V. Terraroli (Milan: Skira, 2003).
[42] E. Hobsbawm, *Age of Extremes: The Short Twentieth Century 1914–1991* (London: Abacus, 1995).

Van Cleef & Arpels
Studies for decorations, 1930s
Van Cleef & Arpels Archives

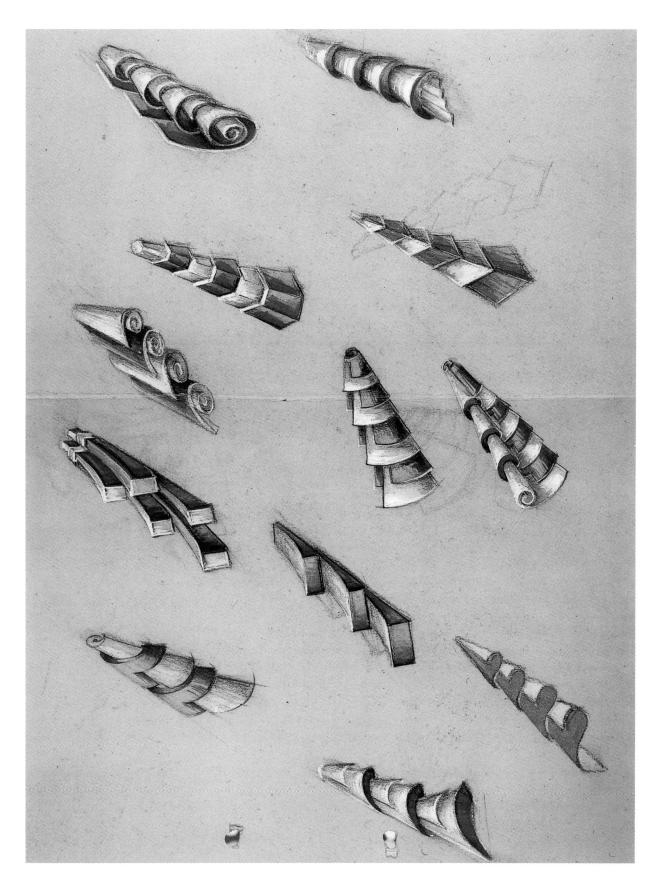

With the war and the Russian Revolution of 1917 the institutions of liberal democracy everywhere disappeared under the advancing boot of fascism[43] and the totalitarian regimes related to it. The economy was on its knees and there had been a large-scale loss of human lives. Only the United States emerged from the World War in almost the same conditions in which they had entered into it, indeed made stronger by it. The revolution in living habits, which radically changed the lives of women and the history of consumption[44] began in the New World. At the same time as the introduction onto the market of the first toaster and washing machine, Rimmel launched their first mascara, while in England Burberry presented its famous check pattern in 1921. In 1922 Chanel introduced its revolutionary No. 5 perfume and Hermes began to diversify production, introducing leather accessories, watches, bags and gloves. In 1923 the first Disney Studios opened in Hollywood and, simultaneously, television made its debut, although the first actual broadcast would only be made in 1936. In 1928 Salvatore Ferragamo transformed the shoe into legend whilst, in the same year, Japan, having survived the terrible earthquake of 1923, discovered its technological vocation when Kazuo Tashima entered into partnership with two German engineers to found a company specialising in cameras: Minolta.

The hardships enforced by the war were replaced by a frenzied *joie de vivre*, generating the madcap, "Roaring 1920s", which went down in history with their cult of luxury and speed. The artistic avant-garde, jazz music, cinema and large department stores generated the "consumer society".[45] France stayed firmly at the helm of elegance and style by means of an aesthetic rather than a distributive model of luxury goods. The vibrant colours of Art Deco were influenced by the Ballets Russes directed by Sergei Diaghilev and Leon Bakst, whose fabrics and sets represented a source of inspiration for every artistic sphere.

Cinemas and magazines popularised a new model of woman in keeping with a more dynamic society than that which had inflicted the torture of corsets and crinolines. On the long road to female emancipation an important role was reserved for Gabrielle "Coco" Chanel who, from her first little black dresses to accessories and perfumes, liberated women from the sartorial scaffolding of the Belle Epoque, restoring to them a freedom of movement which also meant a freedom of expression. Skinny, quick-tempered and sharp-featured, fascinating and non-conformist, Coco Chanel wrote the history of fashion and costume, creating the contemporary idea of style and comfort. This was the great revolution that the porter's daughter bequeathed

to her age. "I wanted lighter clothes for myself, this is why I created a light fashion. My clothes are for women who move."[46] Chanel was inspired by military uniforms, borrowing sports trousers, men's jerseys and the stark silhouettes of workmen's overalls. With Paul Poiret she defined a simple and sophisticated style where dresses shed corsets in order to slip softly over the body, backs were bare, heels were raised and waists were lowered. The diaphanous pallor of face powder provided a contrast to vermilion lips and heavily made up eyes. *A la garçonne* hairstyles led to the disappearance of combs and hairpins. Dangling earrings adorned bare necks, whilst cigarette holders and cigarette boxes became must-haves for the chic woman. Chanel designed every aspect of the new female look, from clothes to accessories, introducing three of what we now consider to be typical features of contemporary fashion: sportswear, lifestyle and range extensions. With her customary arrogance she would often repeat: "other couturiers follow fashion, I have created a style". She was right. The art of understatement introduced by Chanel would become the most powerful and subtle form of Art Deco elitism.

In Le Corbusier's architecture, as well as in Mies van der Rohe's interiors, Marcel Breuer and Gerrit Rietveld's furnishings and Piet Mondrian and Wassily Kandinsky's paintings, the floral effervescence of Art Nouveau was replaced by the Cartesian severity of elementary shapes and pure colours. The *rappel à l'ordre* came, loud and clear, from Adolf Loos who, by banning the inappropriate use of ornament, introduced philosophies that were not pertinent to the sphere of "building" but to the sphere of "living". "The absence of ornament has led other arts to reach unimagined heights", he wrote in *Ornament und Verbrechen* (Ornament and Crime), "Beethoven's symphonies could never have been composed by a man wearing silk, velvet, lace. Whoever wears a velvet jacket today is not an artist but a clown or a house painter. … The absence of ornament is evidence of spiritual strength. Modern man uses ornaments from past ages or foreign peoples as he pleases. He concentrates his inventive spirit on other things."[47]

Loos had understood the key role played by "everyday culture" in the processes of the determination and transformation of civilisation, yet it was Walter Gropius's Bauhaus, founded in Weimar in 1919, that proved that even an item of clothing, a jewel or a rug could be modern, escaping the limited world of cottage industries in order to find a more democratic and "modern" application in mass production (something which in fact never came to pass). This was despite its founder's manifest aversion to the decorative arts, which were erro-

[43] In 1921 Mussolini's Fascist party was founded with three hundred thousand members. In just a few years Italy, like Russia and Germany, became a totalitarian state.
[44] Cf. D. Tirelli, *Il crono dizionario dei consumi* (Bologna: Editrice Compositori, 2002).
[45] During the Weimar period the Institute of Social Research was founded in Frankfurt. It took its name from the Frankfurt School, founded by Karl Grünberg and subsequently enlivened by Max Horkheimer, Theodor W. Adorno, Herbert Marcuse, Walter Benjamin and Erich Fromm. At the centre of their interests lay some themes which began to require urgent attention precisely at this time: the consumer society, mass communication, the crisis of modernity and the idea of progress, the culture industry.
[46] Quoted in A. Cappellieri, "Coco la rivoluzionaria", in *Abitare* 454, October 2005, p. 185.
[47] Cf. B. Gravagnuolo, *Adolf Loos* (Milan: Idea Books, 1981), p. 18.

neously associated with the vilified schools for female dilettantes widespread in the nineteenth century but abandoned a hundred years later. With regard to this, it is worth recalling that, while in Europe the terms *Kunstgewerbe*, applied arts, industrial arts and decorative arts were used, the expression "industrial design"[48] was coined in the United States. In the wonderful clothes, fabrics and jewels of Gunta Stölzl, Carl Fieger, Anni Albers and Naum Slutzky, to mention only a few of the designers of the Bauhaus weaving and metal workshops,[49] the reformist vision of Gropius and the Modern Movement was not dimmed but, on the contrary, shone with new expressive vigour, contributing to the definition and diffusion of the new model. Naum Slutzky especially used chrome-plated brass and silver to make jewellery with architectonic shapes and a minimum of decoration, in keeping with design's "functional" approach.

The artistic avant-gardes and particularly Cubism, Surrealism and Expressionism proved to be just as important, having in common the disassembling of objects as a form of rejection of any realistic representation. Aided by Joséphine Baker, decorators, couturiers and artists drew inspiration from African art, whose geometrical patterns, very similar to abstract act, appeared on rugs, glasses, ceramics, metal objects and jewellery. Elongated forms, zigzags, checks, "V" shapes and sunrays are recurring features in very different works: from architecture to furnishings and other objects of use, from women's shoes to fabric and clothing design. Artists, designers and craftsmen applied the new aesthetics to every sector of the arts.

"Deco is the heir and successor of Liberty", wrote Rossana Bossaglia, "and the direct link between the two phenomena cannot be denied, although the stylistic originality and independence of Deco compared to Liberty should be emphasised."[50] Like Art Nouveau, Deco also flourished in the decorative arts before spreading to the higher arts. The movement derived its name from the *Exposition Internationale des Arts Décoratifs et Industriels modernes* held in Paris in 1925. This date coincided with the full and mature expression of the new style and should not therefore be considered in the sense of it being a period *a quo* as is often suggested. The harbingers of Deco were in fact to be found in the first decade of the century in the works of the Glasgow School, the English Arts and Crafts movement and Wiener Werkstätte, which had, from the start, favoured square shapes and geometrical modules. Once again Paris was established as the capital of excellence, producing extraordinary and unique pieces such as the furniture of Jacques-Emile Ruhlmann and Jean-Jacques Rateau, Eileen Gray's panels, Edgar Brandt's wrought iron, Jean Dunand's lacquers, René Lalique and Maurice Marinot's glass, and Cartier's platinum jewellery. *Grillage*, squares and chessboards also distinguished all of jewellery production in the 1920s.

Deco *imagerie* metamorphosed into jewellery with sober, simple and linear forms, "from which every *impure* attempt at ornament of decoration was banned".[51] Its themes and motifs in fact derived from a dynamic and pulsating reality, from work, sport or the exhilaration of speed, materialising in compositions cadenced by geometrical motifs marked by the choice of clear colour contrasts. As Melissa Gabardi observes, "The air increasingly buzzed with a word – functionality – which appeared to have been created on purpose to seduce that Modern Woman (capital letters are de rigueur) who was then in the limelight, changing her way of dressing and above all of behaving, and forcing jewellers to lower their prices thanks to the use of lacquers, silver, and semiprecious stones which subtracted nothing from the beauty of the jewel but exalted its pure, nude formal invention".[52] This is the reason the 1920s saw the spread of costume jewellery, the favourite of Coco Chanel and Elsa Schiaparelli, no longer seen as a cheap version of costly jewels but original creations, destined, at least originally, for an elite public or the rich bourgeoisie, who considered it more chic to adorn themselves with Bakelite and Galalith jewellery than to replace precious stones with synthetic ones. Howard Carter's discovery of the tomb of Tutankhamen in 1922 unleashed a new wave of Egypt-related mania in all of the arts, including jewellery. Cartier mounted ancient carved scarabs on jewels reproducing Egyptian funeral ornaments whilst funeral symbols characterised a supple bracelet by Van Cleef & Arpels, with two images of Anubis, the god of death, his jackal features flanked by a human-headed falcon with spread wings. Janesich drew on the same influences with a bracelet decorated with stylised sphinxes. In both jewels the design was composed of rubies, emeralds and sapphires, contrasting with onyxes on a background of diamonds. In c. 1925 the decorative motifs became increasingly geometrical and were essentially based on the interplay of flat and compact zones of contrasting colours, mainly black, red and white.

Once the dreamlike plasticity of Art Nouveau had been abandoned, Deco jewellery became sober and neat, with a renewed interest in bright colours and precious stones chosen in response to the privations of war, often combined with semiprecious gems. Three distinct colour trends can be summarised: the white monochrome of

[48] De Fusco 1985.
[49] For a thematic study, cf. A. Baumhof in *Bauhaus*, edited by J. Fiedler and P. Feierabend (Cologne: Könemann, 1999); and *La tessitura del Bauhaus 1919–1933 nelle collezioni della Repubblica Democratica Tedesca*, exhibition catalogue, edited by F. Panzini (Venice: Marsilio, 1985).
[50] R. Bossaglia, *L'Art Déco* (Rome–Bari: Laterza, 1984), p. 1, and also G. D'Amato, *Fortuna e immagini dell'Art Déco: Parigi 1925* (Rome–Bari: Laterza, 1991); Ch. Benton, T. Benton and Gh. Wood, *Art Déco: 1910–1939* (London: Bulfinch, 2003).
[51] M. Gabardi, "L'arte come gioiello", in *L'arte del gioiello e il gioiello d'artista* (Florence) 2001.
[52] Ibid.

haute joaillerie, in the Edwardian version of the white jewel, exalted by the preciousness of platinum and the glow of the *baguette* diamond cut; the black and white of geometrical patterns; and the joyful, multi-coloured *Tutti frutti* introduced by Cartier after his business dealings with India.

Jewellery was light, delicate, two-dimensional and fretworked, made of diamonds and pearls almost always mounted on platinum. The ornamental motif was generally stylised, even in the case of the animal or floral motifs that were the legacy of Art Nouveau. Animals in particular were more stylised and composed compared to Art Nouveau. Some of Art Deco's favourite animals included birds, which adapted well to the mounting of geometrically cut stones, above all on wings and tails, as seen in Janesich's *Heron* brooch, in which the wingtips and tail are made of onyx, in keeping with the custom of using two colours that was so much in vogue in the mid-1920s. In the years immediately following the war, Cartier designers found in panther skin, highly fashionable at the time, a source of inspiration for abstract designs made of onyx and diamonds. The first spotted panther motif, coveted by the legendary Jeanne Toussaint, appeared in 1914 on a woman's watch and from that moment on the panther became the *maison*'s distinctive motif. Americans Udall & Ballou are instead remembered for their running dog, with half its body made of black enamel and the other half made of diamonds, whose dynamism recalls Balla's famous painting. Pets were also the subject of Boucheron's sports themed jewellery. He produced horses ridden by jockeys, dogs, rabbits, fish and birds as well as reptiles, tortoises and snakes, all favoured by Deco jewellers. One of the most popular mythological creatures found in the jewellery of this period was the chimera: this was described in Greek mythology as a many-headed monster with the bust of a lion, the middle section of a goat and the hindquarters of a dragon. Cartier's jewellers revolutionised the look, modelling it on sea monsters of Indian tradition, and used it in bracelets terminating with the twin heads of chimeras with yawning jaws. From the animal to the plant world slender Art Nouveau flowers also flowed into the new style. Boucheron made a spectacular collier with simplified rosebuds in the manner of the Glasgow School for the International Exposition of 1925. Indeed, each rose was divided into three sections of rubies, with a small emerald leaf on the lower tip of the flower. As an alternative to modular decorations Tiffany reconciled the geometrical aspects of Deco with flowing lines in a bracelet where a rose stood out against a background of diamonds under a night sky.

The interest in the "barbaric" Orient of the Ballets Russes and its colour contrasts, captured by the emotional colours of Fauvism, centred on the aesthetic of the ornament which, thanks to materials such as turquoise, jade and coral, contributed to giving the Deco jewel an exotic allure very unlike the pale nouveau enamels. The discovery of platinum revolutionised diamond settings, whilst the creation of new cuts, such as the *baguette*, favoured the establishment of geometrical shapes in design. Uncut, rounded and rough-hewn coloured stones were imported from Thailand, India, Burma and Madagascar, whilst from China came jade rings, bracelets and amulets. African art, through the mediation of Cubism, generated new constructions of geometrical volumes, with stylised decorative motifs and symmetrical shapes. Vertical lines were important, including long necklaces with elaborate pendants and drop earrings, suitable for the new shorter hairstyles. Towards the mid-1920s the fashion for black and white began to spread and black onyx made a comeback, usually matched with pearls, whose market had just been thrown into agitation by Mikimoto's invention of cultured pearls.[53]

Brooches became smaller, with simple and stylised motifs, whilst the elimination of evening gloves encouraged the use of bracelets. The semi-rigid strap bracelet, or *bracelet lanière*, was the most popular typology of ornament during the Art Deco period and every jeweller created different versions to adorn ladies' bare arms. As these bracelets were rather slender, one could simultaneously wear four or five on one's wrist and even when, at the end of the 1920s, they became wider, the habit of wearing more than one remained. Rings in the 1920s were mostly surmounted with a *cabochon* stone, often surrounded by small brilliants or diamonds, whilst wedding rings were made of platinum, used increasingly often for engagement rings with diamond solitaires.

The return of society life and Coco Chanel's fashion made accessories an essential part of the female wardrobe. Preciously decorated evening bags, cigarette boxes and powder compacts burst onto the scene. The habit of smoking and the use of make-up, which had only recently become socially acceptable, were permeated with a sense of daring that made these accessories even more attractive. Jean Dunand began to produce a collection of earrings, bracelets and cigarette boxes made of silver or a low gold alloy named *oreum*. René Lalique presented a collection of glass objects consisting of necklaces made of large beads, glass pendants worked in different ways and even bracelets formed of cylindrical sections of glass joined with elastic strings. The geometrical style of Art Deco adapted well to this typology of

[53] Japanese Kokichi Mikimoto succeeded in producing the first spherical cultured pearl in 1905.

ornament and elegant containers for make-up in enamelled or lacquered gold were produced, sometimes trimmed with decorative panels of carved semiprecious stones or profiles of small diamonds.

Sautoirs made a comeback with the Charleston phenomenon. These were long necklaces hung with pendants – christened "belly button necklaces" by Gabriele d'Annunzio – which set off the neckline or the back, adding a touch of femininity to straight and somewhat severe dresses. Bakelite bracelets, worn not just on the wrist but, above all, in slave fashion, in tune with the fashion of the moment, were also very much in vogue. Boldly coloured and regular shaped gems were favoured, combining colours such as red, black and silver but also brilliant shades such as apple green or orange, which were extremely popular, in order to create striking contrasts. The spectrum of Art Deco colours was both bright and elegant though the sophisticated and elaborate settings of white gold and platinum with turquoise, lapis lazuli and malachite, enormous aquamarines, *cabochon* moonstones, emeralds and *baguette* cut diamonds were highly sought after. The most curious varieties of quartz, found in every shade in nature, were the most popular: milky, pink, tourmalinated. And topaz, long unfashionable, made a comeback.

This trend informed both the masterpieces of the *haute* jewellery of Cartier, Van Cleef & Arpels, Tiffany, Templer, Mauboussin, Boucheron, Fouquet and mass-produced jewellery in which alternative materials such as lacquer, inlaid wood, *galuchat* or zebra-skin were combined with innovative metals such as aluminium and stainless steel, followed by Bakelite and Galatite plastics.

After numerous delays the *Exposition Internationale des Arts Décoratifs et Industriels Modernes*, based on the exposition model for international decorative arts, such as the one held in Turin in 1902, was inaugurated on 25 April 1925 (Boucheron was a member of the jury). Germany was not invited whilst the United States government declined the invitation. Asia was represented by China and Japan (which took the place of the United States) and Africa by the French colonies. The name "Citroën" was vertically illuminated in huge letters on the Eiffel Tower. As in 1900 the Universal Exposition represented a cultural and artistic, as well as a commercial, model and the *Ville Lumière* was its capital. Critic Paul Geraldy[54] noted that the adjective "modern" was used so often it proved inappropriate, whilst the comment of Auguste Perret, interviewed by Marie Dormoy, was strangely intransigent: "In 1900 we saw the triumph of the ornament. Now we claim to have eliminated the ornament but it is merely words. Naturally. We no longer speak of straight lines or of the essential element or of construction. The truth is that today the ornament has become an integrative part of our culture with the result that we have more useless ornaments than we ever did in the past. I would truly like to know who first pronounced the words art and decoration in the same breath. It is a monstrosity".[55] Only Le Corbusier's relived Esprit Nouveau pavilion aroused Perret's interest but the issue was staked on a much smaller scale than that of architecture. As in 1900 the initial aim of the great exposition – international and no longer universal – was to celebrate the triumph of modern decorative arts, where modern meant shunning tradition and folklore as well as the "eccentricities" of Art Nouveau. The license of "modernity" represented a break with the past and the rejection of frivolity. The names of Lalique, Brandt and Ruhlmann appeared again and again in the catalogue. The former, a veteran of the glory days of Art Nouveau, had, after 1914, devoted himself to glasswork, developing his own sophisticated technique of modelling, colouring, carving and sanding objects made of glass. Brandt instead used various thicknesses of iron to create different shades of colour and welding to combine elements of iron, copper and bronze. Ruhlmann produced furniture that many consider to be the quintessence of Art Deco: exotic woods inlaid with mother-of-pearl, ivory and ebony in well-proportioned and elegantly shaped pieces.

There were also important names from fashion, such as Poiret (who exhibited his creations on three barges named Amours, Délices and Orgues), Lanvin, Doucet, Patou and Vionnet. The exposition was organised into five categories, one of which was entitled "Parure", which included the sections of "Bijouterie-Joaillerie", clothes, accessories, flowers, feathers and perfumes, and was located in the right wing of the Grand Palais. The pavilion was designed by architect Eric Bagge, who raised the jewellers' showcases onto a plinth surrounded by lamé curtains. Costume jewellery was arranged along the walls on either side of the plinth. La Maison Cartier instead chose to exhibit in the Elegance pavilion alongside the great fashion *couturiers*. France made a significant contribution to the "Bijouterie-Joaillerie" section with the participation of thirty of their most prestigious jewellers, including Acouc, Boucheron, Chaumet, Dusausoy, Laclöche, Linzeler and Marchak, Mauboussin, Van Cleef, Fouquet, Vever, Sandoz and Templer. Fouquet, who had been the Secretary of the Milan Exposition in 1906, was made president of the jewellery section, flanked by Louis Cartier as vice-president. For the very first time the large

[54] P. Géraldy, "L'Architecture Vivante", in *L'Illustration*, June 1925.
[55] M. Dormoy, "Interview d'Auguste Perret sur l'Exposition Internationale des Arts Décoratifs", in *L'Amour de l'art*, May 1925, p. 174; cf. also W. George, "L'Exposition des Arts Décoratifs et Industriels de 1925 – les tendances générales", in *L'Amour de l'art*, May 1925, p. 283.

maisons revealed the names of their designers and this was certainly thanks to Art Nouveau, which had diffused the culture of design in the sphere of jewellery too. Cartier struck the only discordant note, not only by choosing the pavilion but also by its failure to mention the names of the company's designers. All jewellers were invited to exhibit "only truly original pieces, fused with new sources of inspiration". The results were marvellous Deco jewels and, by extension, accessories. As well as traditional jewels the large *maisons* produced gold, platinum or silver cigarette boxes, carved with the figures of golfers or tennis-players, lacquered with elaborate geometrical shapes or Oriental subjects, mounted with mother-of-pearl and ebony inlays, with glossy black and red lacquers, and precious cigarette holders and accessories such as evening bags, make-up *trousses* and pocket watches. Van Cleef & Arpels created gold vanity cases with individual compartments for various items: lipstick, powder, combs, cigarettes. It was on this occasion that Van Cleef & Arpels was allowed into the empyrean of French jewellers due to the high quality of their designs and technical innovations, and was awarded a Grand Prix for a bracelet adorned with ruby and diamond roses and emerald leaves. Van Cleef's accessories, for which the *maison* invented new typologies, applying them to jewellery, were particularly interesting. In the 1920s they began to produce watches and, in 1930, a mirror with a black and red lacquer handle made with agate and gold. In 1931 they produced a night lamp in gold and green and black enamel. One of their most unusual objects was a cage for a live frog made of agate, jade, coral, lapis lazuli, onyx and gold. However, it was the *nécessaire* which became the icon of Van Cleef & Arpels. This was an object which women began to use after the First World War. The relatively large size of these vanity cases freed the designers of Van Cleef & Arpels from the limitations imposed by conventional jewels. The *nécessaire* lent itself to a wide range of combinations of materials: precious and semi-precious stones, enamels, mother-of-pearl and wrought gold. At the start of the 1930s the *nécessaire* became even more sophisticated. Van Cleef & Arpels invented the *minaudière*, a sleek golden case with a hidden fastening that, once opened, revealed special compartments for powder, lipstick, a tiny comb and small objects indispensable to its owner's glamour. Their success was such that it heralded the decline of the evening bag. The name *minaudière* (simperer) was invented by Alfred Van Cleef who used it to tease his wife. Like the *nécessaire* the *minaudière* offered great artistic scope for designers and craftsmen, who adorned the lids with exotic illustrations.

Vever was one of the great French jewellers to draw attention with his cloud motif bracelets, made to a design by Jules Chadel, and a collection of jewels made of precious stones inspired by Persian miniatures, whilst Mauboussin, who had never succumbed to the charms of Art Nouveau, continued to favour precious stones and *haute* jewellery. Georges Mauboussin was a skilful designer as well as, unusually, a shrewd businessman. Between 1924 and 1931 the company took part in eighteen expositions all over the world: New York, Rio de Janeiro, Buenos Aires, Milan, Paris. With astonishing foresight Georges realised that advertising was the soul of commerce and organised three exhibitions of gems in his atelier, which, due to their cultural rather than commercial nature, stimulated the curiosity of customers as well as the French and American press. The first, held in 1928, was dedicated to emeralds. One of the two hundred and eighty splendid jewels that celebrated the loveliness of this gem was a large emerald weighing more than twenty-four carats that Napoleon had given to Joséphine in 1800. This piece was tremendously successful, as its setting recalled Oriental jewels, which were then extremely fashionable. The second exposition, held in 1930, centred on rubies and gave a clear message to the jewellery market. Mauboussin wanted to denounce and condemn the ill-fated presence and effects of the new, so-called "synthetic rubies" that were starting to circulate. The last exhibition was held in 1931 and was dedicated to the diamond, which had become very popular in the meantime.

Some of the most sophisticated jewels of the decade were produced by Cartier,[56] which combined magnificent stones with extremely elegant motifs. The originality of the design and the quality of the materials and workmanship represented the trademark of the *maison*, together with its ability to be simultaneously "modern" and "traditional". The talent of designer Charles Jacqueau,[57] who had graduated with a diploma from the École des Arts Décoratifs, proved decisive for the success of Cartier and the establishment of Deco in jewellery. At just twenty-three years of age Jacqueau was commissioned to design pieces for the exhibition, for which he originally adopted the Garland style. But his desire for innovation soon led him to invent completely new solutions. Instead, Jeanne Toussaint,[58] Cartier's muse, who had an extraordinary understanding of female tastes and sensibilities, was the person responsible for formal and managerial innovation. In 1923, unexpectedly ahead of her times, Toussaint organised and directed "Department S or silver", dedicated to accessories made of precious metals and materials for men, women

[56] Cf. *L'art de Cartier*, exhibition catalogue, Paris, Musée du Petit Palais, October 1989 – January 1990 (Paris, 1989); M. Jodice, *Capolavori di Cartier: joailliers depuis 1847* (Naples: Electa, 1988).
[57] Cf. H. Nadelhoffer, *Cartier* (Milan: Longanesi 1984).
[58] Hired in 1910, Toussaint reorganised the creative and merchandising department set up by Louis. Her approach was modern, in tune with the new attitude that society was demonstrating towards women. Indeed, she sensed intuitively that jewellery should be calibrated on a new, more dynamic and modern female figure, no longer relegated to the home. Thus Cartier charged Toussaint with keeping an eye on this new woman and looking after the production of jewellery destined for her. "Department S" produced functional yet elegant objects: purses made of gold and silver, crocodile skin or brocades from the Far East; pocket cigarette holders decorated in a geometrical style, frames made of precious metals and semi-precious stones, desk articles.

and the home. On Toussaint's advice Jacqueau drew inspiration for his *haute* jewellery from Indian designs and Moghul jewels and their colourful variety of precious stones. Cartier launched their *Tutti frutti*, a European version of the "tree of life", distinguished by the unusual combination of green and blue created by the presence of rubies, *cabochon* sapphires and diamonds. After all, this coincided with the period when the French *maison* began to trade with India. Following Jacques Cartier's journey to India in 1911 the maharajahs asked him to modernise their extraordinary jewellery. The chromatic quality of Indian workmanship led to the creation of jewels with contrasting combinations of sapphires and emeralds, amethysts, rubies and rock crystals. Jaipur enamels, solid gold settings, large gems, oriental motifs and ornaments for turbans were a Cartier prerogative. The combination of blue and green represented an especially important innovation and *Tutti frutti*'s special feature. Many designs derived from Indian talismans, with crystal or jade charms and the zodiacal stones of local astrology serving as a model for various Art Deco pendants made from jade, amethyst and onyx, inlaid with motifs from Moghul architecture. The fashion for *sautoirs* drew inspiration from the maharajahs' long necklaces, a sign of the intense exchange between the two cultures.

Cartier's ability to interpret the spirit of the times was therefore seen in references to current events – from archaeology to new expeditions – while the use of precious gems innovative in their cut and composition consolidated the positioning of the brand in the eyes of its customers. At the Paris exposition Cartier impressed women by displaying earrings almost eight centimetres long that incorporated cascades of flowers with emerald, lapis lazuli and onyx pendants. The majority of the bracelets exhibited were geometrical, often ring shaped, a fashion that lasted until the Second World War. The most popular rings were those with *cabochon* cut gems, a further distinguishing feature of the *maison*, while the "emerald cut", highly prized for its sparkle, was favoured for solitaires. Brooches were signally innovative, pinned to *revers*, hats, belts and shoes. The double clip buckle inspired most of the brooches of the Art Deco period. Between 1924 and 1925 Cartier produced the *Trinity*, another brand icon. It was a ring consisting of three interlocking ringlets made respectively of polished red, yellow and white gold, whose flawless simplicity enchanted Jean Cocteau, who "adorned it with his ardent imagination".

Boucheron's success was also confirmed by a designer, Lucien Hirtz, who projected jewellery with a strong chromatic impact. Defined by Vever as "an artist of great merit and a hugely talented enameller. A prolific designer, gifted with perfect taste",[59] Hirtz combined fragments of lapis lazuli, onyx, jade, mother-of-pearl and malachite in the shape of palms, shells and spirals encrusted with small brilliants. The brooches shown at the Paris exposition may be considered paradigmatic examples of Deco. Their strict geometrical structure, emphasised by the colour combination of the gems, gives way to the astonishingly soft spiral shape of the shells, creating an ensemble of elegant harmony and vague mystery. The fountain style diadems were presented to complement the fashion for short hair then in vogue. The cascading water effect was created by *baguette* cut diamonds: a line that "made perfect ripples, imitating the small waves of a lake in which the water is barely touched by the wind".[60] The bare neck gave Boucheron the idea of reviving drop earrings, so long they almost brushed the shoulders.

"A jewel must always fit harmoniously with the personality of the woman who wears it and with her toilette." In 1925, just as in 1900, Georges Fouquet[61] continued to produce his independent and original designs, conscious of the changes that had taken place in fashion and society, as described in the volume *La Bijouterie, La Joaillerie, La Bijouterie de Fantaisie au XXᵉ siècle*, which he published at the close of the exposition in order to show the various types of jewellery of the period. Fouquet favoured large, precious and non-precious gems which he mounted in delicate and elegant settings. At that time Louis Fertey was the *maison* designer but, for the 1925 exhibition, Georges Fouquet called on artists such as architect Eric Bagge, artist André Léveillé and poster designer Cassandre (Adolphe Jean-Marie Mouron), who were very much admired by the public. The belief that jewellery should be in keeping with the character and clothes of the wearer was demonstrated with force in 1927 when Fouquet persuaded tailor Jean Patou to show his collections with Fouquet jewels. However, the idea of linking jewellery with fashion was feasible when jewellery was priced low as it was made with inexpensive stones, while a more sober, discreet and lasting style than that required by fashion was still favoured for jewellery made with costly gems. In 1929, on the occasion of a jewellery exhibition, Fouquet said that "Every jewel must be based on an idea, be it made from a single, expensive stone or from many gems. A jewel must not, with the repetitive uniformity of its setting, appear to be the badge of a club".[62]

Fouquet believed in young people, whom he often involved in his work and in the exhibitions in which he took part. These included Paul Brandt, Gérard San-

[59] H. Vever, *La Bijouterie française…* III, p. 450; quoted in *L'arte del gioiello e il gioiello d'artista* (Florence) 2001, pp. 211–12.
[60] Snowman 1990, p. 89.
[61] J. Fouquet, "Bijoux et orfèvrerie", in *Art International d'aujourd'hui* 16, 1931 quoted in *L'arte del gioiello e il gioiello d'artista* (Florence) 2001, p. 154; *Les Fouquet: bijoutiers et joailliers à Paris 1860–1960*, exhibition catalogue, Paris, Musée des Arts décoratifs, 1983 (Paris: Flammarion, 1983).
[62] G. Fouquet, *La Bijouterie, La Joaillerie, La Bijouterie de Fantaisie au XXᵉ Siècle* (Paris, 1925); quoted in *L'arte del gioiello e il gioiello d'artista* (Florence) 2001.

doz and, above all, Raymond Templier,[63] whose work on constructing and defining the *Gesamtkunstwerk* aroused Fouquet's interest. In 1929, Templier founded the "Group of Five" with René Herbst, Robert Mallet-Stevens, Jean Puiforcat, Hélène Henry and Pierre Chareau, who all shared his drive for innovation. His work reached the height of maturity in the period of modernism that followed, the map of which Templier plotted in his jewels.

At the 1925 exposition Austria received a special mention for the jewellery of Wiener Werkstätte. Geometry and polychromy had, as we saw earlier, already been successfully introduced by Hoffmann and Moser in the first decade of the century. Otto Prutscher and Hans Ofner, pupils of Hoffmann at the Vienna School of Decorative Arts also deserve a mention. Belgium too confirmed the skill of the Frères Coosemans and, above all, Wolfers, to whom a Grand Prix was awarded for a large lapis lazuli and brilliant pendant representing a ship's anchor, whilst jewellers Anteloh and Leysen both received an honourable mention. Spain continued to produce jewellery in the spirit of Art Nouveau with jewellers Masrieras y Carreras and Jaime Mercade, as well as numerous jewellers from Barcelona. Switzerland lacked representative *joailliers-bijoutiers* exhibiting only a smattering of enamelled jewels by independent artists. The main attraction was watchmakers, specialists with a centuries-old tradition, who exhibited in a room close to the hall reserved for jewellery. The Grand Palais showcases reserved for Holland contained triangular and diamond-shaped silver *repoussé* jewels such as those created by Laurewick and Zwollo Père et Fils set with coloured *cabochons* or filigree jewels such as those of Citroën and Sheltman. The few jewels exhibited by Japan were unable to render an adequate idea of that country's creativity. All eyes were on Mikimoto's display of cultivated pearls. The jury abstained from making any judgement as their value was clearly attributable to the material.

Great Britain was only represented by Wright and Hadgkiss. In the British pavilion the displays once more imitated the Arts and Crafts exhibition model at the Pavillon de Marsan held in the summer of 1914 and British designers did not stray far from the principles of the Arts and Crafts movement and the Neo-Gothic in particular. The creations of Sybil Dunlop, George Edward Hunt, Henry George Murphy, Dorrie Nossiter and Amy Sandheim breathed new life into Anglo-Saxon jewellery, integrating the teaching of Henry Wilson with examples of the lightness, shapes and colours of Deco.

Denmark exhibited only a few pieces of jewellery at the Grand Palais. Some jewels by Edvald Nielson in engraved gold with slender chains decorated with small flowers are worthy of mention. But it was Georg Jensen[64] who was the undisputed leader of Skonvirke, the Danish equivalent of the Arts and Crafts movement. "Jensen wanted to be an artist, a sculptor, but he was forced to provide for his family", says Isabelle Anscombe. "Well aware of new styles and new movements made popular by the exhibition, he responded wholeheartedly to the artistic questions of his time. In particular the emancipation of the minor arts within a new representation of nature. In his jewellery Jensen showed a sophisticated understanding of abstract naturalism, symbolism and contemporary techniques, without straying from his ideas."[65] Jensen's work decreed the shift from Art Nouveau to Deco, from dreamlike naturalism to stylised nature, according to the principles of Ashbee and the British Arts and Crafts movement. He was mainly interested in silver and semiprecious stones, convinced that harmonious shapes and elegant lines were more important than precious materials. His motto was "those who regard things with simplicity experience the greatest joy".[66] The Danish designer's open and dynamic vision, determined to make objects accessible to the greater public, is also demonstrated in the types of objects he produced: brooches, buckles, buttons, clips, and a wealth of extraordinary lightweight trinkets that highlighted his skills as a sculptor and ceramicist. The partnerships he set up with colleagues and artists, in an attempt not to limit his artistic experience to the single object but to extend it to small ranges to be enjoyed by a greater number of people, were especially interesting. This led to an atelier that soon became an international brand. Christian Mohl-Hansen, creator of the famous dove brooch, Harald Nielsen and Johan Rohde were his closest partners. Jensen's work had an enormous following due to the fact it was sold all over the world. In the United States especially it was much sought after due to its elegant forms, its harmonious blend of colours, the quality of its execution and its low prices, and his work influenced many jewellery designers on the new continent. His presence at the Panama-Pacific International Exhibition in San Francisco in 1915 marked Jensen's entrance into the United States which, as a response to the interest shown in his work, dedicated an exhibition to his silverware at the Art Institute of Chicago in 1921.

With regard to this, it is interesting to note that, despite the United States' absence from the Paris exposition, American jewellery continued on its quest for a global identity independent of European fashions. During the First World War platinum supplies were reduced

[63] L. Mouillefarine and V. Ristelhueber, *Raymond Templier: le bijou modern* (Paris: Norma Editions, 2005).
[64] Cf. D. A. Taylor, *Geog Jensen Jewelry* (New Haven–London: Yale University Press, 2005).
[65] Ibid., p. 65.
[66] Ibid.

to the minimum or stopped altogether in order to back the country's economic efforts which were entirely reserved for the war. This led to the setting up of the "Jewellers Vigilance Committee", which collaborated with the arms industry. "If you mean to be in business when the war is over, you have to stay in business during the war. As a merchant and businessman you have to persevere actively, aggressively".[67] This affirmation is a clear illustration of the condition of American jewellers during the war years. On the other hand, in the post-war period Tiffany, Charlton, Yard and Black, Starr & Frost, along with Udall & Ballou, founded in 1888, and Marcus & Co., founded in 1892, were the most important jewellery brands in the United States. In 1908 Farnham resigned and for Tiffany this meant, as well as wartime preoccupations, a downturn in sales, despite Louis C. Tiffany remaining firmly at helm. Between 1909 and 1914 Tiffany jewels were almost exclusively handmade, going against the current of the industrialised production of Europe.

Italy took part in the exposition with the support of the Fascist regime, which was committed to promoting the national image overseas. The Italian pavilion, a parallelepiped designed by Arnaldo Brasini with the bust of Mussolini prominently displayed, was in a strategic position on the Cours de la Reine just inside the main entrance. What Margherita Sarfatti described as "the artistic Italian soul of classical modernity"[68] contained ceramics and porcelain designed by Gio Ponti for Richard Ginori and, above all, jewellery by Alfredo Ravasco,[69] the undisputed protagonist of Italian jewellery of the period. A goldsmith and enameller, Ravasco, son of famous jeweller Giacomo, made jewels and trinkets consisting of linear and regular shapes with a classical flavour. His production was divided into two parts. The first was his jewellery, which included jewels and objects such as small boxes and knick-knacks, where onyx, coral, precious stones, pearls and enamels adorned gold and silver (it is worth recalling a marvellous pendant made of onyx and coral in pure Deco style, due just as much to its mix of materials as to its play of colour, vaguely inspired by some Cartier models of the 1920s). The second part was instead distinguished by *bibelots* that experimented with new juxtapositions of semiprecious stones, coral, pearls and precious metals. The latter were extremely successful at the 1923 exhibition, so much so that they were mentioned on the pages of the well known magazine *L'Oreficeria Italiana*, the official mouthpiece of the Società degli Orefici, Argentieri e Affini of Milan. Of these creations the small agate ornaments and trays inspired by Renaissance art and, more

accurately, by the jewels of the Tuscan court, revealed Ravasco's remarkable skill as an enameller and engraver.

Past, present and future mingled in the works of Ravasco, determining the Italian oscillation between tradition and progress. Indeed, it is no coincidence that Sarfatti linked modernity to classicism, as this was the oblique trend that held together the decorative arts and the higher arts in the country. Italy preferred respect for tradition and moderation, principles that were taken up by the Novecento Italiano group, founded in 1922, to the homogeneity of an autonomous and original style. Gravitating around Sarfatti, "there emerged in Milan the Novecento Italiano group, whose name was a watchword. It was reproached with wanting to lay a claim to a new century which had just begun. In fact these artists simply wanted to declare themselves Italians, traditionalists, modern. They proudly asserted they wanted to fix in time some new aspect of tradition".[70]

Despite the popularity in Italy of foreign magazines specialising in the creation of jewellery models, such as the French *Art et Bijoux* or the German *Schmuckallerlei*, Italian Deco jewellery did not achieve the same significant levels of innovation and originality as those seen in the sphere of ceramics or furnishings, for instance. Apart from rare exceptions like Janesich of Trieste, the majority of Italian jewellers oscillated between Art Nouveau and Deco producing a tired blend of floral themes and geometrical forms. Art Deco was only experimented with on more simple and less demanding typologies, such as wedding rings decorated with garlands of stylised leaves or the thin bar brooch with its play of geometrical shapes and colours provided by contrasting stones. Nevertheless, jewellers such as Dario Viterbo, one of the major exponents of artistic jewellery in Italy, succeeded in making a name for themselves. Viterbo was awarded a gold medal and produced boxes and cigarette cases decorated with original gold bas-reliefs with enamels and semiprecious stones, and a collection of rings, pendants and brooches depicting acrobats, ballerinas, satyrs, centaurs and lions. He was joined by Aldo Brozzi, a Roman engraver and one of Gabriele d'Annunzio's favourite craftsmen; Borelli and Vitelli from Torre del Greco, with their coral creations; Chiappe jewellers of Genoa, Cusi of Milan, Caderoni, Musy of Turin, Melchiorre & C. of Valenza, Matranga of Palermo and Fecarotta of Catania.

Conscious of lacking their own style, Italian artists and companies organised the editions of the International Biennial of Monza in 1923, 1925 and 1927 (curated by Guido Marangoni) and those of the Milan Triennial, whose aim was to establish an Italian style able to lead Italy to modernity. The jewellery industry took

[67] P. Proddow and D. Healy, *American Jewelry, Glamour & Tradition* (New York: Rizzoli, 1987.)
[68] Margherita Sarfatti (1925); quoted ad vocem in L. Lenti and M. C. Bergesio, *Dizionario del gioiello italiano dal XIX al XX secolo* (Turin: Allemandi, 2005). For some background on Milan Deco, cf. V. Terraroli, *Milano Déco: le arti decorative e industriali tra 1920 e 1930*, in R. Bossaglia and V. Terraroli, *Milano Déco* (Milan: Skira, 1999), pp. 29–117.
[69] Cf. P. Venturelli, *Alfredo Ravasco* (Milan: Skira, 2003).
[70] M. Sarfatti, *Storia della pittura moderna* (Rome: Cremonese Editore, 1930), pp. 123–26. Cf. also R. Bossaglia, *Il "Novecento italiano". Storia, documenti, iconografia* (Milan: Feltrinelli, 1979).

part in the 1923 exposition with the *Mostra degli orafi*, devised with the aim of producing "a collection distinguished by an absolute modernity of forms, even where these prove to be influenced by styles that are already known, both to serve as a guide and lesson to all those young people who are making an effort to learn and improve in this field". At the 1923 exhibition the jewellery section once more included exhibitors who aspired to modernity, or at least claimed to do so. There were works by Milanese Edoardo Saronni, Colombo Gennazzi (a company that had won an award in 1906 and which went on to work with Ravasco), Italo de Bernardi and Mario Restelli. The jewellers of Rome, Venice, Florence and Naples, whose customers were mainly foreign tourists in search of souvenirs, preferred instead to imitate models from the past.

The third edition of the *International Exposition of Decorative Arts* held in Monza in 1927 was organised by Alfredo Ravasco in room 71 of the aristocratic Villa Reale. Here, the Milanese jeweller showed his works, a part of which had already been exhibited in Paris in 1925, together with others produced by the School of Coral Engraving of Torre del Greco, whence came the coral decorations "designed, modelled and mounted" by Ravasco. As Paolo Venturelli observes, "They were mostly illustrations of fish and sea creatures, luxuriant rose buds and fruits, in cascades and bunches, sometimes mixed with seed-pearls, used for decorating boxes, cups and bowls, mostly produced in the square and rationalist forms of Deco".[71]

Ravasco's works acquire sharper contours if observed from an Italian perspective, in the light of the artistic ferment of the lively Milanese scene of the 1920s. Indeed, his compositions constitute a meaningful statement of intent with their reference to the magnificence of classical tradition and their nod to geometries from the Deco period and the turn of the century and Metaphysics, with the outlandish addition of inserts gathered from the ancient world of animal and plant forms. It is no coincidence that Sarfatti was enthusiastic about the creations of Ravasco, whom she considered to be the only jeweller in tune with twentieth-century ambitions. Roberto Papini[72] also admired the works of the Milanese designer, seeing in them the expression of a jeweller able to combine architecture, sculpture and painting in miniature. Indeed, he came up with a definition of Ravasco's jewels as being "far from imitations of museum-pieces, the futurist avant-garde and the Far East", and considered him to be "one of the few genuine Italian success stories in Paris", an opinion shared by the international jury at the Paris exhibition, who awarded him a prize *hors concours*.

III. 1929–46: somewhere between the International Style and organicism

The Spell has been Broken is the name of a painting by Giacomo Balla that beautifully sums up the period between 1929 and the end of the Second World War. On 24 October 1929,[73] which was a Thursday, the Dow Jones index crashed by two hundred points, ruining thousands of savers. It was the beginning of a catastrophic global recession, accompanied by the deadly advance of totalitarian regimes in Europe. The Great Depression marked the decline of Art Deco, whose sophisticated and elite character was incompatible with the straitened circumstances the whole world was suddenly forced to reckon with. Luxury goods consumption fell drastically and everything had to be scaled down, bringing the values of tradition and necessity, but above all the correspondence between form and function, the principle at the root of the Modern Movement, back into favour. This aversion to luxury and decoration became open hostility towards the decorative arts and their products. Before President Roosevelt initiated the New Deal reforms to lift the country out of recession, Henry-Russell Hitchcock and Philip Johnson[74] organised the *Modern Architecture: International Exhibition* "at the newly opened New York Museum of Modern Art in 1932 with the aim of launching the new European avant-garde in America, defining and promoting its distinctive features and paying homage to its exponents, Ludwig Mies van der Rohe and Peter Oud in particular. This generated the International Style, which brought the Modern Movement closer to the United States, ridding it of European ideologies and leading it back to a formal style characterised by the principles of regularity and an emphasis on volume and the intrinsic elegance of material. The Modern Movement, with its rationalist matrix, coexisted with the organic aesthetics of Frank Lloyd Wright in the United States and with those of Álvar Aalto in Europe, which were therefore assimilated into the International Style. The International Style therefore marked the triumph of the Modern Movement in the world, whilst exposing its limits and bringing together categories it had made antithetical: form and function, technique and aesthetics, art and science. Indeed, Johnson and Hitchcock released beauty from functionalism's moral sanctions, bringing the formal aspect of objects closer to industrial manufacturing culture, the only one that could contain the *Zeitgeist* or the spirit of the age.

The flight of the *Norge* to the North Pole, the Zeiss planetarium in Jenae, and Flettner's rotor ship represented the closing stages of the mechanisation of the old world.

[71] Venturelli 2003, pp. 56–57.
[72] V. Terraroli, *Roberto Papini e "Le arti oggi"*, in Bossaglia and Terraroli 1999, pp. 129–55.
[73] Cf. J. K. Galbraith, *The Great Crash 1929* (Boston, Massachusetts: Mariner Books, 1997).
[74] A. Cappellieri, *Philip Johnson: dall'International Style al Decostruttivismo* (Naples: Clean, 1996).

Giacomo Balla
S'è rotto l'incanto (sketch),
c. 1920
Oil on canvas, 44.5 x 32.5 cm
Private collection, courtesy
Galleria Fonte d'Abisso, Milan

The definition of an industrial art that would reflect the demands of the Neue Sachlichkeit, the New Objectivity, became a priority. "Our age is lacking in pathos", wrote Mies van der Rohe. "We do not appreciate grand outbursts, but reason and reality … The individual is increasingly less important. His destiny does not interest us any more. In this the tendency of our age towards anonymity is clearly visible."[75] This led to a re-examination of the role of the artist in industrial production. Indeed, with the demand for technical and economic perfection came a renewed desire for formal beauty. As Walter Gropius wrote "It is clear that the mere material increase of products is no longer sufficient in order to break records in international competition. The technical object, which is everywhere excellent, has to be pervaded by a spiritual aura, by a form that will guarantee it is picked from the mass of products of the same genre. Consequently all of industry must be committed to tackling artistic matters seriously".[76]

On the other hand, "These were the depression years, the early 1930s, when economic paralysis gripped the nation. Manufactured goods served the purpose for which they were intended, but they came off production lines with a stagnant sameness. When business reached bottom, companies began to undercut each other. At the same time, some alert manufacturers came to the realisation that the answer to their problem lay in making their product work better, more convenient to the consumer, and better-looking".[77]

This gave rise to industrial design, favoured by the arrival in the United States of the European artistic *milieu* fleeing from totalitarian regimes. Walter Gropius, Marcel Breur, Ludwig Hilberseimer, Joan Miró, Marc Chagall, Marcel Duchamp, Piet Mondrian, Jean Tinguely, Roberto Matta, Josef Albers, Mies van der Rohe and other Bauhaus maestros, André Breton, Max Ernst with his wife Peggy Guggenheim, as well as philosophers Theodor Adorno, Max Horkheimer and Hannah Arendt moved to the United States, consolidating and spreading the new International Style.

The International Style put paid to the osmotic exchange between various artistic experiments that had characterised Art Nouveau as well as Deco. In the 1930s the distinction between the higher and lower arts had, as we have seen, assumed ideological connotations and the leaning towards a "useful" art definitively established the limits of the arts and with these the decline of decorative arts. The license of modernity therefore implied the necessary abandonment of any ornament or decoration, terms which seemed strictly correlated with the decorative arts, femininity and what Sigfried

Giedion accurately defined as the "decorative vanities".[78] Women's very role in society rejected that breezy boldness that had distinguished Deco, opting for a more conservative and traditional image, with long hair tied back, ankle length skirts and draped garments that emphasised the shape of the body and magnified its movements. This had nothing in common with Matisse's seductive odalisques, the subtle eroticism of Bonnard's bathing women, Chagall's ethereal and unreal creatures. After the androgynous silhouettes of the 1920s breasts and hips were once more valued as emblems of femininity.

At the same time, women's increasing participation in sports activities forced them to choose more comfortable clothing, aided by the spread, in the above-mentioned political climate, of military and party uniforms. In 1926 Coco Chanel launched the sober, practical and chic English fashion with some decidedly masculine touches whilst, in 1933, Elsa Schiaparelli, the most creative and original of the great French designers, introduced dresses with straight and boxy shoulders and shorter hemlines. Jewellery was hit harder by the recession, functionalist severity and "technical reproducibility"[79] than fashion.

"Contemporary jewellery must characterise our times, with its emphasis on space and structure, strong light, open forms, cantilever, floating structures and movements."[80]

With the Great Crash of 1929 jewellery did not merely lose its best customers but also its "aura" of a work of art. The collapse of the economy led to the abandonment of bold, formal experiments and an unexpected return to the value of materials. Jewels were once more easily exchangeable shelter goods, an investment against the fickleness of the stock exchange. The sophisticated innovations of Deco gave way to reassuring forms that held and guarded precious gems, increasingly difficult to find with the threat of war. At the same time, the aspirations of Neue Sachlichkeit were seen in chunky, flashy industrial jewellery, suitable for a vast public who preferred the reassuring value of gems and metals as a commodity to the jeweller's artistry. From the point of view of forms, as Melissa Gabardi notes, "we can confirm the plasticity and three-dimensional structure of jewellery, which increasingly resembles sculpture. The break with the absolute geometry of form is happening. We are seeing the return of the curved line, the circle, scrolls, spirals, and asymmetrical design".[81]

Forms became rounded, larger and gaudier and volumes increased. Purist geometries were replaced by the floral world of brooches and clips. White metals, which

[75] L. Mies van der Rohe, *Architettura e Volontà dell'epoca*, quoted in M. de Benedetti and A. Pracchi, *Antologia dell'architettura moderna* (Bologna: Zanichelli, 1988), p. 402.

[76] W. Gropius wrote an article about "The development of Modern Industrial Buildings" in 1913.

[77] H. Dreyfuss, *Designing for People* (New York, 1955).

[78] S. Giedion, *Bauen in Frankreich, Eisen, Eisenbeton* (Leipzig–Berlin, 1928), p. 49.

[79] W. Benjamin, *The Work of Art in the Age of Mechanical Reproduction*. For Benjamin the work of art at the beginning of the twentieth century, before the advent of the age of mechanical reproduction, enjoyed the status of authenticity and uniqueness. A work was a unique and original piece (not mass-produced) and authentic, or unrepeatable, destined to be exclusively enjoyed in the place where it was found. Benjamin called this *hic et nunc* of the work, its originality, unity, authenticity, uniqueness and exclusiveness of aesthetic enjoyment, its "aura". Otherwise, the work of art in the age of mechanical reproduction undergoes a process that "withers its aura".

[80] Margaret De Patta quoted by Y. Uchida in *The Jewelry of Margaret de Patta: A Retrospective Exhibition*, exhibition catalogue, Oakes Gallery, The Oakland Museum, 1976 (Oakland, California: Oakland Museum, 1976), p. 11; in T. Greenbaum, *Messengers of Modernism: American Studio Jewelry 1940– 1960* (Paris–New York: Montreal Museum of Decorative Arts and Flammarion, 1996), p. 36.

[81] M. Gabardi, *Gioielli anni 40 e 50* (Milan: Mondadori, 1995), p. 12.

had become more precious due to wartime rationing, were only used in the finest jewellery whilst yellow gold was favoured for the middle category, whose consecration arrived in 1937 in Paris at the *Exposition des Arts et Techniques dans la Vie Moderne*. This aesthetic choice was not merely motivated by alternating fashions but also by the changed economic circumstances and by platinum being in short supply. New technologies were introduced in which gold lent itself to being "coloured". Different and unpredictable nuances of gold, from pink to green to blue, were achieved with various alloys. These were mainly juxtaposed with turquoise, coral and rock crystal, in view of the difficulty in finding precious gems. In this twenty-year period jewellery typologies were aligned with various market segments according to the custom of the period: *haute* jewellery for an elite customer base, gold for a broad swath of the market, costume jewellery for the mass market. Eventually there was also art jewellery, transversal to every market, which found a niche of its own in the 1960s.

In jewellery the International Style failed – except in rare cases like that of the artist jewellers of the UAM (Union des Artistes Moderns) – to achieve the stylistic homogeneity and functional "objectivity" of the higher arts and instead oscillated between the decorative richness of *animalier*, the many hues of *Tutti frutti* and the geometrical compositions of Deco, in an abundance of themes and forms that would only be clearly defined in the 1950s. In the post-war period new motifs were introduced such as the "snowflake" (1945), the "marine" motif, which consisted of waves and shells, and gold and platinum meteors. The first of the successful "ballerina" clips of Van Cleef & Arpels was produced in 1945, while in subsequent years birds of every type, from chaffinches to parrots to birds of paradise, became tremendously popular.

At this time technological and typological innovations, such as Van Cleef & Arpels' *pavé secret* or Cartier's *tuyau à gaz* clip and technique, or the transformable jewels (the necklace that divided into two bracelets, the brooch made up of two separate clips, the middle part of the bracelet that could be made into a brooch), variations of which were produced by many jewellers, were more interesting.

New techniques were also discovered for the industrial production of *bijoux*, particularly regarding the fusion of materials (in 1904 Léon Guillet had invented stainless steel and, in 1907, Leo Bakeland had invented Bakelite, the first heat resistant synthetic material), useful for producing finished pieces without welding, and polishing with hot nickel without the need to intervene manually. In 1928 Swarovski imported their crystal into the United States, improving de facto the quality of *bijoux*. On the back of the economic crisis, Hollywood's burgeoning movie industry and new technologies, this proved to be America's most original contribution to the diffusion of costume jewellery.

"In the years following the Great Depression", wrote Deanna Farneti Cera, "the fall in the demand for real jewels forced jewellers and craftsmen to redirect their talents towards the costume jewellery sector, which, although in a critical state, was more commercially viable, partly due to former jewellers and specialised craftsmen taking the quality of the non-precious ornament to extremely high and new levels."[82] Coco Chanel, together with Paul Poiret, Madeleine Vionnet and Elsa Schiaparelli, but also thanks to Auguste Bonaz and Henkel & Grosse's Bakelite creations, cleared costume jewellery of its association with the imitation jewel. "Nothing resembles a fake jewel so much as a beautiful jewel", maintained Coco forcefully. "Why become fixated on a precious stone? It is the same as wearing a cheque around your neck. The jewel has a colourful, mystical and ornamental value. It contains every value apart from those which are expressed in carats."[83] In 1932 the International Diamond Guild commissioned her to make some real jewels for charity. Chanel worked in partnership with Iribe, this time producing strictly precious, articulated and transformable pieces, and declaring that, "In this age of poverty, supreme elegance lies precisely in the unusual exhibition of wealth". Yet her passion for costume jewellery had not diminished and, shortly afterwards, she went back to producing flashy and extrovert *bijoux* designed by Fulco Santostefano della Cerda, Duke of Verdura. Verdura designed for Paul Flato, a renowned New York jeweller, as well as for Chanel. When, in 1937, Flato opened a branch in Los Angeles, he sent Verdura to direct it. Here the designer made some famous friends and customers including Gary Cooper, James Stewart, Marlene Dietrich, Jack Benny, Rita Hayworth, Olivia de Havilland, Katharine Hepburn and many others. Verdura worked with Paul Flato from 1937 to 1939 and then opened his own *maison* in New York. An eccentric character and a Sicilian aristocrat, he drew inspiration for his jewellery from nature's variety and from history. His jewels were always deliberately enormous so as to trumpet their fakeness whilst complementing the simplicity of Chanel's clothes. The pieces were made by Maison Gripoix and were such that they transformed even stones made of coloured glass into luxury items. It is hardly surprising Aldous Huxley described the Chanel look as "rich and sumptuous simplicity", an oxymoron that

[82] *I gioielli della fantasia*, edited by D. Farneti Cera (Milan: Idea Books, 1991), p. 150.
[83] Coco Chanel quoted in E. Morini, *Storia della moda XVIII–XX secolo* (Milan: Skira, 2000), p. 181.

accurately sums up the philosophy of the Chanel *maison*. "I love fake jewels because I find them provocative and I also think it is shameful to go around wearing millions around one's neck just because one is rich. The purpose of the jewel is not to make a woman seem rich but to adorn her. It is not the same thing."[84]

American costume jewellery perfectly epitomises the aspirations of the International Style, due both to the fact that it could be produced serially and to the internationalisation of its applications. This fashion came to North American shores from Paris and made its home there. Favoured by the movie culture of Hollywood and by the extraordinary manufacturing capacity of the district of Providence, as well as contingent economic conditions, costume jewellery soon became a complete expression of the American style. On the other hand the ambition for a better life encouraged many women to identify with movie stars. The accessories of Gloria Swanson, Greta Garbo, Marlene Dietrich and Bette Davis were designed by Miriam Haskell,[85] the great designer of American costume jewellery, who made handmade jewels with infinite patience, as perfect on the back as they were on the front. Starting in 1942 the majority of jewels were made in "vermeil" or gilded silver. This new plating was extremely robust and long-lasting and the new pieces made in vermeil were sometimes produced using the lost wax method until then reserved for precious ornaments. The step from Made in Paris to Made in USA is neatly summarised by tailor Adrian: "I have the impression that the movies are becoming the Paris of America. Consequently women who go to the movies can use stars as their guide to fashion".[86] "For Hollywood everything was larger than life, more than anything that had existed before or since", wrote Diana Vreeland. "Diamonds were larger, furs were plusher, the silks, the satins, the chiffons were richer and shinier. There were thousands of ostrich and marabou feathers, silver fox and sable, miles of coloured beads, paste and sequins. Hollywood was paved with splendor, gloss and glory. Everything was an exaggeration of history, fiction and the entire fantastic world. After all, nothing was too lovely for Hollywood and for Hollywood nothing was too lovely for the people."[87] The dream carried the signatures of Miriam Haskell, Eugene Joseff, Trifari, Coro, Hobé and Boucher, Hattie Carnegie, Mazer, Pennino, De Rosa and Monet. Many jewellery firms, like Eisenberg, switched from jewellery to *bijoux* and the production of costume jewellery catalysed the energies of the best designers in America. Alfred Philippe, after years of collaborating with Van Cleef & Arpels, joined Trifari in 1930

and Boucher left Cartier to devote himself to costume jewellery. Elsa Schiaparelli continued to create *bijoux* designed by Jean Schlumberger, the artist who linked his name to Tiffany in the 1950s.

Hollywood had not just contributed to launching costume jewellery but had also provided new sap for *haute* jewellery. In the 1940s New York became the capital of the new world and Hollywood and its stars determined the fashions. Without the influence of Europe, Americans managed to achieve independence in art and fashion. Above all, fashion was, for the first time, conceived with the sporty and casual American lifestyle in mind, rather than that of the French model of the *haute couture* woman. The ornaments produced in this period, essential for embellishing short, simple dresses, were influenced by topical events. Patriotic brooches (flags, anchors, wings) went hand in hand with brooches illustrating sentimental and naturalistic themes represented by infinite varieties of flowers, hearts and animals. Tiffany was confirmed as a paragon of taste not just in jewels but also in items for the home. In 1940 it moved to its current headquarters to the corner of 57th Street and Fifth Avenue, an eighteen-floor emporium crammed with luxury items, which was defined as the most glittering junction, a "corner of luxury", even before Audrey Hepburn made it a global point of reference. By diffusing the glossy glamour of Hollywood stars the movie industry fuelled its own legend, relying on luxury and opulence. If costume jewellery was large and ostentatious due to movie set demands then so was *haute* jewellery. Tiffany united jewellers Harry Winston, Paul Flato and Trabert & Hoeffer who, as we shall see, had taken over the extraordinary Mauboussin collection. They produced collector's pieces for high society ladies and for movie stars to show off on special occasions.

Floral organicism came back into fashion but stripped of its fantastic references. The American floral was emotive, vibrant and obvious. Arthur Barney, head of Tiffany silver, made two floral jewels for the World Fair of New York in 1939, a two-dimensional orchid made of diamonds and rubies, and an abstract flower made of gold, designed creatively with a *baguette* cut emerald in the centre, topped by white and yellow diamonds, with four gold petals, each of whose tips was decorated with white diamonds, and three leaves of circular cut yellow diamonds and *baguette* emeralds. New York jeweller Seaman Schepps interpreted the modernist style in a simpler and more colourful way with a bracelet made of five flowers with gold petals that surrounded just half of the central *cabochon* sapphires, but anyway creating the impression of whole corollas. The

[84] Ibid., p. 182.
[85] D. Farneti Cera, *I gioielli di Miriam Haskell* (Milan: Idea Books, 1997), p. 14.
[86] Quoted in D. Farneti Cera, *Il lusso della libertà*, p. 161.
[87] Ibid.

realistically designed life-sized flowers, reproduced in every tiny detail, counterbalanced the black/white of Deco and satisfied the now peaceful 1940s' desire for colour. In particular, roses were made to faithfully resemble the actual flower: like Trabert & Hoeffer Inc. Mauboussin's necklace of 1938 made of platinum and diamonds for Queen Nazli of Egypt, with two spectacular rose buds and foliage; Marcus & Co.'s brooch with a rose made of diamonds and another of rubies, with green enamelled leaves: a blown rose accompanied by a bud on a brooch designed by Paul Flato. When worn these brooches created the impression that real flowers had been fixed to the dress. Gardenias were also rather popular. Oscar Heyman designed his first gardenia in 1936, which reflected the credo of the founder of the *maison*: "Jewellery should never be a candidate for redesign but should transcend time like a fine painting, never losing its appeal".

Paul Flato was one of the jewellers most beloved of the Hollywood "starlets". His jewels were a regal homage to their beauty and caprice, like the "corset" bracelet with ruby and diamond garter inspired by Mae West's lingerie, or the "gold-digger" bracelet, one of many made in 1938 for the film *Holiday*, with a gold pick and a black enamel clip with Katharine Hepburn's initials. Flato also took up the abstract floral theme, inspired by current trends in modern art, which was becoming popular with 1940s' *couturiers* as an alternative to the naturalistic rendering. Significant examples are the pieces created by Paul Flato in 1934, including a geometrical brooch decorated with diamond motifs, which, once fastened, could host a bouquet of real flowers. Flato's jewellery was described as follows by his peers: "A jewel of distinctive charm and practicality, combining the luxurious softness of living flowers with the ever enduring beauty of precious stones".

1939 was a year of eccentric behaviour due to the wave of prosperity and the desire to look to the future. The New York World Fair celebrated progress and the most prestigious American jewellers – Tiffany, Black, Starr & Frost-Gorham, Udall & Ballou, and Marcus & Co – displayed their finest pieces. During the 1930s and early 1940s the fashion for customised made-to-order jewellery spread. Julius Cohen devoted himself to creating traditional jewellery with precious stones and introduced an innovation that had more to do with models of distribution than with the form of the jewellery. Although his salon-workshop was in New York, the majority of his work was done at the homes of his customers who relied on Cohen for jewellery designed ad hoc. However, in 1947, on the West Coast, William

Ruser and his wife Pauline launched their company Ruser in Rodeo Drive in Los Angeles, employing forty staff and twenty-two qualified workers to satisfy the demand for the sculpted gold jewels they produced.

"A world was ending, another was about to be born. I was there: an opportunity came up. I took it. I was the same age as a new century which turned to me for its wardrobe. Simplicity, comfort, sharpness were what was required. It didn't know it but I gave it all of this. Real successes are fatal."[88]

In France the last embers of a unique era were dying out. In 1929 French jewellers held an exhibition at Palais Galliera. Deco polychromy was abandoned in favour of black and white, illuminated by *pavé* set or *baguette* cut diamonds. The favoured metal was platinum, contrasted with black onyx. It was the triumph of *mode blanche*, of silver and colourless synthetic stones, of aluminium, steel, nickel, glass and rock crystal. In 1931 Jean Fouquet, Georges' son, published *Bijoux et orfevrerie*, in which he maintained that "The jewel must be something you can see from afar: miniatures are detestable".[89] Curiously, this affirmation of Fouquet, one of the greatest exponents of French Deco, was reciprocated by the large dimension of costume jewellery. As well as the need for visibility, they had research and innovation in common, although in American jewellery the focus was on materials whilst in Fouquet's jewellery it was on forms and compositions. As early as 1925 Fouquet had produced a brooch made of yellow and grey gold, rock crystal and polished onyx, black enamel and diamonds in which the volumes were clearly defined and marked by clear-cut lines and the shapes were emphasised with the contrasting colours of the geometrical elements. Two-dimensional figures gave way to a three-dimensional style and Fouquet was one of the first to propose original jewels, stripped of any superfluous ornament, precious architectures which drew on the International Style's emphasis on volume and dictated the rules of taste for the whole of the 1940s. In 1934 Georges Fouquet coined the term *bijoutiers-artistes* to identify this group of jewellery innovators, the leaders of whom were his son Jean Fouquet, Jean Després, Raymond Templier and Gérard Sandoz, the last great French master jewellers. The career of the latter was extremely short, despite his evident talent. Sandoz renewed the French jewel with the force of his compositional symmetry and his mastery of colour variations. In his works the starkness of the geometry was attenuated by the chromatic softness of the gems, whose reflections could be seen better at close range. Unfortunately Sandoz was unable to weather the economic crisis and in 1931 he

[88] Coco Chanel quoted in Morini 2000, p. 171.
[89] J. Fouquet quoted in Gabardi 2001, p. 154.

retired from the jewellery business in order to concentrate on painting.

A further acceleration of the modernisation of the French jewel came from the Union des Artistes Modernes (UAM), founded in 1929, of which Raymond Templier was a founding member, along with René Herbst, Robert Mallet-Stevens, Jean Puiforcat, Hélène Henry and Pierre Chareau. Like the CIAM (Congrès Internationaux d'Architecture Moderne) for architecture, UAM also aspired to a "truly social art suitable for progress and able to integrate present-day industrial forms and technologies struggling against classicism and tradition".[90] At the first public demonstration, organised by Papillon de Marsan in 1930, UAM reasserted its enlightened desire to break with the past and with tradition. The advocate of this modernisation was Raymond Templier, whose jewellery and attitudes fell in with the principles of the International Style, which would shortly afterwards become established as the dominant aesthetic model. An aesthetic in which functional purity, mechanical geometry and rigorous volumetry made jewellery a paradigm of modernity. Templier's jewels were micro-architectures and, as such, achieved three-dimensionality by means of a clever use of colour. The alternation of volumes and voids, mass and lightness followed the rules of construction in that "learned game, correct and magnificent, of forms assembled in the light", which for Le Corbusier meant architecture. And, indeed, first Templier's and then Jean Després' jewellery recall the rarefied abstraction of Le Corbusier's Ville Savoye or Mies van der Rohe's Barcelona pavilion, where the principle of *nihil addi* reigns supreme. Templier affirmed: "The composition of the jewel must be simultaneously free and bursting forth, closed and concentrated. A found rhythm has something of the absolute, definitive, unmodifiable"[91]; and critic Gastonne Varenne specified "He wants, in short, to create a jewel stripped of superfluous ornaments and decorations in order to produce an object of elegant sobriety which is architectonically constructed and able to arouse more intellectual than emotional enjoyment".[92] Therefore, Templier ruled out using large gems in his jewellery so that the value of the stone would not eclipse the design of the jewel. Equally he avoided animal and plant *imagerie*, drawing inspiration from the aesthetics of the car, sport and leisure. In 1929 he employed designer Marcel Percheron, with whom he collaborated for about thirty years. Templier closed his business for good in 1965.

Jean Després, a member of UAM, was another extraordinary exponent of that aesthetic of function postulated by Adorno in which beauty assumes the forms of truth: a blend of structure and casing, setting and gem, geometry and form, truth unmediated by any decoration, according to the canons of the apostasy of the age. As we read in Melissa Gabardi's fine essay, "It is the biography of the artist that determines his aesthetic choices … And so we see that the designer of airplane engines is the same person who will later design and produce the highly original *bijoux moteurs*: brooches, necklaces and bracelets in the shape of cams, piston rods, gears, wheels, pistons and ball-bearings prevalently made of silver".[93] Després' works have a more timeless elegance than the works of Templier. In them everything, from the choice of colour to the composition of forms, reveals a seamless harmony between the parts, as shown by the 1928 ring made of silver, gold, black and brown lacquer or the tubular silver and gold necklace that dates from the same year. Després was one of the few jewellers who did not hail from a noble dynasty of jewellers and this is why he was usually defined as "the man of metal and hammer". As for his materials, he worked mainly with silver, very much in vogue in the 1930s, combined with onyx, coral, turquoise, lapis lazuli and chalcedony, all at affordable prices consistent with the recession that was underway. Després' work was divided into *bijoux glacés*, *moteurs* and *bijoux ceramiques*, merging the various artistic experiences that he had gained from working with artists such as painters Etienne Cournault and Jean-Claude Mayodon. From his work with the former came the *bijoux glacés*, exhibited in 1930 at the Pavillon de Marsan at the exhibition set up by UAM. These were mainly jewels made of silver, with partially enamelled gold inlays and surrealist inspired glass engraved or painted by Cournault generally placed in the centre. Mayodon, director of the Sèvres factory, supplied him with ceramic elements to include in his so-called *bijoux céramiques*. Nicknamed the "Picasso of jewellery" Després was a clever promoter of his own image, making sure he attended every national and international exposition as well as solo and group exhibitions, and working with artists and colleagues. In this too he was a genius.

At the same time *bijoutiers-artistes* working in France *haute* jewellery *maisons* confirmed their usual levels of excellence, despite the difficulty of finding gems and metals and despite falling sales, above all in the American market. At that time international jewellery of a high standard was the monopoly of Cartier, Van Cleef & Arpels, Boucheron and Mauboussin, whilst domestic markets were catered to by large jewellers who interpreted local fashions, mediating them with French influences. These included Tiffany and Paul Flato in the

[90] Ibid.
[91] R. Moutard-Uldry, "Raymond Templier architecte du bijou moderne", in *Mobilier et Décoration* 8, November 1954; quoted in Gabardi 2001, p. 151.
[92] Ibid.
[93] Ibid., p. 156; cf. by the same author *Jean Després, maestro orafo tra Art Déco e avanguardie* (Milan: Idea Books, 1999); *Jean Déspres, Jeweler, Maker and Designer of the Machine Age* (New York: Thames & Hudson, 2009).

United States, Wolfers in Belgium, Garrard in England, Mario Buccellati and Bulgari in Italy, Bucherer and Gubelin in Switzerland and Germany, and Lacloche in Spain. At the beginning of the 1930s the most sophisticated jewels still came in shades of white and were made of diamonds set in platinum or white gold, where the setting was designed to exalt the beauty and value of the stones. Motifs grew softer with curves, folds and spirals. Long earrings alternated with necklaces with large, boxy links studded with diamonds. In 1935 Van Cleef & Arpels introduced one of the most important innovations in the history of twentieth-century jewellery: *pavé secret*, *serti mystérieux* or "invisible setting", which transformed a technique into a work of art. Lia Lenti correctly defined the *maison* the "Descartes of French jewellery"[94] due to its capacity for wedding tradition and innovation, technology and beauty. The technique consisted in positioning one stone next to another in an extraordinarily uniform monochromatic mosaic without revealing a single trace of the bezel. Rubies and sapphires, perfectly matched in terms of colour and size, had to be cut with enormous precision by a highly skilled lapidary as they had to fit exactly into their slots. A single clip can sometimes require up to eight hundred stones and many may break during the process. This technique added a remarkable degree of flexibility to the aesthetic beauty of the jewel, producing extremely natural results. It generated extraordinary floral compositions with soft petals and furled leaves such as roses, peonies and holly leaves that, despite the recession, sold straightaway. *Serti mystérieux* was also applied to new types of jewellery such as clips, cufflinks, bracelets and boxes, but the floral motif was the most popular, above all in clips and *boule* rings. Floral Van Cleef & Arpels jewels remained fashionable until the 1960s, especially the motif from the *Hawaii* collection with its small sprays of multicolour flowers on clips, earrings, bracelets and necklaces. Another significant invention was the "passe-partout" necklace composed of a "serpent chain" made of yellow gold, to which clips were attached which could be unfastened and applied to hats or clothes, a sign of the interchangeability of evening and daytime jewellery.

Likewise, Cartier continued in the 1930s to develop both the polychromy of *Tutti frutti* and the purity of *mode blanche*, shown by their platinum, polished rock crystal and diamond bracelet dating from 1930. With regard to this Franco Cologni and Eric Nussbaum wrote "the use of different materials led to unusual and very new, even scandalous colour combinations".[95] The blue and green of *Tutti frutti* and the white of the diamonds and platinum were combined in forms which were gentler than those of Deco thanks to the spectacular effects produced by the new techniques. In 1933, in the same year as Van Cleef, Cartier filed a patent for *serti mystérieux*, though this technique did not connote its works as it did the works of Van Cleef & Arpels. Instead, the objects shown at the exposition of 1937 marked the definitive decline of Art Deco and introduced yellow gold together with the *tuyau à gaz* or "serpent" technique, which became one of the most recurring themes in jewellery in the 1950s. The result was flexible jewellery with an emphasis on materials. The same research informed the jewellery of Boucheron, who used the *polonaise* chain on bracelets and watches, rendering them mobile and articulated, with an elegant play of the textures of gold and stones.

Despite their extraordinary creative strength, Mauboussin were unable to avoid closing their New York branch in the wake of the economic crisis of 1929. A part of the collections was sold to Americans Trabert & Hoeffer and from that moment on jewellery with the trademark "Trabert & Hoeffer Inc. Mauboussin" was sold successfully to a vast public. The *Reflection* collection in particular succeeded in blending the sophistication of French jewellery with the vivacity of its American equivalent. The *Reflection* range marked a moment of growth in the history of American jewellery whilst for Mauboussin it signified the capacity to combine art and market. Georges continued on his quest for excellence, purchasing some of the loveliest gems in the world: the *Nassak*, an eighty-nine carat diamond, the fifty-six carat *Porte Rhodes* and the *Beauharnais* emerald. The uniqueness of these stones was reflected in extraordinary jewels destined for an exclusive clientele.

"The history of modern jewellery in Italy is linked to a name: that of Ravasco."[96] This is how Gio Ponti's magazine *Domus* described the works of jewellery presented at the Fifth Milan Triennial exposition in 1933. On that occasion the *saletta degli orafi* regained its dignity at the *International Exposition of Modern Industrial Decorative Arts* revealing, as well as Alessandro Sordelli and Mario Codevilla, the extraordinary talent of Alfredo Ravasco, at the height of his fame, in three showcases, where he exhibited "nineteen pieces: three boxes, two clocks, two magnificent centrepieces, three cups, two necklaces, two clips, a bracelet, two gold cases and a handbag zip fastener, as well as a reliquary cabinet".[97] Alfredo Ravasco may be considered the most important Italian jeweller of the first half of the century, whose participation at international expositions and Triennials proved decisive for the innovation in

[94] L. Lenti, *Van Cleef & Arpels e il gioiello esclusivo*, in *L'arte del gioiello e il gioiello d'artista* (Florence) 2001, p. 225.
[95] F. Cologni and E. Nussbaum, *Cartier, l'arte del platino* (Milan: Mondadori, 1995).
[96] In *Domus* – the renowned magazine published in Milan since 1928, devised and directed by Gio Ponti, which featured a special issue for each Triennial, in which decorative arts finally found a measure of autonomous dignity – an article on the Triennial and, in particular, the "jewellers' room", containing eight works by Milanese Alessandro Sordelli and a jewel created by Mario Codevilla, began by saying, without mincing words, that the state of modern jewellery in Italy was then almost solely identified with the name of Ravasco, who inaugurated "A full, opulent and massy manner with simple and expressive designs"; in *Domus* 66, June 1933, pp. 313–13.
[97] Ibid.

design and semantics of Italian jewellery. He exhibited for the last time at the Seventh Triennial in Milan in 1940. This was also the last Triennial of the Fascist period, where jewellery was allocated a meagre amount of space. In 1936 the Sixth Triennial dedicated an exhibition to ancient Italian jewellery, curated by Franco Albini and Giovanni Romano, memorable above all for its layout, whose ethereal and futuristic *allure* contrasted not a little with the *grandeur* of the jewellery of a bygone age.

The Triennials introduced the new jewellery techniques of the large French *maisons* and the *mode blanche* which was successfully reworked by the major jewellers of the period. Cusi, Villa, Faraone, Bulgari, Settepassi, Janesich, Musy, Missaglia, Masenza and Illario produced jewels in platinum and grey gold plated with sumptuous, symmetrical, geometrical *pavés* of brilliants.[98] Of the models in vogue in Italy it is worth recalling the "plaque" brooch whose generally rectangular or hexagonal structure was unfailingly studded with diamonds. Marilena Mosco has noted that, of the Italians, d'Annunzio's jeweller Mario Buccellati "caught the eye for having imaginatively designed jewels with the most disparate materials, producing classical and neo-Renaissance, Byzantine or barbaric models, continuing to find new formal solutions and, above all, knowing how to work gold and silver using an exclusive technique called *à tulle* or honeycomb".[99] This was a lengthy and complicated technique for working precious metals that used classical Renaissance criteria. Lia Lenti observed that brooches were getting steadily bigger and were even pinned to jacket lapels and shirt collars. Several bracelets with articulated links and *lanière* were worn together at the wrist and over tight-fitting sleeves, in the French fashion. Even larger and more garish dangling earrings were shown off by short, straight and wavy hairstyles. The practical wristwatch, a sign of modernity and emancipation, became a popular feminine ornament. Watch-jewels were worn in the evening and had an all or partially metallic strap, mounted with stones and made up of articulated links in various geometrical shapes.[100] In the 1930s and 1940s, Italian jewellery oscillated between experimental jewels, such as those produced by Ravasco, and traditional jewels, increasingly inclined to favour the value of the material over that of the design. Indeed, curiously, French production was referenced for *haute* jewellery models rather than the experimental jewellery of *bijoutiers-artistes*. The works of master jewellers such as Jean Després and Raymond Templier had no significant impact in Italy but were decisive in an international environment in terms of highlighting the interaction between the artistic object and the plasticity and mobility of the body.

Following their example, art jewellery was making a name for itself in a volatile exchange between artists and jewellers determined to apply their own forms of expression to the jewel as object. In 1926 American Alexander Calder moved to Paris where he made structured toys that no-one bought. In autumn the same year he created *Cirque Calder*, a piece that led him to produce kinetic objects and his first, extraordinary wire jewels. As well as Calder, Harry Bertoia and Margaret De Patta are two of the principal explorers of the points of intersection of art and jewellery, while in Italy it was necessary to wait until the 10th Triennial of 1954, where the jewels of Salvador Dalí were exhibited and where art jewellery became established as one of the most vital expressions of Italian jewellery.

In 1946 MoMA in New York organised an exhibition entitled *Modern Jewelry Design*, which exhibited the works of Calder, Bertoia, José de Rivera, Jacques Lipchitz, Richard Pousette-Dart, Margaret De Patta, Adda Husted-Anderson, Paul Lobel and others. As Toni Greenbaum observes "The approach of Calder and Bertoia to the process of jewelry making was coincidentally akin to that of the tribal smith. Several Modernist jewelers who were to come later displayed the same tendencies. However it is important to note that any metalsmith, whether naïve or sophisticated, who approaches metal in a rudimentary manner by the direct forging of wire will empirically arrive at many of the same conclusions. Modernist jewelers were, therefore, not necessarily intent upon creating jewelry in a primitive manner. They were, in fact, like the tribal metalsmith, actually evolving pieces with technique as content".[101]

Calder's influence also extended to fashion, with his famous collection of clothes inspired by the circus, which Elsa Schiaparelli presented in Paris in 1937. The circus clothes were complemented with metal jewels designed by Jean Schlumberger. These were simple, cheerful, new and witty ornaments mainly inspired by Dadaism and Surrealism. Compared to Chanel, Schiaparelli's fashions were decidedly more eccentric, especially the jewellery designed by her surrealist friends, such as Jean Clément's electrically lit pieces or Louis Argon's aspirin necklace. Christian Bérard, Salvador Dalí and Jean Cocteau also designed pieces for Schiaparelli, including earrings in the shape of telephones, necklaces hung with peapods and brooches in the shape of ostriches, skates, eyes, insects, bagpipes and even the pattern of moles on her cheek. Fashion and art met in jewellery

[98] Cf. I. de Guttry, M. P. Maino and M. Quesada, *Le arti minori d'autore in Italia dal 1900 al 1930* (Rome–Bari: Laterza, 1985).
[99] After the design was indicated by the jeweller, materials were chosen, followed by expert craftsmen tracing it onto metal plates and then, with a small hand drill, making a hole in the centre of each "beehive" template. The pentagon shape of the hole was made with a tiny saw. This was followed by cleaning, done by pulling a cotton thread impregnated with pumice stone through each hole. This required skilled labour, experts in the most up-to-date techniques.
[100] L. Lenti, *Gioielli e gioiellieri di Valenza. Arte e storia orafa 1825–1975* (Milan: Allemandi, 1993).
[101] Greenbaum 1996, p. 25.

and the major artists of the age, though not jewellers themselves, took an interest in the theme of the ornament. These artists included Calder, Picasso, Max Ernst, Jean Arp, Dalí followed by Man Ray, Giacometti, Arman, Lichtenstein, Fontana and Niki de Saint Phalle.

Oscar Wilde wrote "The only thing that can console one for being poor is extravagance", and were this true one might be able to understand why this period, which was certainly one of the least happy in history, was so crammed with pomp and fake glitter. In 1940 "L'oiseau en cage", the symbol of occupied France, appeared in the windows of Cartier in rue de la Paix and Madame Toussaint was summoned by the Nazis.

IV. 1947–67: from the New Look to Pop

The ideological rigour of the Modern Movement clearly revealed its weakness in the post-war period, when the "economic miracle" (the *Financial Times* definition of 1959) of the 1950s generated a frenetic desire for consumption whose explosive force swept away any functionalist reluctance. Industrial reorganisation and the start of free trade with the United States were at the basis of the economic wellbeing that determined mass culture, which was defined by Edgar Morin as *L'Esprit du Temps*.[102] The nations hardest hit by the war aimed to once more take up their rightful place in the sphere of global commerce, whilst reconstruction brought with it a revival of the arts, fashion and design. The latter especially became the most complete expression of the new society; it developed as industrial design in the United States but design linked to culture and lifestyle in the case of Italy. The aura of "Made in Italy", the most important brand in the world, which combined product quality with a taste for *la dolce vita*, was thus born. The driving force behind growth was, principally, the growth of the consumeristic middle class in those years, which was celebrated the Pop Art of Andy Warhol and Roy Lichtenstein. Between 1950 and 1955 MoMA of New York and the Merchandise Mart of Chicago organised a series of exhibitions entitled *Good Design* with the aim of showing that "Good Design is Good Business",[103] and that a partnership between art and commerce was not only possible but also mutually beneficial. The austere face of modernity, in which form had to bow to function, therefore gave way to comfortable, seductive, and playful "good design", with evident repercussions and elements of innovation for jewellery too. Georg Jensen, in particular, exhibited furniture, glass, ceramics and fabrics made of light silver, in addition to his jewellery, showing Americans and, therefore, the world the commercial potential and design quality of Scandinavian design.[104]

The world economy picked up speed again and the West rediscovered the fun and joys of a happy-go-lucky society life. Theatres reopened, parties and balls returned and there were many opportunities for entertainment. This was the decade of Marilyn Monroe, Elvis Presley, James Dean, Billy Wilder, the Duke and Duchess of Windsor, Truman Capote and the Beat generation, household appliances, the discovery of leisure time and the bikini, "today's myths" analysed by Roland Barthes in 1957. This was followed by the subversive 1960s, which were destined to shatter the peace of the previous decade. It was the era of Swinging London, Mary Quant's miniskirts, Kerouac and the culture of "On the Road", youth demos, rock and unisex, consumerism and pop. The swinging 1960s "were a period of major political, social and cultural revolutions. Relationships between races, generations, classes, sexes, society and politics were changed forever, becoming more open, tolerant and democratic".[105] Art, literature and music underwent profound innovations and adopted new expressions. Television brought new ideas and new lifestyles into people's homes. Pacifist and non-violent ideals spread amongst young people, along with a new sexual freedom encouraged by the contraceptive pill, which became available in 1960.

Luxury reverted to being a factor of capitalist growth and a spur to modernisation. It was no coincidence that the American Diners Club introduced the first credit card in 1950, announcing the birth of virtual money. The 1950s were the last great decade for Paris *couture*, whose fashions were decidedly more thrilling than its accessories, jewellery included. In the post-war period neither art nor architecture made the same explosive impact as fashion and its high priests. Pierre Balmain, Jacques Fath, Cristobal Balenciaga, Pierre Cardin, Yves Saint Laurent, Chanel (who had closed the *maison* in 1939 and reopened it in 1954) soon made people forget the horrors of war. Christian Dior uniquely satisfied women's desire for new luxuries with his *New Look* of 1947 which harked back to the splendours of the *Belle Epoque*. It was a dream in which soft shapes and the generous squandering of fabric symbolised optimism and opulence and, above all, redress for the dullness and poverty of wartime fabrics. The New Look was seen as a promise of wellbeing, elegance and *joie de vivre*, and represented the most complete expression of the new frenzy for sumptuary consumption. The notion of plenty was manifested physically with the arrival of buxom women. Sophia Loren, Elizabeth Taylor and, above all, Marilyn who, with her platinum blonde hair, consecrated the unforgettable *Gentlemen prefer Blondes*

[102] In 1947 Theodor W. Adorno and Max Horkheimer published *Dialectics of Illuminism* in which the term "culture industry" was used instead of "mass culture" to prevent the latter being confused with a contemporary form of popular art. The Marxist critique of the production of commodities was also applied to symbolic goods and the cultural industries were seen as an extension of other capitalist industries. The new cultural forms were determined not by artistic logics, but by the simple motivation of accumulation of capital, where the only effect cultural products had was to manipulate desire and attract consumers. In 1962 a French sociologist, Edgar Morin, in his most famous work, *L'Esprit du Temps*, re-evaluated mass culture instead, taking a stance which was almost directly opposed to that of the Frankfurters. Morin set himself the goal, not to exalt, but to put the role of high culture back into perspective.

[103] J. Loring in *Tiffany's 20th Century: A Portrait of American Style* (New York: Abrams, 1997), p. 201.

[104] The exchanges between the United State and Scandinavian countries were particularly intense at this time. Between November 1956 and January 1957 an exhibition entitled *Young Americans–Young Scandinavians* was staged at the Museum of Contemporary Craft in New York to bring the two cultures closer to good design.

[105] L. Cocciolo and D. Sala, *Storia illustrata della moda e del costume* (Verona: Demetra, 2001), p. 260.

and the nipped-in waist and tight-fitting sweaters that showed off generous forms exalted by highly architectonic lingerie. From vamp to angel at the hearth, the difference was a matter of degree since both aspired to a coordinated lifestyle: from "twin sets" to "matching sets", from the blender to the sofa, the rule was a harmony of references that linked fashion to living. And it was this association that enabled the fame of "Made in Italy" to spread across the world.

"Our age of anxiety is, in large part, the result of trying to do today's work with yesterday's instruments and concepts".[106]

In the 1950s and 1960s there was no formal harmony of stylistic features, such as might furnish an unequivocal definition of a style, and neither, interestingly, was there any local specificity of excellence but rather underlying themes that sinuously intersected in a play of references between the higher and lower arts. Jewellery felt the organic influences that were developing in the United States and the Scandinavian countries, just as it clearly held vestiges of the modernity of the International Style, yet none of these trends was as gripping as those found in fashion, whose shockwave proved to be devastating in jewellery as in clothes. Jewellery docilely complied with the dictates of *couturiers*. Never before had jewellery so evidently been an accessory. Which did not – and does not – detract from its artistic value. Nor, much less, did it represent a renunciation of quality in favour of the transitory nature of fashion. It was rather an awareness that society was changing and was therefore a manufacturing response to mass consumption, whose boundaries were and are clearly distinct from the elite ones of art, to which traditional jewellery and more daring designers answered and still answer. Women had changed and so had their clothes and habits. Cocktail jewellery emerged at the same time as the cocktail dress. Costume jewellery, which flaunted its design rather than the material it was made of more than Art Nouveau jewellery, played an important part in this. And while it is true that costume jewellery did not seek innovation, having never entirely abandoned its attempt to revive "haute" references, it is also undeniable that its evolution from "appearance to use"[107] was instead heavily influenced by technological innovations linked to materials. These ranged from Swarovski's paste, adored by Marilyn, to the fake diamonds discovered in 1955 by American physicist Percy Bridgman,[108] Nobel prize-winner in 1946, or the introduction of plastic (created in 1954 by another Nobel prize-winner, Giulio Natta, with the first polypropylene fibre), widely used to produce jewellery in tune with the new fashion aspi-

rations, as shown by the models that followed in the 1970s. According to Roland Barthes, "...more than a substance, plastic is the very idea of its infinite transformation. As its everyday name indicates, it is ubiquity made visible. And it is this, in fact, which makes it a miraculous substance".[109] As in both Kartell furniture and costume jewellery, plastic represented an opportunity to experiment with the formal potential of material, bestowing on it artistic dignity, expressive beauty and flexibility of use. In the 1960s the order of society changed radically as did the role of women in society. From the perfect housewife à la Doris Day, women became tireless workers, with a tempo that required versatile *bijoux* such as those "from desk to dusk" advertised by Trifari.

"1960s design is a journey into the world of youth and adventure. Nothing is considered over the top and jewellery has become increasingly large and crazy. The visual impact and the cult of image means that the driving force of the decade is innovation and change. And since jewellery is so cheap to produce and to buy, it is also easy to throw away."[110] In 1953 Mamie Doud Eisenhower wore a matching set of pearls by Trifari to her husband's Presidential inauguration ball. It was a sign of change, a turning point when costume jewellery succeeded in combining tradition and innovation, progress and elegance. Moreover, it signalled the adoption of new materials and technologies and the democratic aspirations of *prêt-a-porter* fashion. Perhaps more than any other designer of costume jewellery, American Kenneth Jay Lane was to combine many of the various components of 1960s taste in a coherent and original way. Lane adored Cartier jewellery of the 1930s and 1940s designed by Jeanne Toussaint, especially the "big cat" baubles created for the Duchess of Windsor, but he perceived that it was possible to reinvent them in ways that would match the taste for the fun and unexpected that was so typical of the 1960s. "I made white leopards with polka dots and I got away with it because it was costume jewellery."[111] The animal theme appeared in the majority of Kenneth Lane's creations and, as in traditional jewellery, catered to consumers' tastes. Tigers, rams and snakes' heads decorated bracelets in gilded or enamelled or paste-studded metal bracelets, whilst Lane's 1960s' interpretations of Van Cleef & Arpels' lion's head earrings are still highly sought after today.

Another extraordinary costume jewellery designer was Roger Scemama, who debuted with Elsa Schiaparelli in the 1930s. His collection of ornaments was characterised by juxtapositions of elegant colours, such as rose with aubergine or white with beige, and new materials, such as boxwood combined with pearls. More

[106] M. McLuhan in *Bruno Munari, Artista e Designer* (Rome–Bari: Laterza, 1971), p. 50.
[107] Roland Barthes tackled the issue of the development of modern plastic materials in his 1972 essay "Myth Today", from which this quote has been excerpted.
[108] In partnership with researchers from General Electrics the first artificial diamond was created from carbon, as we see in nature, but thanks to a device invented by Bridgman which enabled pressures of 20,000 atmospheres to be reached.
[109] Barthes in "Myth Today".
[110] T. Tolkien and H. Wilkinson, *A Collector's Guide to Costume Jewelry* (London: Thames and Hudson, 1997).
[111] Quoted by Deanna Farneti.

artist than businesswoman, Lina Baretti invented extraordinary, exquisitely original *bijoux de mode* in the 1950s and 1960s in which she combined natural materials such as cork or straw, feathers and shells, moss and raffia, which, braided together with metal and fabric, inspired unusual sets of unparalleled beauty. This was costume jewellery destined to stun and grab the attention and women's magazines confirmed the increasing importance these jewels gained over time. The role of Italy as a country that led the way in taste was an important factor for Italian costume jewellery in the American market. Neiman Marcus organised the *Italian Fortnights,* an event dedicated to the promotion of Italian products in Dallas in 1960. Two Italian jewellers, Lynda Coppola and her brother Bruno, towered above the rest of those present. The United States, the uncontested leader in costume jewellery, thus decreed that Italian costume jewellery could operate on an international level, acknowledging its independence and style. Neiman himself announced "Madame Coppola has come for our Fortnights with her collection of the most inventive hand-manipulated artistry in crystal … No wonder we sought her out in Italy just as we do all the best fashion houses of Europe". The Dallas event represented the high point of the long trade partnership between Italy and the American market that had begun in the 1950s. As regards the materials of that period, faceted jet and ostrich feathers were hugely popular. In 1962 Madame Gripoix presented a sumptuous collier with paste, pearls and emerald green gems, edged with a *collerette* of ostrich feathers.

"The customary role of the jewel is to put the finishing touch to the transformation of woman into idol", wrote Simone de Beauvoir. Traditional jewellery also followed the stylistic evolutions of the day dress and the evening dress, accessories included. Decorations of *haute* evening jewellery consisted mainly of bouquets and vases of flowers, such as those by Cohen and Bulgari, "cascade" motifs and starbursts like "fireworks", with showers of brilliants and *baguettes*, the most famous of which came from Van Cleef and Cartier. As for the day jewel, while it is true that the type and decoration of 1940s jewellery survived intact into the following decade, it is equally true that a feature of 1950s production was again shiny yellow gold, found in the form of smooth wires or twists, braided like rope or twine, worked like matting or "herringbone" or "fishnet" fabric. Moreover, the thin twine proved to be extremely useful in the production of fringes, bows, pompons, pendants and charms, evoking braiding, which created the idea of movement, very popular in

the arts. After ten years of absence the palm came back into fashion, no longer represented in an abstract way, as it had been in the 1940s, but in all its decorative and naturalistic fullness, as seen in the models of Cartier and Bulgari. This fashion was clearly seen in the two recurring typologies of the season, which were colliers made ample and luminous so as to fill generous, plunging necklines, and brooches and clips decorated with cascades of stones which perfectly suited the ubiquitous *tailleurs*. The *parure* made a comeback for the same reasons, with jewels that could be detached and reassembled in different combinations.

There was a leaning towards naturalistic themes, made lighter and more sophisticated by the *pavé secret* technique. In particular, Van Cleef & Arpels' holly leaf represented one of the season's triumphs. But it was Fulco di Verdura who introduced some of the most interesting forms of the post-war period. The pine cone brooch, especially, became an icon that was copied straightaway, followed by mushrooms, branches, trees, amoebas, starfish and shell valves. The predilection for soft, flowing shapes, typical of this twenty-year period, was matched by the organic research that many architects and designers, from Wright to Saarinen, were carrying out at that time. Scandinavian design, in particular, sparked a great deal of interest in the American circle thanks to Georg Jensen's silvers. In 1960 the Metropolitan Museum in New York held the large exhibition *The Arts of Denmark: Viking to Modern*, introducing Scandinavian design to the Americans. Georg Jensen's jewellery was designed by Arje Griegst and Viviana Torun Bülow-Hübe and they must take the credit for transferring the stark lines of Nordic design to the jewel, thus decreeing its success. The works of Torun were especially eye-catching, due to their elegant shapes and colour combinations, as seen in the famous clock made of gold and silver which became an international bestseller.

Together with organic forms, colour represented the common denominator of jewellery production in the 1950s and 1960s. The oppressive dreariness of the war dissolved in the cheery colours of Pop. From tablecloths to bed linen, from clothes to lamps, from jewellery to sofas, everyday life became imbued with a post-war euphoria and the new plastic materials. In jewellery, and, above all, in French jewellery, everything turned into a glittering kaleidoscope, with large citrine quartzes, aquamarines, turquoise, corals, amethysts and synthetic rubies. Colour reigned supreme in the precious jewel just as it did in costume jewellery. In Van Cleef & Arpels' *Grand bouquet parure*, dating from 1947, we can see the polychrome glint of the gems reflected in the sparkle of shiny yellow gold. Another *maison* distinguished for their clever use of colour was Boivin, with Germaine Boivin, René and Jeanne Poiret's daughter, taking over the reins of the *maison* after her mother's death in 1959. Germaine created jewels characterised by unusual colour combinations, including showy orchids, shy primroses, bouquets of violets and, for her mother's eightieth birthday, a brooch in the shape of a cedar, complete with a series of foil strips engraved with the names of the designers, master jewellers and partners who had worked with her parents over the years. The tree was highly symbolical, with amethyst roots symbolising her parents and a trunk made of *pavé* amethyst with different shades of pink tourmaline, and garnet needles, from which the pink tourmaline pine cones grew. The use of colour brightened up day suits and cocktail dresses and so characterised *prêt-à-porter* jewellery and costume jewellery. The latter was now designed by *couturiers* themselves, as well as by large American brands, as accessories for their clothes. However, at this time colour also distinguished evening jewels. Cartier preferred the polychromy of *Tutti frutti* to the monochromy of *mode blanche* pursued by the likes of Harry Winston with his spectacular diamonds. In the *Draperie* collier, designed for the Duchess of Windsor in 1947, the large *ramage* of turquoise, amethysts and diamonds crystallised the contemporary desire for colours as well as for large, obvious forms. Cartier also stood out in this period with its extraordinary and unusual pieces that lay outside the habitual scope of jewellery. This is the case of the dress sword of the Academy of France made in 1955 to a design by Jean Cocteau: the hilt reproduces the profile of Orpheus, whose myth had heavily influenced the work of Cocteau, and is surmounted by a lyre set with a 2.84 carat emerald. The French *maisons* of *magnificent jewellery* were joined by other names such as Pierre Sterlé who, three times winner of the Diamond International Award, possessed a bold talent and an extraordinary ability to create fantastic and dynamic forms of outstanding workmanship. It is enough to recall his numerous brooches with birds that seem genuinely poised to take flight.

The United States was the leading country for both traditional and costume jewellery in the 1950s and 1960s, just as Italy took the lead in the field of design. One of the protagonists of this colourful period was Jean Schlumberger, whom we have already come across in his role as *bijoux* designer for Schiaparelli. But the turning point for him came in 1956 when Walter Hoving, the chairman of Tiffany, persuaded him to go and work for them, dedicating to him a new salon for his jewellery

and collectibles. On 23 March the *New York Journal* reported that "Some women want to look expensive, I would prefer to have them look precious".[112] In the same year the photograph of Julie Andrews, who was winning over the American public in the stage production of *My Fair Lady*, appeared in *Town & Country*, portrayed wearing Tiffany jewels designed by Schlumberger. Liz Taylor and Jacqueline Kennedy were also loyal customers of his. His jewels were three-dimensional, sculptural and colourful, with a precious yet unconventional allure, and became a status symbol for high society ladies. In 1957, in an interview given to Daniel Burnham of *Realities*, Schlumberger stated "I make jewels but I hate modern jewellery and I can't tell people I make antique jewels".[113] For him modern jewellery meant precious gems and ostentation – Chanel's cheque worn around a neck – whose value still stemmed from the material and not the design. Like Verdura, Schlumberger also drew inspiration from nature, flowers and sea creatures. His enchanting jellyfish encrusted with diamonds, exotic parrots and luxuriant fruits beautifully represented the strength of expression of 1960s jewellery. He loved yellow gold, coloured stones and bright, intense, translucent enamels, especially on bracelets made of *paillonné* enamel, favourites of Jacqueline Kennedy. The *Trophy* brooch created for Diana Vreeland, legendary director of *Vogue America*, was particularly significant. It was a piece of warrior armour complete with a shield of oval amethysts and rubies, whilst the bow, arrows and sword were made of blue lacquer. Just as significant was the *Night of the Iguana* brooch made for Liz Taylor in the 1960s, where the body of the iguana is studded with brilliants and imprisoned by a gold honeycomb cage, a complex structure with cabochon sapphire eyes and emerald lips in which the *torchon* movement of the flexible tail lends the object movement and three-dimensionality. Like Cartier's dress sword, Schlumberger's *Goldfish* cigarette lighter also marked an important moment in the history of the American *maison*. This goldfish, with its flexible tail and eyes made of gems, transposed the language of jewellery to accessories. It was followed by treasure chests, starfish, shells and bouquets of flowers. The years he worked for Tiffany, from 1957 to 1987, were the artist's most prolific. He said himself, "I try to make everything look as if it were growing, uneven, at random, organic, in motion. I want to capture the irregularity of the universe. I observe nature and find verve".[114]

In the 1960s it became fashionable to portray pets as ornaments. Many *maisons* followed this trend – Van Cleef & Arpels with brooches in the shape of cute poodles, Boivin with a huge variety of dog breeds, and Ver-

[112] Loring 1997, p. 171.
[113] Cf. E. Nidy, *Bejeweled* (New York: Abrams, 2001), p. 101.
[114] Snowman 1990, p. 188.

dura with cocker spaniels, poodles and cats. Wild beasts and fantastic creatures were the subjects preferred by David Webb, Jacqueline Kennedy's favourite designer, who concentrated on zoomorphic jewels, reintroducing bracelets with animal heads on their tips that resembled jewels of antiquity. The favoured subjects for this typology of jewel were horses, zebras, elephants, fish, bulls, rams, frogs and lions. One of Webb's most famous works was his bracelet with a vine motif, with bunches of *cabochon* emeralds alternating with leaves of *pavé* diamonds, accompanied by gold curlicues at regular intervals, creating a sophisticated and elegant composition. Raymond Yard, one of the most important jewellers on the American scene, was someone who managed to introduce the whimsy of the period into his jewellery. Raymond Yard[115] worked as an assistant in the jewellery department of Marcus & Co. until John Rockefeller advised him to open his own store. He took up the suggestion and became one of the best New York jewellers. His precious jewels were traditional but whimsical and took their cue from events of the period. In particular there were his brooches, such as those with rabbit waiters carrying trays of drinks to exorcise the ghost of prohibition, or those with the little coloured houses in the 1960s, celebrating new-found affluence. Julius Cohen, who opened his New York store in 1956, also made fantastic and bizarre jewels, such as the brooch with the weeping willow made of gold wires welded together to create roots, trunk and branches, and laden with heavy peridoti foliage. For the 1957 Diamond International Award, Cohen designed another jewel consisting of a vase of flowers in which a series of U-shaped gold stalks supported leaves and buds made of diamonds. The outstanding feature of this jewel was the vase, made of a 4.15 carat diamond cut into a highly original shape, that won the jeweller an award. In Italy Bulgari created beautiful vases of flowers, with precious stones arranged *en masse* and juxtapositions of rubies, sapphires and diamonds. It was precisely in those years that the Roman *maison* began to use *cabochon* cut coloured stones as a distinctive element of its style and *tremblant* brooches that beautifully conveyed the dynamism of the times. Another morphology popular in 1950s and 1960s jewellery was the posy and, particularly, the posy of violets, flowers that had symbolised loyalty throughout the nineteenth century. Verdura designed a posy of this type made of diamonds and tourmalines and Boivin created two versions of it, one with oval amethysts and one with pink tourmalines. Tiffany produced a classic bouquet of flowers, in which the corollas were made of rubies and white diamonds, with an elegant touch provided by a brown yellow dia-

mond at the centre of the composition and a leaf that entwined around the stalks. Sterlé produced a dahlia, which, instead of being shown frontally, was three-quarter framed, its mother-of-pearl petals stirred by the wind.

At the same time, Russia began to revive its prestigious goldsmith tradition. In 1947 it began to embrace jewellery when Maria Tone's pieces were exhibited at the *All Russia Art Exhibition*. From that moment on an increasing number of artists like Zinaisa Zenkova, Sergei Budanov, Vera Povolotskaya, Vladislava Khramtsov, Taisia Chistyakova, as well as the leader, Maria Tone, explored the world of jewellery, curiously without any links with industrial reality. This is probably why their production proves to be as harmonious in its forms as it is in its references to classical art. As Taisia Chistyakova said: "We studied original works, the History Museum's exhibits, stylistically we went all the way back to old Russia to Baroque, to late Classicism and to Art Nouveau".[116]

In Europe the opportunity to learn about new areas of research was favoured by the activity of specialised institutes as well as by artists' increasing interest in jewellery. A few cities emerged as major centres for the promotion of contemporary jewellery, thanks mainly to the busy activity of schools and academies: the Fachhochschule für Gestaltung in Pforzheim, the Akademie der Bildenden Künste in Munich, Saint Martins College of Art, the Central School of Arts and Crafts and the Royal College of Art in London, the Gerrit Rietveld Academie in Amsterdam and Escola Massana in Barcelona. In 1961, the *International Exhibition of Modern Jewellery 1890–1961* was held in London, promoted by the Worshipful Company of Goldsmiths' in partnership with the Victoria and Albert Museum. It was the first international exhibition dedicated to modern jewellery since the Second World War. As well as the creations of the most famous *maisons* there were jewels designed by young people, proof of the innovative changes that were taking place in this field. The new headquarters of the Schmuckmuseum in Pforzheim was inaugurated in the same year. This was one of the most important institutions dedicated to jewellery and combined its museum activities with the intense activity of promoting and advertising mostly original and artistic contemporary jewellery.

"Art is something one can always get away with."[117]

In Italy too, jewellers of consolidated fame, such as Bulgari, Mario Buccellati, Cusi, Faraone, Fasano, Petochi and Settepassi, were being joined by other exponents of the 1950s style. Particularly worthy of

[115] Cf. Nidy 2001, p. 69.
[116] A. Karpun, *Russian Jewellery* (Moscow: Beresta, 1994), p. 17.
[117] McLuhan 1971, p. 13.

mention are Enrico Serafini of Florence, who made sculptural pieces inspired by flowers and exotic animals, and Rino Frascarolo, who specialised in the creation of jewels and precious enamelled objects in the shape of animals. The 1960s encouraged points of contact between artistic experiments and traditional jewellery. Moreover, while it had mainly been artists – from Calder to Picasso – who approached jewellery in the 1940s, now it was jewellers who were approaching art, changing both its plastic and its semantic features. In a climate of profound technological-industrial innovation and in a culture increasingly oriented towards mass consumption, "art jewellery" drew attention to the jewel as a sculpture and to its unique status. Whilst Margaret De Patta,[118] Peter Macchiarini, Merry Renk, Irena Brynner, Frances Spensen and Bob Winston founded the San Francisco Metal Arts Guild (MAG) in the United States in 1951, thereby introducing jewellery into the arts, there were signs of semantic renewal in Italy at the Triennial expositions, an effective freeze frame of the artistic production of the period. If jewellery was absent from the 8th Triennial of 1947 for evident reasons linked to the recently ended war, Mario Pinto, an artist from Padua, drew attention to himself at the 9th Triennial of 1951 by presenting an embossed gold leaf bracelet and an engraved casting of a bunch of plants. These were deliberately unfashionable works with an archaic, ancestral flavour, containing those embossments which, highlighting the simplicity of the forms, the materials and the light, created a close dialogue between the elements. Pinton's jewellery, unlike art jewellery, did not convey the strength of a symbol but that of a material that had been shaped, tamed and controlled. Pinot, who was the founder of the School of Padua, the only school in Italy to energetically promote art jewellery, knew everything there was to know about gold. His medium was the metal and he was not interested, unlike many artists such as Dalí, Fontana, Man Ray and Max Ernst, in the miniaturisation of an artistic expression already encoded in painting or in sculpture. Pinton did not exhibit ideas and manifestos but a material – gold – that represented the *incipit* of his creative process. At the Triennial there was also a costume jewellery section where the various pieces exhibited included the embossed necklaces and brooches of Genni Mucchi and the enamelled necklaces of Paulo de Poli. The 10th Triennial in 1954 was dedicated to the unity of arts and the partnership between the world of art and industrial production or, in other words, industrial design. These were the years when the Italian furnishing industry saw the most growth and the Triennial became its favoured showcase, a place where

new products were tested and where the modern aesthetic of homes and lifestyles in the new affluent society was anticipated. In the jewellery section Pinton's works were joined by those of other countries. Spain, in particular, exhibited twenty-one unique pieces of jewellery designed by Salvador Dalí and made by Alemany & Ertman of New York. Referring to his jewels Dalí said, "Without a public, without the presence of spectators, these jewels would be unable to absolve the function for which they were created. Therefore, it is the spectator who is the ultimate artist. It is the eyes, the heart, the mind – to a greater or lesser extent able to understand the artist – that breathe life into a jewel".[119] In the midst of the various hearts and crosses, there were also the famous *Los labios de rubí* (ruby lips), a brooch shaped like a mouth and made from pearls and rubies; *Los pendientes telefónicos* (telephonic earrings), earrings in the shape of a telephone, made of gold, diamonds, rubies and emeralds; and *El ojo del tiempo* (the eye of time), a clock in the shape of a human eye made of diamonds, enamel and rubies. The section dedicated to German jewellery, which displayed silverware and fabrics in marvellous showcases fitted out by graphic artist Wolfgang Nicolaus and architects Rossana Monzini and Giuseppe Terragni, was also worthy of interest. This was the most important exhibition dedicated to jewellery in Italy.

The jewellery section of the 11th Triennial of Milan of 1957 was curated by brothers Giò and Arnaldo Pomodoro. The Pomodoros had noted how Italian jewellery was unable to keep up with the international race for innovation and the increasingly pressing request for "up-to-date jewellery". For this reason they involved jewellers from Valenza Po and some "avant-garde artists" in setting up an experimental production of "modern jewellery" which, however, had to possess the characteristics of genuine jewellery. In other words they had to be made of precious materials and unique. Major Italian artists including Enrico Baj, Sergio Dangelo, Aldo Bergolli, Gianni Dova, Cesare Peverelli, Ettore Sottsass, Emilio Scanavino, Lorenzo Guerrini, Francesco Assetto, Ada Minola, Bruno Martinazzi, Francesco De Cal and Mario Pinton were invited to take part. The experiment consisted of an exploration of the potential of jewellery and its meaning in terms of the goldsmith's art, combining artists and jewellers for the first time in Italy. The Pomodoro brothers exhibited a gold and jade ring and bracelet by Giò and a gold necklace with turquoise and gold earrings with rubies and sapphires by Arnaldo. Their ornaments were designed as organic encrustations, created by layers of elements encircling a nucleus fused with cuttlebone. For the Pomodoro brothers

[118] Cf. Greenbaum 1996.
[119] L. Vinca Masini, *L'arte del Novecento. Dall'Espressionismo al Multimediale* (Florence: Giunti, 1998).

the making of jewel represented a marginal and incidental aspect of their production. As Lara Vinca Masini wrote "Arnaldo and Giò Pomodoro have experimented with the force of their creativity on jewellery, which they have then developed and applied to their sculpture".[120] This affirmation was confirmed by Arnaldo Pomodoro himself who in 1965 declared, "My work on new jewellery began as a study and apprenticeship of the art".[121] On the contrary, for a designer like Sottsass, the Pomodoro brothers' invitation to the Triennial was the first opportunity he had been given to approach jewellery. He created an egg-shaped brooch made of gold, divided into two equal parts, one with small, round holes, the other with small, square holes and an embossed gold necklace with mobile spheres and rings: the work was dedicated to his wife, Fernanda Pivano. Sottsass's predilection for simple shapes underlined his aim to make ornaments using archetypal forms that would satisfy the need for decoration, with symbols to be worn as "offers for a thrilling journey through life". Emilio Scanavino, an informal artist, transposed his poetics of sign and material to two embossed gold leaf brooches adding wires, whilst Lorenzo Guerrini, an expert in embossing and engraving, exhibited a necklace with a gold-plated pendant. Bruno Martinazzi was a novice jeweller when he arrived at the 11th Triennial yet his talent was immediately evident in his gold leaf bracelet with its three articulated pieces, which beautifully expresses his study of movement. Martinazzi exhibited other pieces made of gold leaf: earrings with hanging squares, a rectangular-shaped embossed brooch and a stiff circular collar with four articulated elements. An entire display case was reserved for master-jeweller Mario Pinton, in which there was a gold and turquoise ring, a turquoise necklace with a pendant, a gold leaf brooch with embossed centaurs and earrings also made of gold leaf with embossed figures. These jewels made with the embossing technique, typical of Pinton's work, depicted motifs that can be traced back to the time of the Etruscans, Egyptians and Greeks.

The affluent and exuberant climate of the 1960s soon dissolved with the assassination of John Kennedy and Martin Luther King, the war in Vietnam and the May protests in France, the student uprisings and colonial wars. Absolute certainties were swept away and, with them, the great philosophical currents of the post-war period. As Michel Foucault put it, it was the end of "bourgeois humanism".

V. 1968–78: from *radical* to *global*

The 1970s was a decade of tough transition, which saw the utopian ideals of changing the world, the subject of peaceful demonstrations in the 1960s, go up in smoke. After the fever for technology, which culminated in the moon landing in 1969, this was the decade that witnessed the war in Vietnam, the Watergate scandal, the Russian invasion of Afghanistan and the coup that toppled president Salvador Allende in Chile. But Europe too was shaken by waves of violence with the terrorist attacks of the IRA, the Baader-Meinhof gang in Germany, the Red Brigades in Italy and the carnage in Piazza Fontana. Art and, above all, architecture took refuge in large-scale technological, urban and energetic utopias whilst young people shouldered the burden of building a new society.

London became the centre of music and fashion whilst Italy was the centre of design. In 1972 Italian design enjoyed international success with the exhibition curated by Emilio Ambasz at MoMA in New York, whose title was *Italy: The New Domestic Landscape*. This exhibited works by Gae Aulenti, Ettore Sottsass, Joe Colombo, Alberto Rosselli, Marco Zanuso and Richard Sapper, Mario Bellini, Gaetano Pesce, Ugo La Pietra, Archizoom, Superstudio, Enzo Mari and Gruppo 9999: "Italy has become a micromodel" – reads the curator's essay – "in which a wide range of the possibilities, limitations and critical issues of contemporary design are brought into sharp focus. It is possible to differentiate in Italy today three prevalent attitudes toward design: the first is conformist, the second is reformist and the third is, rather, one of contestation, attempting both inquiry and action."

Italian design principally addressed the bourgeoisie with its sophisticated furnishings, whilst young people were the absolute protagonists of fashion. Clothes became a palette on which to experiment the boldest patterns and combinations of colours and fabrics, the new textures of Optical Art. Fashion discovered legs to be a new focus of seduction. The miniskirt was worn with boots, which were no longer thought of as rainy day footwear, and the use of synthetic materials, such as vinyl, allowed a far wider choice of shapes, colours and lengths. Nylon tights became must-haves and were colourful, flashy, and brightly patterned. *Haute couture* could only adapt to the spirit of the times and the go-ahead atmosphere was found in collections influenced by space exploration, a style with a strong visual impact, combining art and science, past and future. Stylists like Cardin, Courrèges and Rabanne drew inspiration from astronauts for their "architectural clothes", which were geometrical and modular, with visible structural features, made of new materials such as plastics, steel and mirror glass held together by bolted stitching and welding, in homage to technological progress.

[120] L. Vinca Masini, *Gioiello d'artista, gioiello d'autore*, in *L'arte del gioiello e il gioiello d'artista* (Florence) 2001, p. 350.
[121] A. Pomodoro in *Progettare con l'oro*, exhibition catalogue, Florence, Palazzo Strozzi, 1979–1980 (Florence: Nuova Vallecchi, 1979), p. 36.

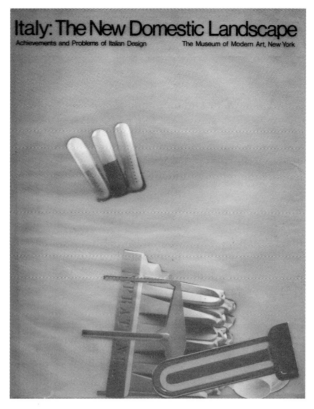

Italy: The New Domestic Landscape
Achievements and Problems of Italian Design   The Museum of Modern Art, New York

"The Old Guard no longer decides fashion. The watchword is youth, youth youth!" wrote *Women's Wear Daily.* And youth it was. Hippies and flower children were succeeded by rock and punk, underground culture, the music of the Ramones, the Sex Pistols and the Clash. Maxi skirts were replaced by tight leather trousers, flowers by studs, platform heels by chains. And if the bon ton of Jackie Kennedy enchanted shabby chic ladies all over the world with its understated and cosmopolitan elegance, the punk aesthetics clearly made it understood that, in the words of Johnny Rotten "being a punk means being a fucking son of a bitch, someone who has made the pavement his dominion, the cursed son of a jubilee nation shamed by the Monarchy, with no future and the desire to smash the face of his charitable neighbour".

The *trait d'union* between the various artistic experiences was the body. Released from hippie prudery it became the domain of the artistic experimentations of Vito Acconci and Dennis Oppenheim's Body Art, and pierced by punk safety-pins and studs. Paco Rabanne's idea of "body jewellery", inspired by medieval chainmail, now came to life, transforming jewellery into clothes and costume jewellery into *bijou de couture.* The Spanish stylist had already created his first collection of "anti-jewels" made of shiny plastic in the 1960s, commissioned by Balenciaga, Dior and Givenchy. Made in squares, circles and spirals, Rabanne's jewels were totally and boast-

fully lacking in economic value. The stylist explained that he wanted to create something totally crazy and wild, which would constitute a clean break with the rules of the past: "I wanted to produce jewellery that would recall the paintings of that period, oversized, mad and uninhibited. Women too wanted to change, rejecting the traditions of the past. Their jewellery had to belong to the new aesthetic. I made jewellery for the alternative side of a woman's personality, for her madness". Rabanne experimented with new materials, from wood to paper to aluminium and PVC. He chose neon colours and dazzling black and white for swirling spirals and concentric circles. Together with Cardin and Courrèges, he exerted a powerful sway on popular fashion, to the point that his jewellery was slavishly imitated in the world of bijoux. In the United States Trifari launched a youthful range of jewellery, including bracelets in the shape of cages, necklaces like broken spider-webs, with intersecting squares and spirals, and a bolero made of gilded warp thread like Rabanne's "fake chainmail".

Unisex was born at this time, with men and women wearing the same clothes, symbolising the equality which had now been won. Ungaro and Lanvin also promoted geometrical ornaments, covering them in white leather or moulding plastic into forms which recalled the design and architecture of the period. Yves Saint Laurent too created a series of *bijoux* using non-precious materials, including daisies, blocks like Lego and multicoloured fish hanging from a necklace. Another element very much in vogue in this decade was enamel, which inspired the production of brightly coloured jewellery, ostrich feathers and the new Swarovski "pagoda" cut, which allowed the stone to be turned upside down. The influence of art was felt through Pop Art, Abstract Art and Optical Art, which made "Op" *bijou* popular. This was geometrical and principally based on the opposition of black and white. *Bijou de couture* was now sold from the boutiques of stylists who were increasingly turning from clothes to accessories.

In Italy Walter Albini was a precursor of Italian *prêt-à-porter.* In an interview he gave to *Corriere della Sera* in 1976 he declared: "In Italy there is a lack of real cooperation between those who make fabrics, those who make accessories or buttons, and those who design clothes. Our stylists, unlike their French counterparts, are unwilling to launch a fabric, a line, a colour together". *Bijou de couture,* which integrated with the line, becoming a part of it and not merely an accompaniment, fitted this perspective. An advocate of the *total look,* Albini looked for a common style that he could adapt to clothes, accessories, furnishings and fabrics. He designed his *bijoux* and had them made up by skilled artisans. They included bracelets, necklaces with gold, black and white coloured beads made of semiprecious stones or glass, earrings, and diamond-shaped and pendant brooches in glass or paste.

This policy of brand extension also characterised the large jewellery *maisons*, who brought no major innovations to the jewellery sector other than this new model of building up the brand and distributing its products. In 1973 Cartier entrusted Alain Dominique Perrin with a sector that proved to be decisive for the future of the company: marketing. Perrin's strategy was to make sure new products would capitalise on the tradition and excellence of Cartier. To this end the trademark "Les Must de Cartier" was created, consisting of watches and lighters until 1974, when Cartier presented their new range of burgundy leather goods, causing a huge scandal at the Comité Colbert, then controlled by the Place Vendôme jewellers. 1976 was the year of the pen. The door was now open to accessories since, as chairman Robert Hocq observed, "In 1898 Cartier sold between one and three diadems a day. Now, in 1970, with a bit of luck, we can sell one a year".[122]

In the decade of ideologies, any show of wealth or luxury as an end to itself was banned. Art and jewellery were combined in a less casual and sporadic way than in the past, encouraging exchanges between various artistic experiences. This was indubitably the decade of art jewellery and experimental jewellery, the decade of those who challenged the richness and preciousness of materials and the social symbolism of jewellery, making it instead a form of research or experimentation unlinked to manufacturing logics and market demands. The experiments of Surrealism, Kinetic Art, Informel, and Pop Art, like the CoBrA group, had evident repercussions for the jewellery sector, and many of the principal exponents of these currents made jewellery. They were, in the main, episodic experiments, a kind of manifesto that could be worn to strengthen artistic ideology. Except for rare exceptions, like Calder, who continued to make jewellery, or Pol Bury of the CoBrA group,[123] who stopped painting in 1953 and, after 1968, applied his research on electromagnets to jewellery, it was principally a matter of jewellers transferring their values and the plasticity of visual arts to the art of jewellery. If, therefore, as the School of Toronto maintained, *the medium is the message*, the message of jewellery in the 1960s became that of repudiating luxury by means of using alternative materials and a revisitation of the relationship with the body. This followed the direction art was heading in, to the extent that in 1971 Reinhold Reiling, professor of the art of

jewellery in Pforzheim, wrote a book entitled *Jewels as Artistic Testimony of our Age*, in which he vindicated the artistic origins of jewellery and its ability to testify to its age. For Enrico Crispolti "the comparison between artist-jewellers and jeweller-artists has its own precise motivation. The leap in invention, which made avant-garde jewellery prestigious in the first decades of the second half of the twentieth century, is indubitably owed to the influx of plastic artists (or artist-jewellers) beginning with sculptors, in the field of jewellery design, introducing new inventive perspectives and production methods with unusual boldness. However, it is just as indubitable that in the last two decades of the twentieth century a new creative reality of jeweller-artists, that is artists trained in sculpture, who have chosen to work mostly in the field of jewellery, has begun to establish itself. Their purpose is avant-garde experiment, disassociating themselves from an albeit high level of jewellery production preciously aimed more at the prestige of the target than at formal and material innovation".[124]

The work on materials, evaluated in terms of their expressive strength and not in terms of their exchange value, informed most of the activity of the artist-jewellers and jeweller-artists of the 1960s, as we can see in the works of Slovakian Anton Cepka and Yugoslavian Peter Skubic, who was equally successful in extending his light compositions from jewellery to sculpture by treating them as *objets trouvés*. The Dutch School played a leading role in this period and was represented by Emmy van Leersum and Gijs Bakker with their idea of "wearable sculpture", the title of the 1966 exhibition in Amsterdam, which then changed to "objects to wear" in 1969. It was curated by Jean Leering, director of the Van Abbemuseum of Eindhoven, and Wil Bertheux, curator of the department of Decorative Arts of the Stedelijk Museum of Amsterdam. Both declared that "in the total picture of Dutch art the making of jewellery, an activity which in the past would have come under the head of applied art, claimed a special place".[125] Bakker's lively and restless talent led him very early on to design abstract and pure lines that showed his skill in forging gold and silver into completely new forms, revealing a close interest in the constructive element and focusing especially on the jewellery-body relationship. The designer soon turned his back on tradition by choosing alternative materials (aluminium, steel, chrome, wood, leather, linen, cotton, PVC, paper) and developing unusual shapes. Bakker is, first and foremost, a designer, whose works clearly reveal the shift from the traditional to the contemporary concept

[122] F. Cologni and E. Mocchetti, *L'oggetto Cartier* (Milan: Mondadori, 1992), p. 198.

[123] The CoBrA group was a movement founded in Paris in November 1948 by a group of artists from Northern Europe concerned with geometrical abstraction and socialist realism. The name is made up of the first letters of Copenhagen, Brussels and Amsterdam, capitals of the countries of the major artists involved, including Asger Jorn, Karel Appel, Pierre Alechinsky, Jean-Michel Atlan. Although trained differently, they shared the same aspiration to a "natural" and spontaneous art, leading them to reject every type of theoretical intellectualism and dogmatism in favour of the free experimentation of direct and intuitive means of expression. Their art was provocative and asserted the right to the hedonistic pleasure of the artistic gesture resolved into an exasperated highly tactile neo-expressionism. Their favoured themes were the woman, the child, the bird, the sun and the moon and, above all, the mythological bestiary which was a cross between the fantastic and the naïf.

[124] E. Crispolti, "Appunti per una storia del gioiello d'arte in Italia nel secondo Novecento", in *Gioielli d'autore. Padova e la scuola dell'oro*, edited by M. Cisotto Nalon and A. M. Spiazzi (Turin: Allemandi, 2008), p. 59.

[125] From the catalogue of the Eindhoven exhibition (1969); quoted in *Gijs Bakker and Jewelry* (Stuttgart: Arnoldsche, 2005, p. 22).

of jewellery. "I like jewellery", he has written, "because it is absolutely superfluous. I like jewellery because it is never a priori functional. I like jewellery because, like clothes, it is closest to our body and says something about the wearer. A painting is hung on the wall and can be ignored. A piece of jewellery is worn and creates an impression."[126]

His interest in design, understood as a process and not as a stylistic reference, makes him one of the most interesting designers of the period. Popular jewellery of this time included large, transparent plastic collars with inserts of photographs, flowers or gold leaves. Emblematic of this sensibility was the *Circle in Circle*, "an ornament for neck and shoulder", consisting of a flat disc with a wave in the centre. It was a jewel designed by a part of the body. His method of design also drew attention to the industrial process which, although it did not obtain the success it deserved, remained the basis of his design choices, as he himself declared in 1978: "When designing jewellery I have always had the industrial process in mind. I have never been interested in handmade things and I am, in fact, suspicious of the charm. It is the idea that matters, and whether it's produced by me or by a machine, nothing must detract from the idea".[127] His position was out of step with that of jeweller-artists, above all in terms of his indifference towards the artisan's handmade product and his decision to reject reproducibility as a method. While the work of Van Leersum contained something akin to sculpture and an extraordinary grace of forms, her husband Gijs Bakker's work was sensational in how it revealed new ways of approaching materials and the very concept of jewellery.

And so we have the *Shadow Bracelet* of 1973, a gold wire that marks the skin and decorates it, or the *Profile Ornament* for Emmy van Leersum, or the irony of the *Alexandra* collars of 1977, and *Pforzheim 1780* of 1985, which alludes to the precious jewel, locking it into laminated photographs. Bakker's work marked the beginning of the contemporary jewellery period. His reworking of the principles of design was also vital to the success of Dutch design. As he wrote in 1969, "To me, the creative process equals research: the form should be created but it should come forth naturally as a result of research. After all the form is just a wrapping of an idea".[128] In those same years in Holland we also find Robert Smit, whose use of colour recalls Japonisme and De Stijl abstractions. Instead, the influence of the CoBrA group is clearly seen in his treatments of surfaces, saturating the object with colour by painting over it and thus negating the preciousness of the material, which is only visible from beneath.

In Great Britain Graham Hughes, director of The Worshipful Company of Goldsmiths, organised the first *International Exhibition of Modern Jewellery* in 1961. Interesting and original lines of inquiry were emerging from the ranks of British jewellers that were subsequently confirmed by 1970s' production.

Some of the major exponents of the British *nouvelle vague* were Andrew Grima, John Donald, Gerda Flöckinger, David Thomas, Wendy Ramshaw and David Watkin. Andrew Grima had studied engineering and this interest in structural aspects and the experimentation of new techniques is seen in his works, as does his willingness to compete with industrial production. Indeed, Grima made watches-jewels for Omega, where the focus on mechanics generated precious and futuristic textures. The surface work developed by Grima also characterised the work of John Donald, who preferred the artistic-craft dimension to the industrial component. Donald was an expert in glasswork and innovative in the way he used scraps from gold production, which he made into organic and suggestive forms. David Thomas's work was oriented towards the production of jewellery made of micro-soldered wire, which he experimented with a new technique that consisted of plunging the wire into the cast of a wax model. The jewels were thus produced in limited series, combining mass production with painstaking detail. Instead, Gerda Flöckinger produced delicate and elegant jewellery. The first woman to have a solo exhibition at the Victoria and Albert, Flöckinger used fretwork and filigree, the same techniques used by Stuart Devlin, with finesse and grace. The work of Wendy Ramshaw, who explored themes such as the modularity and portability of jewellery with originality and innovation, was more oriented towards the geometries typical of the 1970s. Her five rings of different widths, which produced different designs depending on how they were put together, won recognition from the London Design Centre.

As in Andrew Grima's work, the ability to combine manufacturing requirements with the aesthetics of the jewel was also the underlying theme in the work of Swiss Gilbert Albert, who worked for Omega and Patek Philippe, as well as Jean Lurçat, who produced a magnificent collection of jewellery for the latter.

In the United States, jewellery was oriented towards both tradition and the experimental nature of art jewellery. In the 1960s Tiffany once more demonstrated its shrewd head for business by commissioning Elsa Peretti to design their jewellery. The formal elegance and rarefaction of Peretti's designs made them an extraordinary emblem of the culture of their time. In 1972 Joan

126 Ibid., p. 190.
127 Ibid., p. 120.
128 Ibid., p. 146.

Sonnabend's Sculpture to Wear Gallery presented the art jewellery of GEM Montebello in the Plaza Hotel in New York, with works by Man Ray, Roy Lichtenstein and Alexander Calder, and young, emerging artists such as Cara Croninger and Robert Lee Morris. The latter, in particular became one of the most influential American designers and was an advocate of jewellery inspired by natural objects such as wood and stone, ancient talismans, Celtic crosses and African tribal artefacts. His jewels were always highly distinctive, thanks to their clean, organic and sculptural lines. Usually made without gems, they were simultaneously bold and elegant. In 1977 Morris opened his own gallery in New York called Artwear, where he exhibited his own creations alongside those of other young artists, who were working with unusual materials such as rubber, silicon, silk and resins, and were attempting to come up with a new concept of experimental jewellery. This work was especially admired by the world of fashion and Donna Karan often used Artwear jewels for her fashion shows.

The German School centred on Pforzheim, which was famous for its jewellery industry. It was interesting as it actively involved production, an element which was a matter of indifference to the majority of artist-jewellers of the age. The works of Reinhold Reiling were some of the most interesting with their highly geometrical shapes imitating contemporary trends. Then there was the work of Friedrich Becker, whose kinetic jewellery elegantly interpreted the aesthetics of the machine that Becker had studied as part of his training as an aeronautical engineer. Unlike Kinetic Art, where the object was constructed so that its lightness and the arrangement of its components, or the nature of its materials, would allow it to move by itself, movement to Becker meant technical-technological virtuosity, the result of skilful construction.

In Japan, as Clare Phillips notes, "a small group of young jewellers emerged, both influenced by European trends and, at the same time, permeated by national, cultural themes".[129] Yasuki Hiramatsu was its principal exponent along with Kazuhiro Itoh. Their jewellery was connoted by its three-dimensional spatiality and by the lean austerity of its forms. Itoh then introduced alternative materials, such as marble and bamboo, in small plastic bags, confirming a new consideration of materials used in jewellery in the 1970s.

Nordic jewellery recalled the magnificence of Georg Jensen in the creative vigour and talent of Tone Vigeland, Nanna Ditzel and Toril Bjorg. Norwegian Vigeland was particularly successful in reviving the Viking tradition of steel and hammered silver, bringing it elegantly up to date with unexpected lightness and grace. Born in Oslo in 1938, Vigeland trained at Oslo's National College of Arts, Crafts and Design. After an apprenticeship at Plus, a centre of applied arts in Fredrikstad, he opened his own studio in order to better explore the relationship between sculpture and jewellery. For Vigeland too the design *incipit* came from the body and its forms. In the 1970s Vigeland began to explore techniques that would enable him to make his large pieces of jewellery, combining plain, corrugated metals such as iron with the luminous preciousness of gold, resulting in an extraordinary strength of expression and formal elegance.

As was already the case with design Italy proved to be a leader in jewellery production in the 1970s. Having nothing in common with the kind of experimentation that characterised Dutch jewellery production, it still produced excellent art jewellery, excelling in both design, with GEM Montebello of Milan and Masenza-Fumanti of Rome, and in training, with the School of Padua. More than any other country Italy was able to harness the energy of the exchange between various artistic disciplines and to emphasise their modernisation and innovation. The modernisation of art jewellery had begun with the works of sculptors Mirko, Dino and Afro Basaldella, Fausto Melotti and the Roman milieu of Mario Masenza, who perceived, with astonishing clear-sightedness, that "the lack of competition in art jewellery specifically, a number of willing customers and the chronic lack of money that afflicts artists"[130] represented favourable conditions for proposing artistic masterpieces in the form of jewellery to the aristocracy and to Roman collectors. His gallery in Via del Corso was a meeting point for the major artists of the age, including Giuseppe Capogrossi, Mirko and Afro Basaldella, Fausto Melotti, Pietro Consagra, Carla Accardi, Getulio Alviani, Franco Angeli, Gino Marotta, Mario Ceroli, Franco Cannilla, Renato Guttuso, Giuseppe Uncini and many others. Masenza's gallery became a "Last Supper of artists" devoted to what he defined as "*il gioiello d'autore*". Masenza asked artists for a sketch of their design, whilst production was taken care of by jewellers Fumanti who organised the exhibition *Contemporary Artists' Jewellery* in their shop in 1970. Although this formula led many artists to approach jewellery, it did not raise the hoped for profits, forcing the Fumanti to close their business in 1986.

GEM Montebello, founded in 1967 by GianCarlo Montebello and Teresa Pomodoro, who, conscious of the world opening up, focused on international artists

[129] C. Phillips, *Gioielli, breve storia dall'antichità a oggi* (Milan: Skira-Rizzoli, 2003), p. 230.
[130] F. Romana Morelli, "I gioielli indiscreti", in *Ori d'artista* (Cinisello Balsamo: Silvana Editoriale, 2004), p. 22.

and distribution, were more successful. Their idea was to apply the reproducibility of design to the art of jewellery and, in particular, to produce beautifully made multiples from the artist's sketch, which would be accessible to a vaster public than the limited public interested in collector's pieces: "The intention behind our plan", said Montebello, "was to turn these isolated and intermittent episodes into an 'event', organizing both the productive work and publicity and distribution in such a way that our choices might become part of the normal (not the on-again, off-again) scene, with the prominence that is the artist's birthright. So our task was 'getting the works out there', by means of an entirely independent operation at the service of the artist".[131]

Advertising and distribution were highly innovative for the age. GEM Montebello did not have its own sales outlet but distributed its works through international galleries, relying on the most powerful form of advertising: word of mouth.

The artists invited to design for Montebello included major exponents on the international scene: Alighiero Boetti, Rodolfo Aricò, Arman, Pol Bury, César, Pietro Consagra, Bill Copley, Allan D'Arcangelo, Sonia Delaunay, Lucio Del Pezzo, Amalia Del Ponte, Piero Dorazio, Erté, Lucio Fontana, Alex Katz, Claude Lalanne, Richard Lippold, Peter Lobello, Milvia Maglione, Ronald Mallory, Man Ray, Livio Marzot, Matta, Lowell Nesbitt, Niki de Saint Phalle, Gastone Novelli, Meret Oppenheim, Harold Paris, Arnaldo and Giò Pomodoro, Hans Richter, George Rickey, Larry Rivers, Lidia Silvestri, Richard Smith, Kenneth Snelson, Ettore Sottsass, Jesús Raphael Soto, Joe Tilson and Jack Youngerman, who transposed the extraordinary richness of their respective figurative languages to jewellery. The theft of the entire collection in 1978 during an exhibition in Udine meant the end for GEM and pushed GianCarlo Montebello to the other side of the fence, where he became an artist-jeweller.

One of the artistic trends to have the most impact on jewellery was Kinetic and Programmed Art, which only became an important phenomenon in the mid-1960s when art Informel had exhausted its potential. The early signs of this new aesthetics date back to 1952 when Bruno Munari wrote the *Manifesto del macchinismo*, in which he predicted a society of machines. Artists would have to abandon canvas, paints and chisel and begin to make art with machines. This is what happened with Kinetic and Programmed Art, whose major exponents were Enrico Castellani, Enzo Mari, Getulio Alviani, Dadamaino, the British artist Bridget Riley, Israeli Agam, Argentinean Soto, GRAV, the N Group,

the T Group, the Uno Group and the Zero Group. Out of the exponents of Kinetic Art who took an interest in jewellery, Bruno Munari, Gabriele De Vecchi and Alberto Biasi all deserve a mention. In 1975 Bruno Munari, artist, designer, graphic artist, pedagogue but, above all, design genius, whose motto was "Production without appropriation, action without self-imposition, development without oppression", produced *Costellazioni*, a series of pendants of signs of the zodiac of a rare delicacy, with small perforations illustrating the sign of the zodiac, as bright as gems. Architect Gabriele De Vecchi was close to the T Group. His experiments range from *Argenti Interattivi* ("interactive silvers"), in which silver and the environment limit each other, to the production of jewellery, first for Danese and then for himself. Examples of the body-jewel-movement relationship are the *Libro* brooch, the *Turchese* ring, the *Blink* ring and the *Tourné* ring. His jewellery encapsulates and exalts movement, designed, as shown by his most recent collections, for day and evening use. Alberto Biasi instead belonged to the N Group from Padua, whose members claimed that movement is given by the spectator changing his position, and therefore favours objects that can be moved or rather which acquire particular characteristics thanks to outside intervention. Biasi created kinetic works, dynamic photo-reflections and fluctuating environmental and perceptual projects.

One of the most interesting innovations in the world of Italian jewellery in the 1960s was the Padua School, so-called as it centred on the teachings of Istituto Statale Pietro Selvatico of Padua. "The Padua School", wrote Graziella Folchini Grassetto, "is the name given to a group of artists who, alternating in the roles of pupil-teacher, have promoted an original and harmonious jewellery culture that today counts spans generations."[132] Despite its geographical closeness to the jewellery district of Vicenza, the Padua School did not become rooted in the industrial *humus*, as had happened in Pforzheim or Providence, nor in the technical training of vocational schools, but in an artistic tradition handed down from teacher to pupil in the classrooms of Selvatico. As Fritz Falck observes, the Padua School is "an artistic identity, a school in the sense of artistic community".[133] The paternity can be traced to Mario Pinton, director of the institute from 1969 to 1976, who then handed over the reins to his pupils Francesco Pavan and Giampaolo Babetto, both co-opted in Selvatico's teachings. The *incipit* of the Padua School was, in Pinton's words, "the evocative value of the material, which should be listened to as an expression of its metallic nature". Gold here becomes a pulsating, plastic mater-

[131] GianCarlo Montebello in L. Somaini and C. Cerritelli, *Jewelry by Artists in Italy 1945–1995* (Milan: Electa, 1995). The unabridged text was kindly supplied by GianCarlo Montebello himself.
[132] G. Folchini Grassetto, *Gioielleria contemporanea. La Scuola di Padova* (Stuttgart: Arnoldsche, 2005), p. 12.
[133] F. Falk, "Per la gloria della città. La scuola di Padova", in Cisotto Nalon and Spiazzi 2008, p. 41.

ial, released from the symbolism of gems, softly caving in to the will of geometry, transforming itself into a song of abstraction, as shown in the graffiti of the sapphire brooch of 1979.

From the 1970s on, the Padua School became linked with Programmed Art and the N Group in particular, where Francesco Pavan approached problems of perception, enriching formal sensibility. "Pavan's geometry", noted Folchini Grassetto, "is expressed through primary forms of white or yellow gold…. He uses flat, square or circular shapes which, galvanised by clever articulations, are transformed into masses, cubes or spheres, whose shaky equilibrium tends to lead them back constantly to their original two-dimensional forms".[134] The precision of Cartesian geometries also connotes the work of Giampaolo Babetto, whose restlessness makes it indomitable and passionate. Babetto is the most pervious to the teachings of the Padua School and his curiosity towards the world outside is only matched by his ability for introspection, which takes the form of an absolute creative and productive self-sufficiency. Babetto is a law unto himself and yet, for some bizarre reason, he is simultaneously the most powerful sounding board of the Padua School. His work finds an efficient exegesis in the internal/external exchange to which there is a corresponding entrance/exit. This capacity for osmosis made a decisive contribution to broadening the operative and cultural vistas of the third generation of the Padua School. Babetto was excited by the kinetics of geometrical structures of mobile and rotating elements, such as the extraordinary ring made of thin plates in 1970, followed by long, elastic and extensible chains composed of modular elements, like the yellow gold necklace of 1977, consisting of a series of parallelepipeds, or the necklace of triangular elements made of white gold dating from 1973. Babetto introduced new materials such as ebony and resin, boldly combining them with gems, rightly convinced that they would not look out of place. Art, architecture and jewellery meet in Babetto who, as Germano Celant poetically puts it, "aspires to re-establishing the tie between spirit and matter combining, in the purifying vortex of gold, male and female, natural and artificial, past and present".[135]

VI. 1979–2008: from Materialism to Minimalism

The 1980s was the decade of the "material world" Madonna sang about, a period of excess and ambition. It was the decade of the yuppies, careers, mad spending, the fitness craze, discos and pop stars, stylists and top models and the discovery of the brand.[136] On one hand, style was discreet and almost formal, whilst, on the other, there were also signs of opulence and extrav-

agance. "Perestroika and break-dancing, Live Aid and the Berlin Wall, CDs and CND: a bit of everything, of everything a bit", as Charlotte Seeling put it in a nutshell. "These were the years of high-tech aesthetics, widespread affluence and its ostentation, individualism and hedonism and the rule of the image. Perhaps never before to the same extent had the economic system stimulated, exalted and invented new needs for the individual, projecting him into an illusory dimension in which happiness equalled success and economic affluence."[137] In March 1982 *Time* dedicated its famous cover story to Giorgio Armani, consecrating Italian fashion on a global level. Art and history once more became an element of inspiration for fashion, substituting the movies that had, until then, represented its principal stock of references. The recovery of the folk memory was also a theoretical principle of Postmodernism, the movement launched in 1979 by Philip Johnson in the United States which, in 1980, found a distinguished and cultured Italian exponent in Paolo Portoghesi and his Biennial. Theorised by philosopher Jean-François Lyotard in *La Condition postmoderne. Rapport sur le savoir* of 1979, followed by *The Language of Post-Modern Architecture* by Charles Jencks, the postmodern represented the beginning of the contemporary age due to its decisive break with the rigours of function and its free and de-contextualised use of history. Fashion, architecture and design were thus united in the freedom of drawing their own expressions from the ornamental album of history.

Architecture, design and fashion converged in the pastiche at an alarming speed. As did jewellery. Working on the scar tissue that forms on the boundary between academic theory and popular culture, in the words of Omar Calabrese,[138] the notion of author, which replaced that of genre, became established. With austerity now just a memory, the 1980s consumption of luxury goods skyrocketed, confirming the dawn of a brand-name as an added value of any acquisition. The frenzy for "designer" goods extended to all product categories, starting a process of "democratisation" of luxury by means of shrewd marketing and brand extension strategies. But the collapse of the New York Stock Exchange in 1987, the fall of the Berlin Wall in 1989, the Gulf War in 1991 and the Tangentopoli storm in 1992, not to mention the World Trade Center attacks in 2001 and the Iraqi War, were unequivocal signs that the opulence of the 1980s was irretrievably drawing to a close. The climate of uncertainty determined a return to values such as spirituality whilst postmodern addition was replaced, in fashion as in design, by the austere and rigorous minimalism of the

[134] Folchini Grassetto 2005, p. 42.
[135] G. Celant, *Giampaolo Babetto* (Milan: Skira, 1996), pp. 9–10.
[136] Cf. A. Cappellieri, *Moda e Design: il progetto dell'eccellenza* (Milan: Franco Angeli, 2007), p. 36.
[137] Cocciolo and Sala 2001, p. 288.
[138] *Il modello italiano. Forme della creatività*, edited by O. Calabrese (Milan: Skira, 1998).

Giorgio Vigna
Sketches for a platinum
wedding ring, 2008
Platinum Guild International
Italy Collection

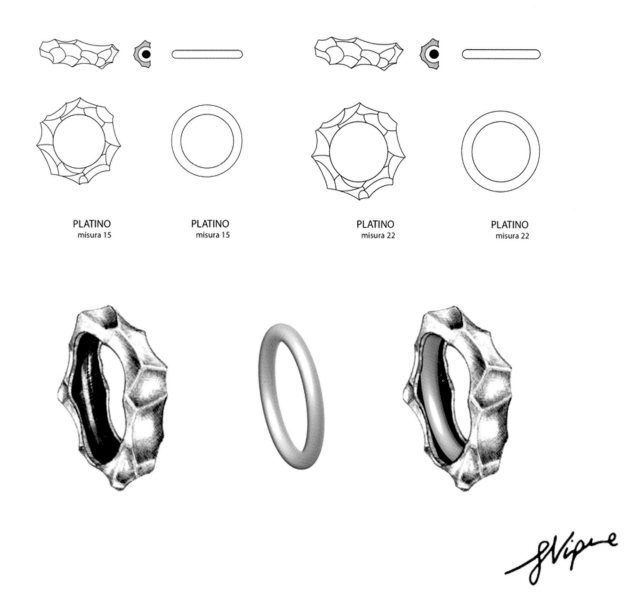

PLATINO
misura 15

PLATINO
misura 15

PLATINO
misura 22

PLATINO
misura 22

1990s, with the monastic shapes and colours of the collections of Jil Sander and Calvin Klein. In the new millennium, notes Enrico Cisnetto,[139] minimalism, low profile and understatement remain some of the most solid pillars of the lifestyle and aesthetics of the well-to-do class, despite going hand-in-hand with luxury choices and consumption.

Jewellery imitated the new luxury,[140] from the 1980s' obsession with the logo to the advertising bombardment of the 1990s, going on to embrace the polysensorial luxuries of the new millennium. Borders came tumbling down. Jewellery *maisons* merged with fashion *maisons* and became "brands", choosing the global market as their stage. In the wake of Cartier big names in jewellery began making accessories, from scarves to perfumes, from handbags to soaps, backing the production of magnificent jewellery. With the introduction of marketing, new ground was broken, such as Bulgari's B.Zero1, a collection that, in 1999, radically changed the perception of brand jewellery.

The contemporary jewel found a pertinent key to its interpretation in the Lyotardian fragment that led to the coining of the term *a quo* in 1979.[141] In fact, what seems evident is that the unitary nature of the jewel now began to be challenged in favour of a diehard multiplicity, which is the chief characteristic of the contemporary jewel. A multiplicity of meanings as well as forms, for which the salad bowl metaphor proposed by Giampaolo Fabris is a good example of the coexistence of diversities. In modernity the term jewellery indeed indicated an object made of precious metals and gems, and this preciousness represented an inviolable and non-negotiable line of demarcation. The same cannot be said now, when the status of the jewel has lost its "aura", to echo Walter Benjamin, and when its bordering on being an accessory requires terminological acrobatics.

[139] *Capital*, March 2001.
[140] Cf. A. Cappellieri, F. Celaschi and A. Vasile, *Lusso versus design* (Milan: Franco Angeli, 2004).
[141] Cf. *Gioiello italiano contemporaneo. Tecniche e materiali tra arte e design*, exhibition catalogue, edited by A. Cappellieri, Vicenza and Milan, 2008 (Milan: Skira, 2008), p. 14.

Whether we like it or not, contemporary jewellery is founded on the simultaneous presence of different values, where the preciousness of metals and gems is no longer, apart from a lexical level, a necessary and sufficient condition for establishing the value of an object and making the difference between a jewel and a non-jewel exhaustive. In the post-materialist contemporary, the quality of the material has been summed with the quality of the design which, while it is clearly not enough to make an object "precious" in terms of its exchange value, does, in fact, give it its plurality of meanings, as Bruno Munari clarified once and for all, strangely enough, back in 1978. And so the break-up of the contemporary is reflected in a pluralism of expressions, a pandemonium that is deliberately ignored in the sphere of jewellery, but whose cheerful promiscuity represents an evident sign of innovation.

To sum up, the contemporary jewel may be retraced to *exempla* identified by its design coordinates: artist's jewel, jeweller's jewel, architect's jewel, industrial designer's jewel, fashion designer's jewel, and why stop here? Or in terms of production parameters: unique piece, limited series, mass production, the latter further divided into high, medium and low mass-production, whilst the traditional jewellery categories of precious jewels and jewel-accessories, where the value came from the materials, have, as we mentioned earlier, been rendered obsolete by the importance of design. Large jewellery *maisons* like Cartier, Van Cleef & Arpels, Tiffany, Harry Winston, Seaman Schepps, Chaumet, Chopard, Bulgari, Mario Buccellati, Damiani, Garrard and Stern, sell the same jewellery from Milan to Shanghai to Dubai, in stores that are all alike, creating an international brand identity.

The work of companies such as Ciro Cacchione's San Lorenzo are more oriented towards research. Since 1970 they have tirelessly investigated crossovers between design, architecture and jewellery, commissioning jewellery designs from major contemporary architects and designers such as Franco Albini and Franca Helg, the Vignellis or the Scarpas, whose design talent, combined with Cacchione's production, have generated awe-inspiring and innovative objects, such as Massimo and Lella Vignelli's *Endless* of 1992, Franco Albini and Franca Helg's *Triangles*, and Afra and Tobia Scarpa's necklaces. This was the first systematic exploration of design jewellery, which was then extended to other objects in everyday use, from the bowl to the saucepan, from the golf putter to liturgical furnishings, proving that a designer's vision, combined with technological expertise, can presage beauty and innovation. The work

of San Lorenzo opened the door to design jewellery which, in 1984, inspired Cleto Munari to invite the empyrean of contemporary architecture to design for him. It was the debut of the postmodern in jewellery, or, as Barbara Radice says, "the first real figurative update of jewellery as an applied art since the 1920s–1930s".[142] Paolo Portoghesi's facades of the Strada Novissima were miniaturised in splendid rings and the Ionian columns of Stanley Tigerman's buildings lay languidly in rings designed to be worn on two fingers. Peter Eisenman's jewels were dynamic stratifications of geometries just like his houses, while those of Arata Isozaki "were models of architecture. Everything I do is close to my architecture. I have used vaults, cubes, pyramids, occasionally cylinders. They are architectonic volumes".[143] Portoghesi is just as explicit: "My jewels are micro-architectures, archetypes of ancient and somewhat sacred architectures. I have dealt with the theme of the house just like children".[144] Whereas Portoghesi reduces the scale of his facades in his jewellery, Sottsass investigated the colours and overlapping of volumes and geometries just as he did for Memphis. Sottsass's marvellous jewels are, as he said himself, "more or less the reproduction of what I think one can do in architecture, formal exercises of architectonic composition". In jewellery architects prefer volumetric strength to "wearability", the equivalent of "functionality" in architecture. With regard to this Mendini observed that he had designed jewellery "in an abstract way, independently of the presence of a body". And this is one of the biggest surprise elements. The form freed itself from function in order to become sign, and what matter if the pieces were so very impractical to wear. The process that Eisenman had defined as "a progressive continuum from the ring to the building" was the same process that had characterised art jewellery in the previous decade, the difference being that the subjects being mimicked were, in the case of architects, their buildings and, in the case of the artists, their paintings or sculptures. Curiously, German jeweller Dieter Roth had achieved the same results ten years earlier. After moving to Reykjavik, he sent a five-page letter with designs of rings to Langenbacher and Wankmiller, his producer in Lucerne, on 30 May 1971, asking to have them made up. These rings were very similar to those of postmodern master-jewellers in terms of their aesthetics and materials, containing geometrical elements with coloured reliefs. In the same year it was a ring with interchangeable hats (*Chapeau*), ironic and iconic objects that confirmed the stature of Roth as a precursor of a language that would soon emerge as the ruling aesthetic.

[142] B. Radice, *Gioielli di architetti dalla collezione di Cleto Munari. Gioielli di Mario Bellini* (Milan: Electa, 1987), p. 7.
[143] Ibid., p. 46.
[144] Ibid., p. 64.

In making it easier for artistic experiences to penetrate each other, Gijs Bakker became established as the true innovator of the contemporary jewel. With his collections *Chi ha Paura..?*, which he began to design in 1996 in partnership with Marijke Vallanzasca, the brilliant Dutch designer and Paduan gallery director involved leading industrial designers and international jewellers in creating serial and not too costly jewels made from gold, silver and alternative materials (though not gems) using advanced technologies.[145] Ron Arad, Pauline Barendse, Dinie Besems, BLESS, Onno Boekhoudt, Tord Boontje, Lin Cheung, Warwick Freeman, Marijke de Goey, Martí Guixé, Konstantin Grcic, Ineke Hans, Dick van Hoff, Esther Knobel, Matijs Korpershoek, Otto Künzli, Sofie Lachaert, Emmy van Leersum, Michael Leung, Charles Marks, Alberto Meda, Ramón Middelkoop, Marc Newson, Ted Noten, Ruudt Peters, Katja Prins, Rolf Sachs, Constanze Schreiber, Peter Skubic, Studio Job, Wieki Somers, Frank Tjepkema, Marcel Wanders, Hannes Wettstein and Mina Wu revisited the concept of the jewel confirming that polyphonic choral nature which is precisely the distinctive mark of contemporary jewellery. With his customary vision Gijs Bakker circumscribed not so much the themes and materials of jewellery as the difference between artist and designer, independently of what products are being designed, decreed by the reproducibility of the object. Mass-produced pieces, though not necessarily a large number, for the designer, or collector's pieces for the artist. What changes is the design method defined by the limits imposed by production – industrial or semi-artisanal – which become themes for the designer. On the other hand, these limits do not invalidate the work of the artist who has the faculty to choose the design limits he prefers, be they material, technological, formal or temporal. Moreover, the designer has to take into account the "wearability" of his jewels, while the artist, producing sculptures of the body, can choose to ignore this. In 2004 the results of this study were highlighted by the exhibition *Il Design della gioia*[146] at the Triennale in Milan, where the jewellery of designers – from Sottsass to Dalisi, Portoghesi and De Lucchi – was exhibited together with that of sculptors, artists-jewellers, collector's pieces, fashion jewels and manufactured jewels.

The new millennium began with an offensive from fashion designers, whose entrance into the arena of jewellery production threw the jewellers' distribution system into disarray, while the horizontal levelling of the age of access[147] expanded the market. Fashion lowered the buying threshold of jewellery, summing it with an added brand value that previously only the large jewellery *maisons* had enjoyed. The general interest shown by fashion designers in jewellery – from Gucci to Dior, from Versace to Prada to Calvin Klein and so on – englobed the jewel in the colossal sales network of mono-brands and in the universal advertising of fashion. In the new millennium the jewellery industry, founded on practically no advertising whatsoever and a network of small local distributors, reacted to this colossal blow by engaging stars and starlettes for advertising campaigns at a cost equal to half of their turnover or by borrowing fashion instruments such as the trend book without having any designers able to transform them into products.

Globalisation favoured the circulation of ideas and talents, with the advantage that many countries, historically oriented towards considering the jewel as something of a local craft, succumbed to the charms of the goldsmith's art. One of these countries was Israel which, in just a few short years, developed a school consisting of mostly female jewellers who have produced stunning results. The catalyst was Esther Knobel, whose contacts with the British milieu and, above all, with Gijs Bakker, led her to develop an interest in contemporary jewellery, favouring experimentation. This openness towards other cultures can be seen especially in Knobel's lovely *Immigrant Brooches* of 1990, where the designer cut out pictures of people, tigers and rabbits from boxes of Chinese tea, producing awe-inspiring effects. Knobel experiments with different materials, which she combines with metal, exalting the lightness and structural boldness of the composition. The same goes for Deganit Stren-Schocken, who creates dreamlike landscapes out of metal wire. Her 1980s' brooches highlight movement, underlining, as the artist says, that "jewels are miniatures of architectures on the body".[148] And so we have her *City* of 2003, a convulsive tangle of chains confirming Stern-Schocken's interest in the context that surrounds her. The strength and lightness of wire mesh also characterises the work of Vered Kaminski, whose works of the 1990s explored the lightness of wire combined with piles of pebbles like his *Baskets* of 1991–92. In his more recent creations, such as the exciting *Stacking Stools* of 2004, the metal wire has become texture in broad bangles, but also a boundary between the body and world, an interior/exterior in which the jewel is a go-between. On the contrary, there is Bianca Eshel-Gershuni, whose jewellery contains the bright colours and naturalism of plant forms. Her jewels are made of yellow gold, whose softness and warmth is enhanced by the small flowers, animals and leaves of the compositions, as shown by the brooches she made in

[145] Cf. *Il Design della gioia. Il gioiello tra progetto e ornamento*, exhibition catalogue, edited by A. Cappellieri and M. Romanelli, Milan Triennial, November 2004 – February 2005 (Milan: Charta, 2004), pp. 18–19.

[146] Ibid.

[147] Jeremy Rifkin, in *The Age of Access*, maintains that the impact of new technologies is radically changing the shape of society and our ways of living. In the immediate future property will be replaced by paid access to every kind of commodity, service or cultural experience.

[148] D. Stern-Schocken in *Women's Tale: Four Leading Israeli Jewelers*, exhibition catalogue, edited by D. S. Taragin and A. Ward, Jerusalem, The Israel Museum and The Racine Art Museum, 2006 (Manchester, Vermont: Hudson Hill Press, 2006), p. 100.

the 1990s. Eshel-Gershuni's jewels are intense, reminding us that the stories and encounters of a life are glued together in the addition of material.

Another interesting surprise was Russian jewellery,[149] which energetically modernised itself within the context of an important jewellery tradition. After the pomp of Fabergé and the czars, Russian jewellery managed to find an original and innovative contemporary form of expression in the works of Natalya Bykova, Gennady Bykov, Vladimir Goncharov, Felix Kuznetsov, Olga Kuznetsova and Dmitri Popov who, at the end of the 1970s, conceived the jewel "as a means of reflecting life. The peculiarities of contemporary jewellery art are manifested in the broadest range of technologies and materials, a wealth of imagination and experimentations. Traditions can be continued through new approaches to designing rather than through interrelations of forms alone".[150] Therefore, contemporary fragmentation was also an efficient magnifying glass for Russian jewellery as it began to explore the evolutions of geometry, in Goncharov or Mikhail Borschchevsky, or Vera Povolotskaya's rings, and, especially, Felix Kuznetsov's interesting *Polycentrum* brooches of 1985, tradition in the filigrees and granulations of Popov's bracelets, Jutta Paas-Alexandrova's earrings and Ivan Shedov's rings, and the textures of materials, in Tatiana Belkina's beautiful necklace of 1979, made of silver chain mail, or the marble streaking of Vladislav Khramtsov's bracelet. There are echoes of Kinetic Art in Felix Kuznetsov's *Eternal Motion* titanium brooches of 1983, in Dmitri Popov's elegant *Flight* brooches and in Andrei Selivanov's *Topology Sketch* earrings of 1985. Natalya Bykova's enamel, copper and bronze *The City Garden* brooches of 1988 also deserve a mention, as do Viktor Anipko's *Little Birds* rings, small birds made of enamel dating from 1988, a reminder that there can be no future without the past.

Contemporary American jewellery was extraordinarily vital and oriented towards both tradition and innovation in equal measures. One of the underlying themes linking *haute* jewellery, *prêt-à-porter* and experimental jewellery was the world of nature which, after a phase of minimalism and austerity, came back into fashion. The timeless marvels of Tiffany and Harry Winston were joined by the jewellery of Neil Lane and Martin Katz of Los Angeles. Both began their careers selling antique jewellery and went on to include the seductive forms of nature in their jewels, characterised by tulips made of sapphire, amethyst, diamond and garnet *pavé* with coloured leaves and flowers. In the last two decades New York has been the major centre for jewellery design. Here many designers reinterpret the past in order to create jewellery for the new millennium. Some of the most interesting are Christopher Walling, Marilyn Cooperman, Henry Dunay, Ella Gafter, James de Givenchy, David Yurman and Sorab Bouzarjomehri. Californian David Freda makes enamelled orchids in the spirit of Art Nouveau and, in order to make his pieces realistic, uses real flowers as a model, which he plunges into hot wax to produce the mould. Artist-jeweller Michael Good experiments with new treatments of gold wire which he twists into fascinating combinations, while Arline Fisch makes soft mesh bracelets by hand. William Harper has specialised in *cloisonné* enamel with raw gold, while Jamie Bennet has developed a granular, opaque enamel. The works of Douglas Bucci, Cappy Counard, Sharon Church, Sandra Enterline, Steven Ford & David Forlano, Matthew Hollern, Ron Ho, Daniel Jocz, Robin Kranitzky, Sondra Sherman, Stanley Lechtzin and Daniella Kerman, Keith Lewis, Linda MacNeil, Richard Mawdsley, Bruce Metcalf, Hellen Shirk, Marjorie Schick and Zandra Zilker are particularly interesting.

In this period the large French jewellery *maisons* – Cartier, Van Cleef & Arpels, Piaget and others – merged with the Richemont group, which thus became the largest company to produce *haute* jewellery. In the 1980s Parisian *maison* Boivin continued to produce fanciful and astonishing phytomorphic jewellery according to the dictates of Jeanne Boivin. Even the humble radish was considered a subject worthy of *haute joaillerie*. The same themes also characterised the *haute* jewellery of big name fashion houses such as Chanel and Dior. The freshness of floral polychromy distinguished jewels designed by Victoire de Castellane for Dior whilst Chanel opted for the sophisticated monochromy of *mode blanche,* reediting some of the *maison*'s celebrated pieces such as the *Comet*, the *Fringe* or the *Fountain* collection. Within the sphere of *haute* jewellery we also find JAR, Joel Arthur Rosenthal, who sells jewellery from his boutique in Place Vendôme made of iridescent oxidised titanium overlaid with floral motifs, such as the *Moghul Flower* bracelet. Two of the most interesting designers on the French scene, generally oriented more towards traditional than experimental jewellery, are Françoise and Claude Chavent, who combine metals such as steel, gold and silver, modelled in geometrical shapes, small cubes, pyramids, rectangles and circles. Their aim is "to bring volume and movement to forms to make them light and ambiguous. To do so we avoid using perspective and trompe l'œil. Hammering thins the metal and gives it sharp edges. When the piece is flat, the illusion is created by the reflection of light on

[149] Karpun 1994.
[150] Felix Kuznetsov in Karpun 1994, p. 19.

the different surfaces. We tend to simplify more and more to shorten the distance to be travelled from the concept to the object". Their minimalism has nothing in common with commercial fashions but, on the contrary, emphasises the void as the essence of purity.

In 1998 Garrard's splendid masterpieces merged with those of Asprey to generate the British pole of luxury. However, eight years later, in 2006, they separated. Garrard and Asprey represent the two pinnacles of British jewellery. However, Anglo-Saxon jewellery has little to do with the crown jewels, characterised as it is by experimentation and innovation rather than traditional luxury. Vivienne Westwood's punk ornaments exerted a greater influence on British jewellers than the glittering *Star of Africa*, favouring the communicative aspect over the ornamental or geological features of the jewel. Great Britain has numerous institutions involved in the promotion of jewellery, from the Victoria and Albert Museum to London schools, such as the Royal College of Art and Central Saint Martins College of Art & Design. These schools, examples of an educational system that counts numerous sectors dedicated to jewellery, have ensured a constant stream of trained jewellery designers. Among the protagonists of the British scene a prominent place is reserved for David Watkin, director of the department of the Royal College of Art from 1984 to 2006. Watkin led Britain to experiment with materials thought to be somewhat unconventional or anyway not greatly in keeping with the sphere of jewellery. Thanks to his ideas and position, a wide range of materials was introduced, such as plastic used creatively, acrylic combined with delicately worked precious metals, corrugated Perspex coating photographs enclosed in silver pendants, or paper, one of the most ephemeral materials, with which he and Wendy Ramshaw produced a powerful collection at the end of the 1990s. As he himself has explained "I explore the potential of new technologies, processes and materials to contribute to the aesthetic and formal development of jewellery artefacts. This involves the appropriation of industrial techniques and their integration into studio practice". Peter Chang's marvellous jewels also draw their expressive strength from materials: acrylic, polyester resin and PVC create a kaleidoscope of fantastic forms in his jewellery, emblems of that liquid modernity that Zygmunt Bauman speaks of. Chang is one of the few who have managed to make a poor material such as plastic precious. His creations are unique and delicately combine sculpture and jewellery. He is indifferent to labels and says: "The pieces I create can be sculptures or they can be worn as jew-

ellery. Each individual will have a different response to them and I like that".

The use of plastics is also seen in the gorgeous pieces of Roger Morris, Susan Heron and Nual Jamieson. Susan Heron has made a study of perspex with her work entitled *Boomerang*, Jane Adams anodised aluminium, Edward de Large and Clarissa Mitchell titanium, Michael Rowe coated brass, Susan Cross crochet wool, Ester Ward steel wire and Jane Short enamel, whilst Catherine Martin has instead adapted the Japanese technique of braiding known as *kumihimo*.

The Dutch school of jewellery is, like Dutch design, one of the most innovative on the international scene. Heavily influenced by Gijs Bakker who, in the meantime, founded Droog Design, one of the truly original design companies of the contemporary age, it has no internationally important jewellery firms but can count on the sound training provided by the Gerrit Rietveld Academie of Amsterdam. Major Dutch jewellers have taught here, including Ruudt Peters (to whom we owe the introduction of a mystical symbology where esotericism concerns the transformation of matter), his pupil Iris Eichenberg, and Truike Verdegaal, a lover of Japanese culture, which she reworks in jewels of extraordinary and fantastic richness. Another interesting professor is Hilde De Decker, originally from Belgium, who is known for including vegetal and natural elements in her works. For instance, in her 2004 collection, *For the Farmer's Market*, peppers, aubergines, tomatoes and other vegetables are incorporated in rings to represent gems. De Decker does not succumb to the usual mimetic or naturalistic visions of nature typical of traditional jewellery but rather exalts the fragility and unparalleled beauty that precedes its decay.

One of the features of the Dutch School is its rejection of the statute of the precious jewel through the use of material. This is seen for example in Nel Linnsen's paper jewellery, pleated collars which have an extraordinary expressive strength, but also in the use of colour in the work of Ralph Bakker, who says "Working as a jewellery-artist is a matter of attitude, a conscious choice for a certain way of working; a mentality. It is of no importance to me whether the piece of jewellery I make exceeds boundaries. My aim is to make a good piece of jewellery and whether it is defined as art is up to others. In making my jewellery I am in search of answers to questions I cannot or will not ask myself, hoping that my jewellery can show me both the questions and the answers".[151] Ted Noten's work is innovative and groundbreaking. He casts traditional jewels in Plexiglas cases, like *Agata Aussteuer*, a bag containing fifty-eight rings belonging to relatives of the person the object is des-

[151] http://www.ralphbakker.nl/

tined for, or *Bagfromretiredjewellerymaker*, a case for a retired jeweller who does not want to be separated from his beloved tools.

In Germany Stefan Hemmerle of Munich has changed *haute* jewellery with his New Objectivity: "I want to tread a middle path between the decorative art and the severe", he says, "I wanted my clients to feel that they have found someone who can bring essential to the fore – but with imagination!"[152] His jewellery, like *Fern* of 2004, finds a harmonious and elegant formal reference in nature. One company that has contributed to the innovation of the contemporary jewel is Marc-Jens Biegel's *Biegel*. Above all there is Niessing, which systematically explores the frontiers of design since, as they say, "Design at Niessing results from ongoing evolution. The fundamental concept has always remained unchanged. Each piece of jewellery embodies an idea, an underlying principle. The design concentrates on this principle. This design idiom characterises Niessing. It remains unchanged and is independent of the particular individuals who work on it. Niessing has established organisational conditions and a personnel basis to ensure this".[153] Today Niessing jewellery, which combines the beauty of the form with the beauty of technology, is designed by major German jewellery designers – Susanna Loew, Mathias Moennich, Norbert Muerrle, Marion Roethig, Dorothea Schippel, Petra Weingaertner, Susanne Arusha Winckler – just as, in the past, it was designed by great professionals such as Friedrich Becker, Juergen Braeuer or Herman Hermsen, to mention but three. This successful formula is rooted in an unusually reactive territorial system. There is the industrial district of Pforzheim which, in time, has also been transformed into a cultural district, thanks to the museum and its activities, and schools such as the Akademie der Bildenden Künste of Munich and the Hochschule of Pforzheim, which have favoured that exchange between academia and the professions which is crucial for the renewal of both. Its protagonists include Hermann Junger, who followed in the footsteps of Franz Rickert, whose best work is his combinatorial, modular jewellery in which "miniaturised figurations, often raised from the surface of the surrounding support, divide the spaces up between tangled linearities, pointillism like throbbing matter, a minimum of pigmentations, jutting gems, always small and varied, bright and many-hued".[154] He was succeeded in 1991 by Otto Künzli, who re-elaborated the geometries and colour variations typical of the 1980s to produce an original and autonomous style. At the beginning of the 1980s Otto Künzli created polystyrene brooches covered with wallpaper, stirring a lively and fertile debate on how far a jewel could travel in form and function from tradition while retaining its definition as a jewel. The German School has always generated, and continues to generate, an abundance of ideas. There is the mixture of materials – as in Claus Bury's jewellery which combines acrylic with precious materials to produce brooches, rings and pendants in abstract shapes with mechanical components. Then there is the body – for Gerd Rothmann the body becomes a digital print, a sign of distinction, but also a decorative motif. Rothmann plays with the personalisation of some parts of the body, the nose, the heel, the finger, in order to load the jewel with affective and aesthetic values. Then there is nature – Onno Boekhoudt experimented with sections of tree trunks but his work on the "house" – which is reflected like an inner space in the rings, a piece of steel into which the finger is inserted, or the same form, consisting of numerous layers, regulated fluidly around the finger – is also interesting. The works of master-jewellers Rudolf Bott, Michael Becker, Bettina Speckner, George Dobler, Iris Eichenberg, Ingrid Gossner and Falko Marx are also fascinating.

Scandinavian jewel has evolved in the last twenty years towards a radical experimentation whose fulcrum remains the geometrical silver jewellery of Georg Jensen and the expressive strength of Tone Vigeland's work. The simplicity of forms and shapes is the underlying theme linking the works of Danish Agnete Dinesen, Helga and Bent Exner, Poul Sorresiig and Willy Palden. The jewellery of Swedish Ohl Ohlsson, AnnChristine Hultberg, Eric Robbert and Theresia Hvorslev, more oriented towards organic forms and heterogeneous materials, is more diverse. The intense activity of Finnish design is also seen, though with less expressive vigour, in the jewels of Mirjam Salminen and Björn Weckström. Recent works deserving of a mention include those of Sigurd Bronger, Juhani Heikkilä, Helge Larsen and Darani Lewers, Margaret Sandström, Tore Svensson, Terhi Tolvanen and Mona Wallström.

As well as the international *maisons* Chopard and De Grisogono, Swiss *haute* jewellery is distinguished by the zoomorphic jewels of Emmanuel and Sophie Guillaume for ESG Jewels of Geneva, made of a platinum alloy. Naturalism also permeates Austrian *haute* jewellery. Schullin's creations are distinguished by their extravagant shapes and colours, such as the collier made of thin twigs of coral, arranged like bunches of chilli pepper. Artist jewellers include Eva Tesarik, Margit Hart and Fritz Maierhofer. The latter in particular, after experimenting with colour in the 1970s and with synthetic materials in the 1980s, has now cho-

[152] Quoted in J. Dormer, *Stefan Hemmerle: Art of Nature* (New York), p. 7.
[153] http://www.niessing.com/
[154] G. Folchini Grassetto, "Il binomio-artista docente nelle scuole orafe europee", in Cisotto and Spiazzi 2008, p. 79.

sen the following direction, as he explains himself, "I was expressing my ideas in tin and gold. Pure tin is very soft and the person using it as jewellery can wear it in numerous different positions. I worked small segments of gold, the function of which was to hold the jewellery in place, into each piece. I create my works as independent as small sculptures and to be hung on the wall to bring them closer to their audience. Jewellery should not be put away in cases, but kept where it is visible when not being worn. The relationship between an item of jewellery and the wearer is intense, which means that it is worn both consciously and with emotion at the right moment. Thus it passes on its signals and messages".[155]

In South America jewellery is interesting from the point of view of both production and design. In Brazil, the company Stern has succeeded in establishing itself as an international player thanks to its shrewd blend of tradition and innovation. It has combined top- and medium-range jewellery with the works of designers such as the Campana brothers, who have revisited forms and materials with far-sightedness. The work of Jorge Castañon of Buenos Aires is also worthy of interest. In Spain it is the Escola Massana[156] of Barcelona which represents the hotbed of Spanish jewellery and the centre of jewellery culture, originally under the direction of Manuel Capdevila, then succeeded by Ana Font in 1972 and by Ramón Puig Cuyàs, in 1977. Catalan jewellery is profoundly tied up with the extraordinary artistic experiments of the twentieth-century avant-garde, as seen in the creations of Cuyàs, who uses painting combined with assemblages of a variety of materials. The work of Valencian Antonio W. Rodríguez also deserves a mention. Portugal has a surprisingly lively contemporary jewellery scene, in terms of both production and the circulation of ideas.[157] The delicate handwriting of Alexandra Serpa Pimentel, the thimbles of Catarina Silva, Cristina Filipe's readymades, Diana Silva's corals, Dulce Ferraz's encrustations, Leonor Hipolito's pralines, Manuela Sousa's keepsakes, and Margarina Matos and Susana Rezende's light projections are highly prized.

In 2008 the exhibition *Il Gioiello Italiano Contemporaneo*[158] showed that in the contemporary age Italian jewellery has moved towards a plurality of expressions and fields, with corresponding markets and customers. High level production finds its principal international exponents in Mario Buccellati, Bulgari and Damiani, followed by Crivelli, Hafner, Mikimoto, Scavia, Salvini, Visconti, Villa and Pasquale Bruni. The most interest-

ing contributions to new expressions in *prêt-à-porter* jewellery come from Vhernier, Pomellato, Mattioli, Mattia Cielo and Antonimi, who have brought their knowledge of transversal disciplines such as fashion, design, art and architecture to bear in an attempt to innovate Italian jewellery whilst retaining its traditional features of beauty and quality. Equally interesting are the ideas of Marco Bicego, Nanis, Roberto Coin, Chimento, Uno A Erre, Carità, Ascione, Chantecler, Ponte Vecchio and Garavelli, representing excellence in Italian jewellery. In the same market segment we find the jewellery of Italian fashion companies such as Ferragamo, Gucci, Armani, Versace and Cavalli, whose recent forays into jewellery have been encouraged by the extensiveness of their sales network and by advertising campaigns. Breil, Miluna, Rosato, Morellato and Nomination deserve acknowledgment for bringing young people closer to jewellery by introducing alternative materials such as steel at affordable prices. Sharra Pagano, Donatella Pellini and Maria Calderara produce accessory jewellery which is extraordinary in terms of taste and materials.

Except for the case of San Lorenzo described earlier, Italian contemporary jewellery lacks solid partnerships between designers and producers, something that is needed if there is to be any kind of innovation and renewal. It is an astonishing fact that two centres of Italian jewellery excellence such as the School of Padua and the industrial district of Vicenza have not managed to establish any form of communication despite being just thirty-five kilometres apart. The short geographical distance between the jewellery district in Vicenza and the School of Padua has unfortunately not led to the "happy marriage" theorised by Vico Magistretti that nicely sums up the reasons Italian design is so successful.

Designers who take their cue from the limits imposed by manufacturing include Giorgio Vigna, with his awe-inspiring glass jewellery, James Rivier, with his titanium jewellery, Fabio Cammarata, who has worked with important fashion companies, Massimiliano Bonoli, Stefania Lucchetta, Manuela Gandini and Alessia Ansaldi. The extraordinary legacy of Italian traditional techniques has been revisited producing astonishing results by Rossella Tornquist, Patrizia Bonati, Carla Riccoboni, Jacqueline Ryan, Giovanni Corvaja, Maurizio Stagni and Elisabetta Dupré. Roberta Bernabei is one of the most sensitive interpreters of materials, as well as Marco Borghesi, Rita Marcangelo, Barbara Uderzo, Isabella del Bono, Milli de Maria, Margherita Marchionni, Tramontano, Sandra di Giacinto, Barbara Paganin, Nathalie Jean and Ute Kolar. Italian con-

[155] http://www.fritz-maierhofer.com/statement-en.htm
[156] For an in-depth study of the school of European jewellery, cf. Folchini Grassetto 2008, pp. 79–83.
[157] Cf. *4 punti di contatto tra Roma e Lisbona*, AGC, Pin, October 2006.
[158] *Dizionario del gioiello italiano contemporaneo* 2005.

temporary master-jewellers include GianCarlo Montebello, who has demonstrated the elegance and lightness of steel with his *Superleggeri*; Alba Lisca, whose work on plate has reached magisterial levels of compositional harmony; Karl-Heinz Reister, whose sophisticated colours recall Deco elegance; Fausto Maria Franchi, who has cleverly used the strength of gold; Gabriele De Vecchi, whose lust for movement has been sated by splendid reversible jewellery; Riccardo Dalisi, whose ultra modest jewellery has revealed beauty in the poverty of its materials. Some of the Italian master-jewellers are exponents of the School of Padua we remind Graziano Visintin, Alberto Zorzi, Renzo Pasquale, Giorgio Cecchetto, Maria Rosa Franzin and the younger Stefano Marchetti, Annamaria Zanella, Alberta Vita and Lucia D'Avanzo.

The relationship with production, deliberately neglected by the School of Padua, has instead been seized upon by the Lombardy system of jewel, crystallised in the acronym SIGILLO, distinguished by its systemic vision of combining design, production, advertising, training and promotion, considered to be complementary aspects of the contemporary jewel. The Lombard jewel is aware that a jewel is not just a masterpiece to be admired but an object to be experienced, accompanying our life and adorning it, an ornament which has to address the dynamism of the body, the world and its commodities. Milan has given a shape to the Italian jewellery establishment deploying major industry players: in design, in production, in training – Milan Polytechnic and Domus Academy; in promotion – the Triennale, the Milan Trade Fair, Associazione Orafa Lombarda, Associazione Gioiello Contemporaneo, and the galleries of Deanna Farneti Cera and Milli de Maria; in advertising – *Vogue Gioiello* and trade magazines. Its aims are to prove the existence and coherence of the system of Lombard jewellery, to document the multiplicity of the contemporary scene by observing transversal environments, and to testify to an acceptation of jewellery where preciousness does not come from materials but from design, since, as Enzo Mari maintains, "the quality of a design depends on the degree, albeit minimal, of the cultural change it triggers".

Works

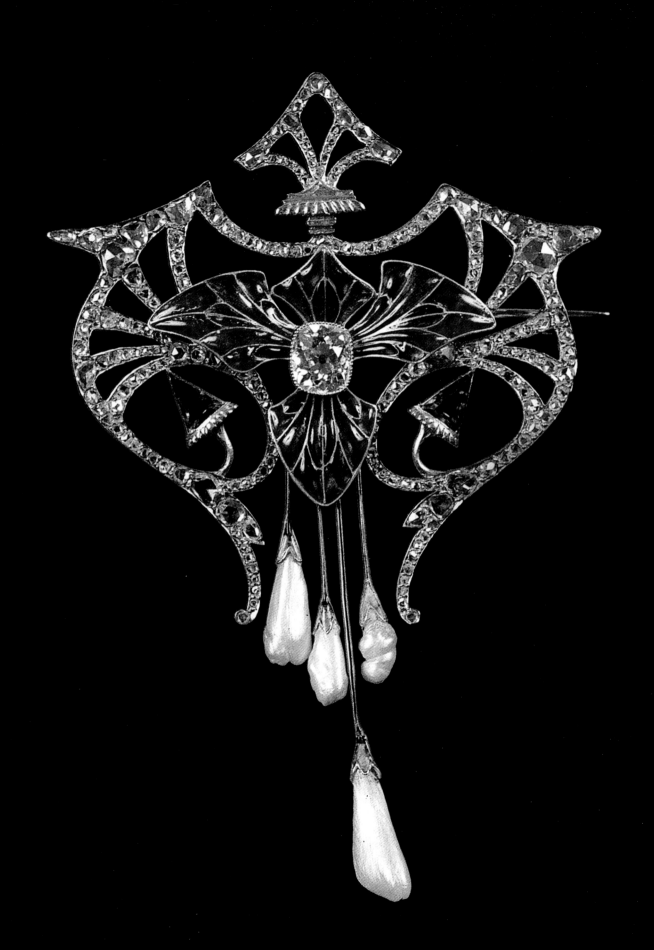

Georges Fouquet
Brooch-pendant, 1895
Gold, diamonds, emeralds,
freshwater pearls, enamel
Private collection

Georges Fouquet,
designed by Alphonse Mucha
Chain with pendant,
1899–1900
Gold, mother-of-pearl,
tourmalines, garnets,
sapphires, emeralds, pearls,
freshwater pearls, enamel
London, Mucha Trust
Foundation

Georges Fouquet
Chain with pendant, c. 1900
Gold, freshwater pearls,
enamel
Private collection

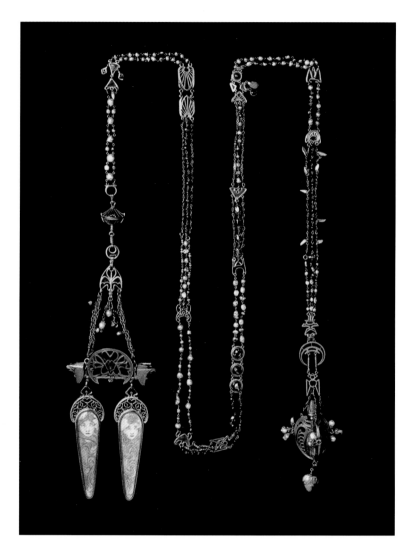

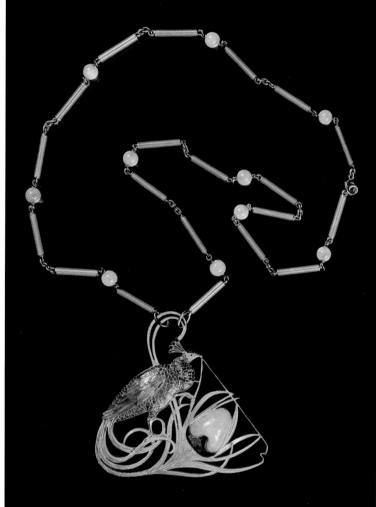

Georges Fouquet
Hair ornament, 1905–06
Horn, enamel, diamonds,
freshwater pearls
Paris, Petit Palais, Musée des
Beaux-Arts de la Ville de Paris

Georges Fouquet
Brooch-pendant, 1902
Gold, enamel, amethysts, opal,
freshwater pearls
Private collection

Georges Fouquet,
designed by Alphonse Mucha
Slave bracelet made
for Sarah Bernhardt, 1899
Chased gold, enamel, opals,
rubies, diamonds
Private collection

René Lalique
Serpents corsage ornament,
1898–99
Gold and enamel
Lisbon, Museu Calouste
Gulbenkian

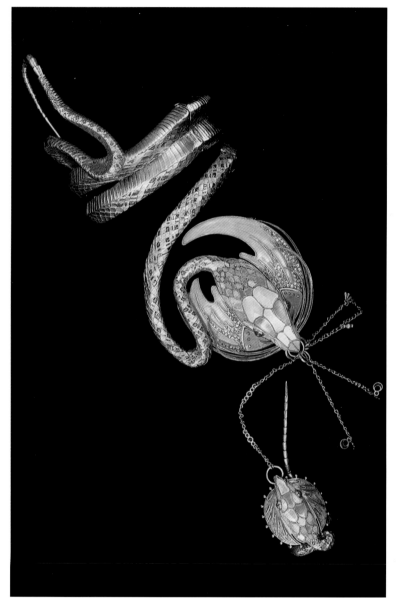

Georges Fouquet
Fuchsia necklace, c. 1905
Gold, enamel, opal, pearls,
diamonds
Paris, Petit Palais, Musée des
Beaux-Arts de la Ville de Paris

Vever, designed by Henri Vever
Perfume pendant, 1900
Chased gold, opal, enamel
Paris, Musée des Arts
décoratifs
Photo: Georges Fessy

Vever, designed by Henri Vever
Bees belt buckle, 1907
Chased gold, enamel,
diamonds
Paris, Musée des Arts
décoratifs

Vever, designed
by Eugène Grasset
Apparitions brooch, 1900
Gold, ivory, enamel
Paris, Musée des Arts
décoratifs

Vever, designed by Eugène
Grasset
Omphale necklace, 1900
Gold, silver, enamel, jasper,
rubies, emeralds, opals,
turquoises, diamonds
Paris, Musée des Arts
décoratifs

Vever, designed by Henri Vever
Sylvia pendant, 1900
Gold, enamel, agate, rubies,
diamonds
Paris, Musée des Arts
décoratifs

Lucien Gaillard
Hair ornament, 1904
Carved horn, gold, diamonds
Paris, Musée des Arts
décoratifs

Lucien Gaillard
Sycamore hair ornament, 1906
Horn, gold
Paris, Musée des Arts
décoratifs
Photo: Les Arts Décoratifs /
Laurent Sully Jaulmes

René Lalique
Two Women pendant,
1898–1900
Gold, enamel, pearl
Hakone, Japan, Lalique
Museum

René Lalique
Pendant, 1898–1900
Silver, vitreous paste, baroque
pearl, enamel
Lisbon, Museu Calouste
Gulbenkian

René Lalique
Grasshoppers necklace,
1902–03
Horn, tin foil, baroque pearls
Lisbon, Museu Calouste
Gulbenkian

René Lalique
Insect Women and Black Swans necklace, 1897–99
Gold, Australian opals, amethysts, enamel
New York, The Metropolitan Museum of Art

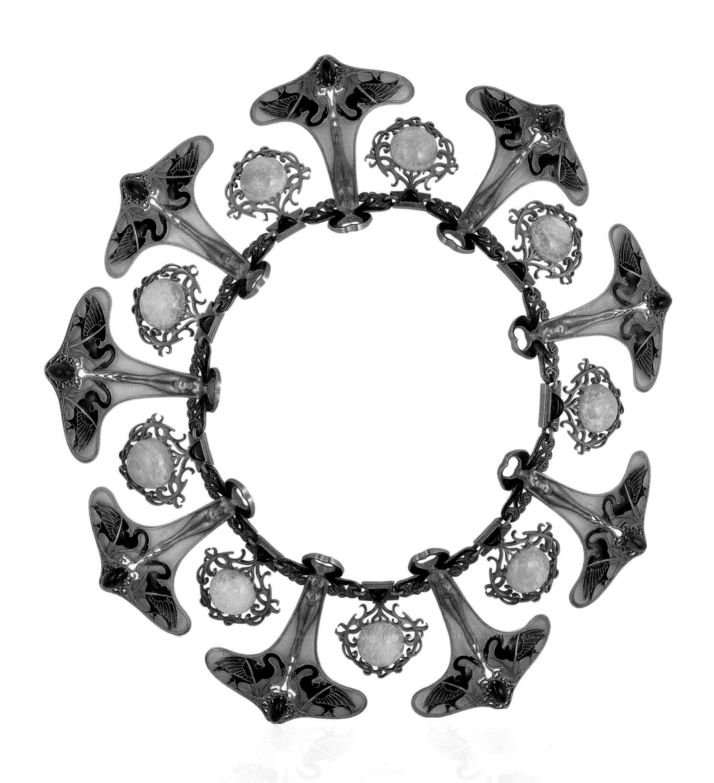

René Lalique
Wisteria bracelet, 1900–02
Gold, enamel, vitreous paste
Lisbon, Museu Calouste
Gulbenkian

René Lalique
Owls bracelet, 1900–01
Glass, gold, enamel,
chalcedony
Lisbon, Museu Calouste
Gulbenkian

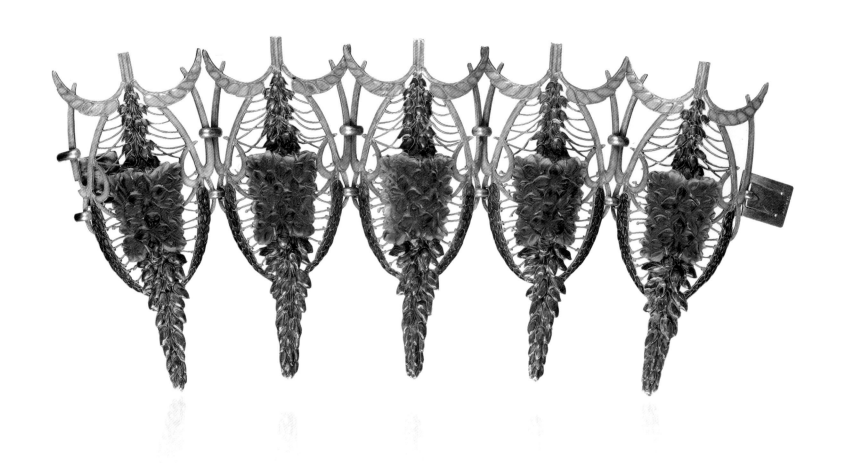

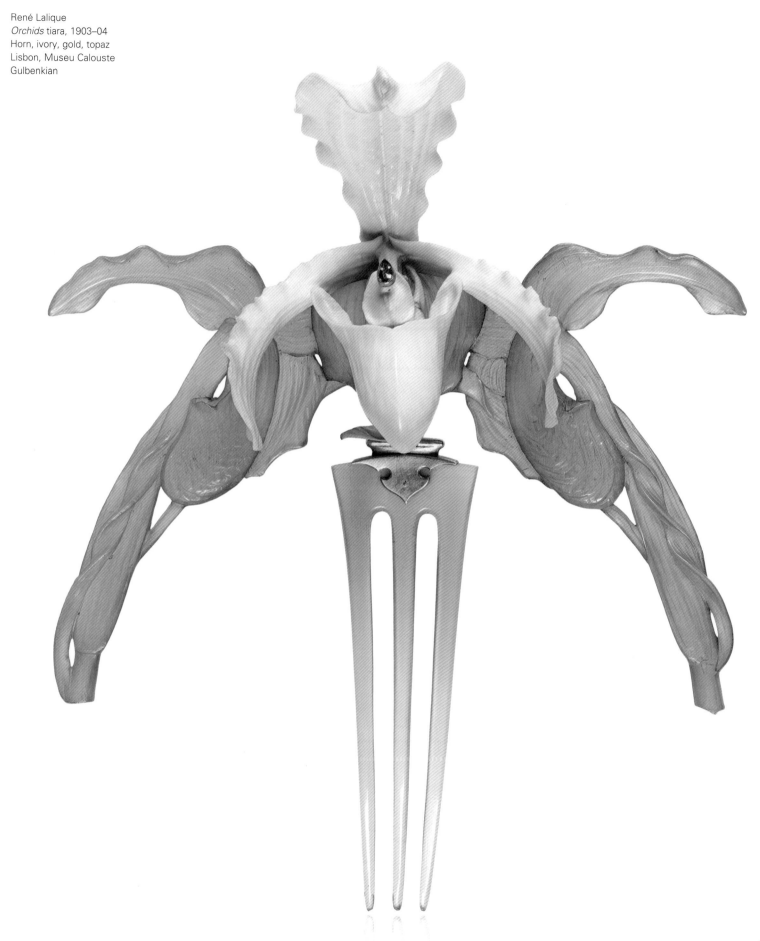

René Lalique
Wasps brooch, 1899–1900
Gold, enamel, opal, diamonds
Copenhagen, Det danske
Kunstindustrimuseet

Boucheron, designed
by Lucien Hirtz
Buckle, 1908
Gold, cornelian, jade
Boucheron Collection

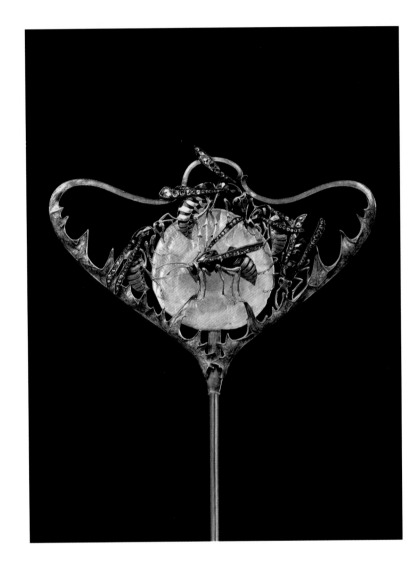

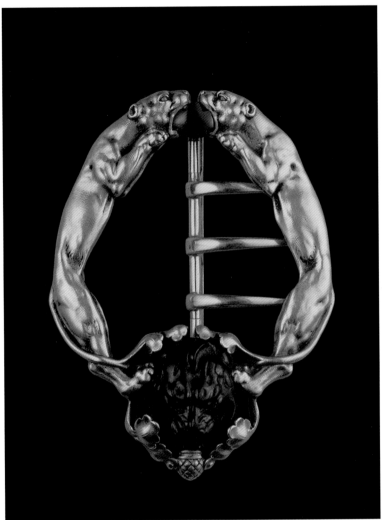

René Lalique
Dragonfly Woman corsage
ornament, 1897–98
Chased gold, enamel,
chrysoprase, chalcedony,
moonstone, diamonds
Lisbon, Museu Calouste
Gulbenkian

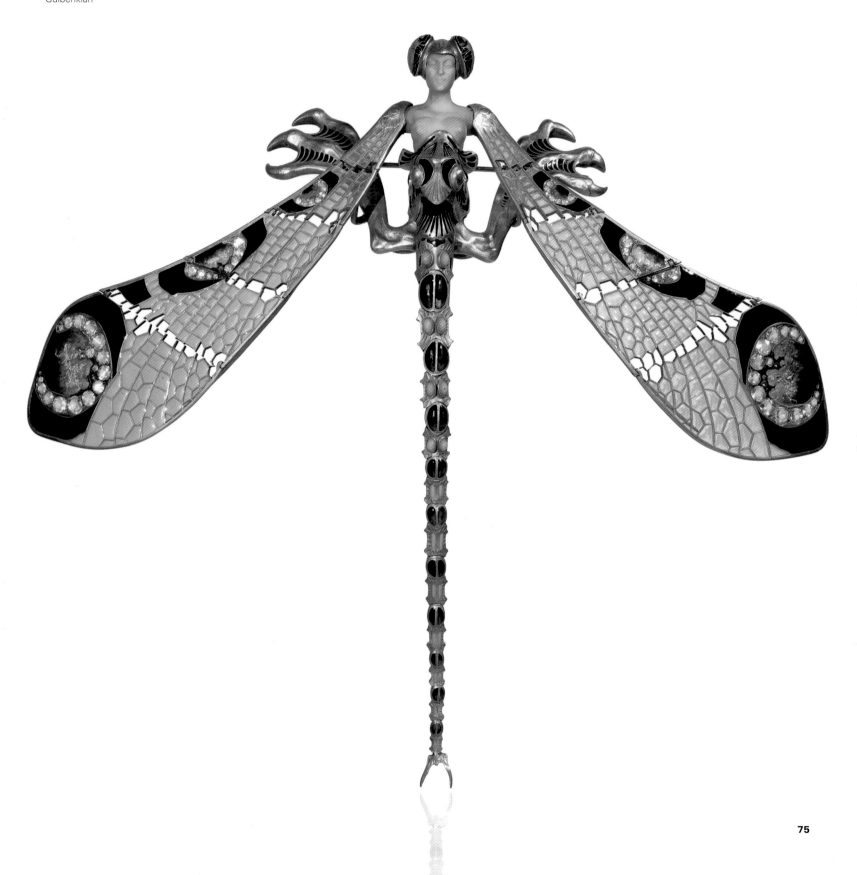

Georg Anton Scheidt
Buckle, c. 1900
Silver
Private collection

Marcel Bing for La maison
de L'Art nouveau
Woman-Peacock pendant,
1900–01
Chased gold, enamel, ruby
Paris, Musée des Arts
décoratifs

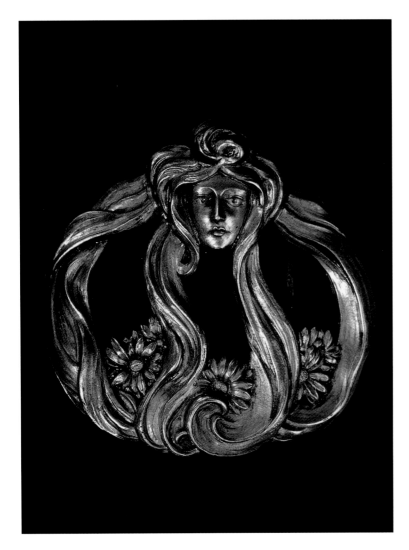

Edward Colonna, attributed
Buckle, c. 1900
Chased gold, natural pearls,
rubies, opal
New York, Cooper Hewitt,
National Design Museum,
Smithsonian Institution

Wiener Werkstätte
Brooch, 1905
Silver, topaz, citrine
London, Tadema Gallery

Wiener Werkstätte,
designed by Josef Hoffmann
Buckle, 1910
Copper, enamel
Vienna, Asenbaum Collection

Wiener Werkstätte,
designed by Josef Hoffmann
Necklace, 1909
Hammered and gilded silver,
topaz
Private collection, courtesy
Neue Galerie New York

Philippe Wolfers
Swan with Serpents pendant,
1898
Opal, gold, rubies, diamonds,
pearls
Private collection

Theodor Fahrner
Brooch, c. 1900
Gilded silver, onyx
New York, Chazanof Collection

Philippe Wolfers
Day and Night buckle, 1897
Chased silver, amethysts
Private collection

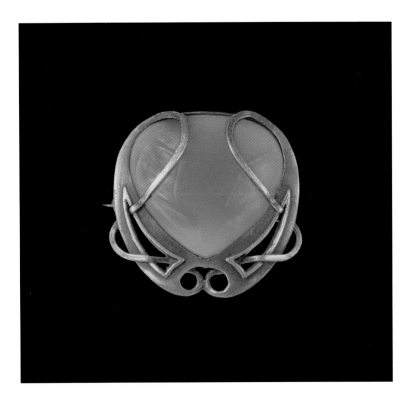

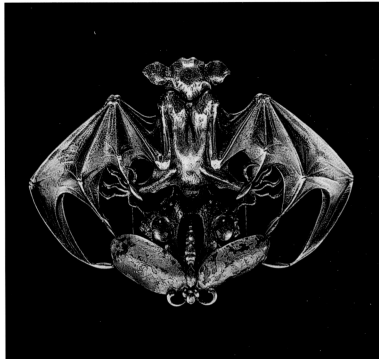

Philippe Wolfers
Victoria pendant, 1902
Chased gold, enamel, rubies,
emeralds, diamonds,
tourmaline, freshwater pearls
Private collection

Philippe Wolfers
Large Dragonfly pendant,
1903–04
Gold, opal, enamel, rubies,
diamonds, Mexican opal
Private collection

Henry van de Velde
Brooch, c. 1898
Gold, rubies, diamonds
London, Tadema Gallery

Henry van de Velde
Necklace, c. 1900
Gold, sapphires, emeralds
Munich, Museum für
angewandte Kunst, die Neue
Sammlung

Theodor Fahrner,
designed by Franz Böres
Necklace with pendant, c. 1905
Silver, enamel, pearls
Private collection

Theodor Fahrner,
designed by Franz Böres
Necklace, c. 1904
Silver
Private collection

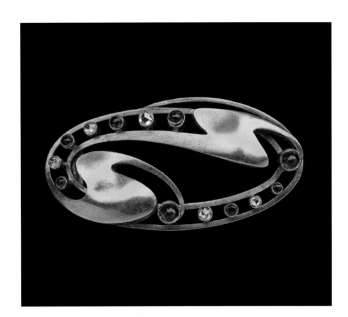

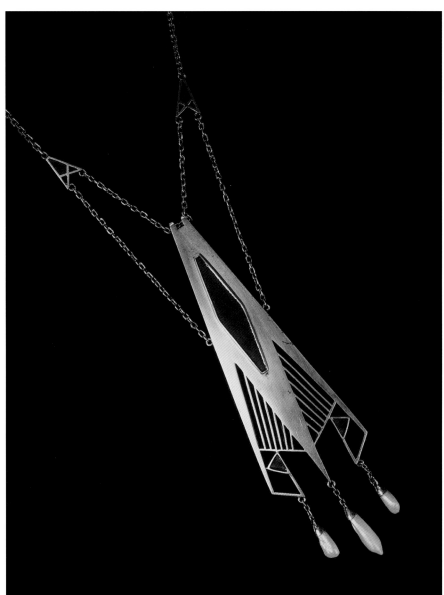

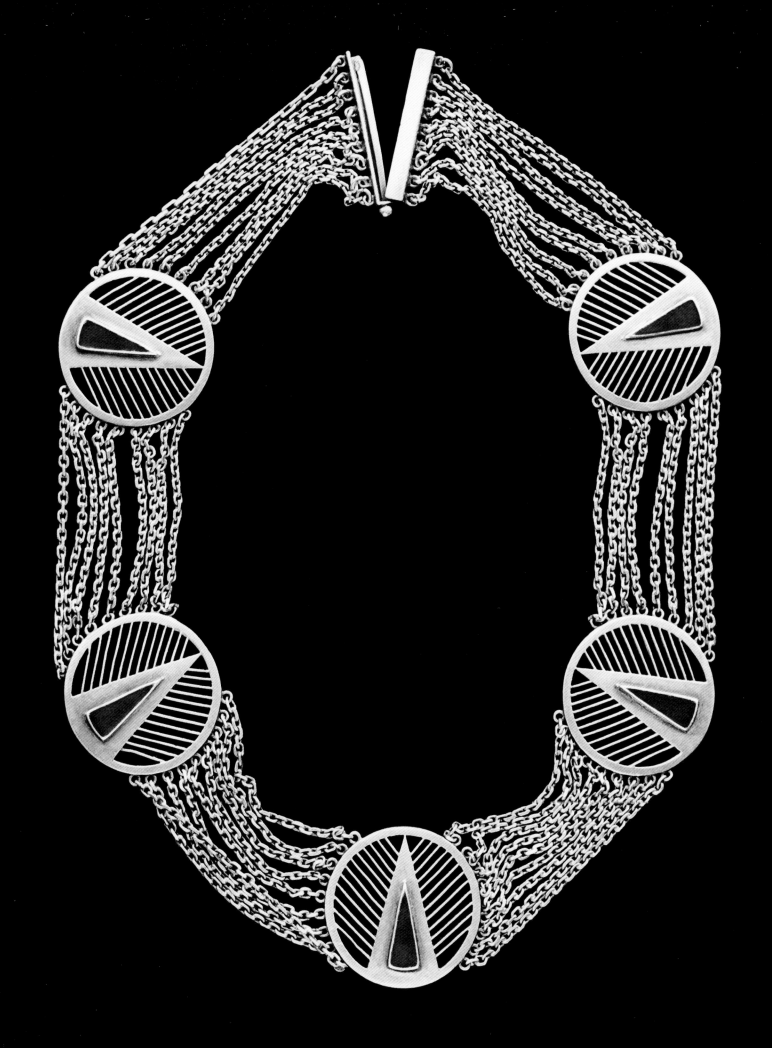

Liberty & Co., designed
by Jessie M. King
Necklace, c. 1900
Gold, pearls
Private collection

Liberty & Co., designed
by Archibald Knox
Pendant, c. 1900
Gold, opal, pearls
Private collection

Liberty & Co., designed
by Archibald Knox
Buckle, 1903
Silver, turquoise
Cheltenham, Gloucestershire,
Cheltenham Art Gallery &
Museum, The Hull Grundy Gift

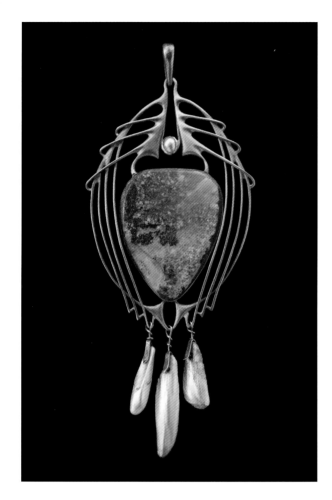

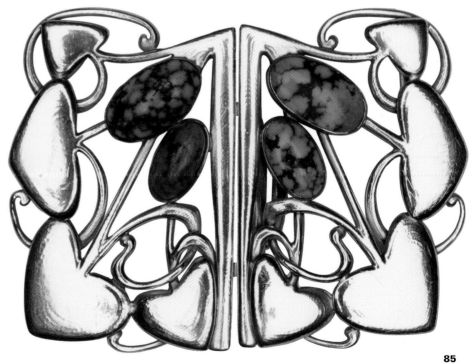

Charles Robert Ashbee
Snowdrop pendant, c. 1900
Gold, yellow topaz, aquamarine
London, Tadema Gallery

Frances McNair
Brooch, c. 1900
Silver, enamel
Royal Museum of Scotland
Collection

Henry Wilson
Ring, c. 1905
Gold, pearls
Private collection

John Paul Cooper
The Kingfisher necklace, 1906
Gold, emeralds, rubies, pearls
London, Tadema Gallery

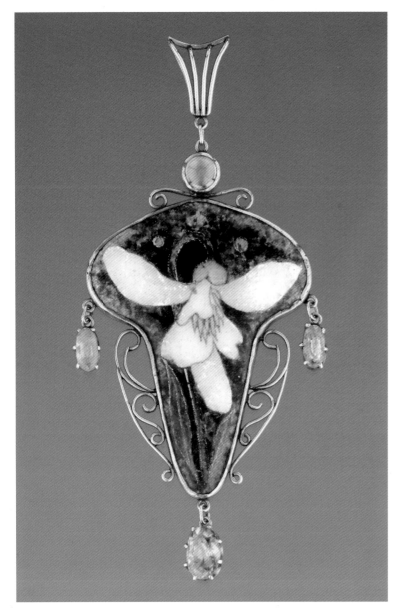

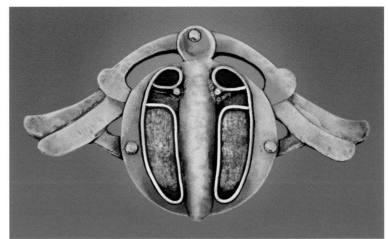

Melchiorre
Necklace, 1910–20
Platinum, brilliant cut diamonds
Alessandria, Vincenzo
Melchiorre Collection

Carl Fabergé
Nobel necklace-bracelet, 1912
Platinum, silver, diamonds,
rock crystal
The Link of Times Foundation

Mikhail Perkhin,
workmaster to Carl Fabergé
Lilies of the Valley egg, 1898
Enamel, diamonds, rubies,
gold, pearls
The Link of Times Foundation

Mikhail Perkhin,
workmaster to Carl Fabergé
Coronation egg, 1897
Enamel, gold, diamonds,
rubies, platinum, rock crystal
The Link of Times Foundation

89

Tiffany & Co.,
designed by G. Paulding
Farnham and Louis Comfort
Tiffany
Perfume bottle, 1900
Gold, platinum, glass, Mexican
opal, rubies, emeralds,
diamonds, enamel
Ralph Esmerian Collection

Tiffany & Co.
Iris brooch, 1900
Gold, silver, platinum,
sapphires, garnets, topazes,
diamonds
Baltimore, Walters Art Gallery

Tiffany & Co., designed
by Louis Comfort Tiffany
with Julia Munson
Fringe necklace, 1905
Gold, amethysts, nephrite
Private collection

Tiffany & Co.
American Flag brooch,
1900–10
Platinum, gold, rubies,
sapphires, diamonds
Private collection

Tiffany & Co., designed
by Louis Comfort Tiffany
Dragonfly brooch, c. 1904
Gold, platinum, opal, cornelian
Ralph Esmerian Collection

Cartier
Hair ornament, 1902
Platinum, diamonds
Cartier Collection

Cartier
Two Fern Sprays brooch, 1903
Platinum, diamonds
Cartier Collection

Cartier
Lilies brooch, 1906
Platinum, diamonds
Cartier Collection

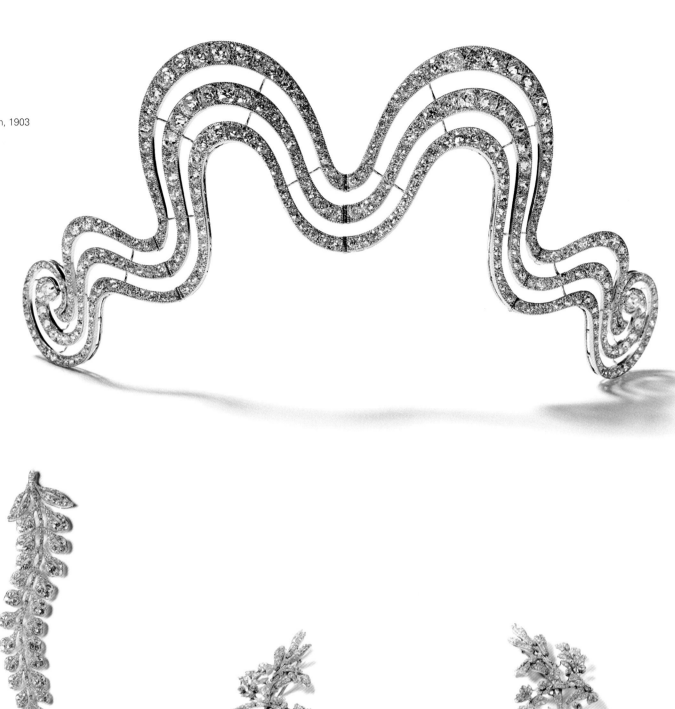

Cartier
Tiara, 1905
Platinum, diamonds
Cartier Collection

Cartier
Serpent necklace, 1919
Platinum, diamonds
Cartier Collection

Cartier
Corsage ornament, 1907
Platinum, diamonds, sapphires
Cartier Collection

Boucheron
Pocket watch, 1925
Gold, sapphire, enamel
New York, private collection

96

Cartier
Pendant, 1913
Platinum, onyxes, diamonds
Cartier Collection

Cartier
Dragon pendant, 1922
Platinum, onyx, pearls, coral,
diamonds, emerald, silk cord
Cartier Collection

Cartier
Arc de Triomphe brooch, 1919
Gold, platinum, sapphire,
emeralds, rubies, topazes,
diamonds
Cartier Collection

Cartier
Pendant, 1921
Platinum, rock crystal, emerald,
diamonds, onyx, silk cord
Cartier Collection

Cartier
Brooch, 1922
Platinum, emeralds, diamonds,
onyx
Cartier Collection

Cartier
Scarab brooch, 1924
Platinum, quartz, turquoise
faience inlays, emeralds,
enamel, diamonds
Cartier Collection

Cartier
Bracelet, 1924
Gold, platinum, coral, mother-
of-pearl, diamonds, enamel
Cartier Collection

Cartier
Signet watch, 1924
Platinum, gold, jade, rubies,
diamonds, onyx, enamel
Cartier Collection

Cartier
Signet watch, 1925
Gold, platinum, diamonds,
onyx, coral, enamel, silk cord
Cartier Collection

Cartier
Brooch, 1922
Platinum, emeralds, diamonds,
onyx, coral
Cartier Collection

Cartier
Brooch, 1925
Platinum, emerald, diamonds,
coral, black enamel
Cartier Collection

Cartier
Nécessaire, 1925
Gold, platinum, sapphire,
emerald, diamonds, enamel
Cartier Collection

Cartier
Chinese Vase nécessaire, 1927
Gold, platinum, onyx, cabochon
emerald, coral, sapphire,
diamonds, enamel
Cartier Collection

Cartier
Nécessaire, c. 1926
Gold, platinum, jade, onyx,
diamonds, enamel
Cartier Collection

Cartier
Tutti frutti bracelet, 1928
Platinum, rubies, emeralds,
sapphires, diamonds
Cartier Collection

Cartier
Tutti frutti bracelet, 1925
Platinum, sapphires, rubies,
emeralds, onyx, diamonds,
enamel
Cartier Collection

Cartier
Tutti frutti necklace, 1936
Platinum, rubies, emeralds,
sapphires, diamonds
Cartier Collection

Cartier
Chimera bracelet, 1928
Gold, platinum, emeralds,
sapphires, diamonds, coral,
enamel
Cartier Collection

Cartier, designed
by Jean Cocteau
Trinity ring, 1924
Gold
Cartier Collection

Cartier
Bracelet, 1926
Platinum, ruby, diamonds, rock
crystal, onyx, enamel
Cartier Collection

Cartier
Bracelet, 1930
Platinum, rock crystal,
diamonds
Cartier Collection

Cartier
Bracelet, 1930
Platinum, rock crystal,
diamonds
Cartier Collection

Harry Winston
Necklace, c. 1940
Platinum, diamonds
Private collection

108

Mauboussin
Panier Fleuri brooch, c. 1928
Platinum, diamonds, onyx,
emeralds, rubies, amethyst,
citrines, enamel, sapphires
Photo courtesy Sotheby's
Genève

Mauboussin
Necklace, c. 1925
Platinum, emeralds, sapphires,
diamonds
Mauboussin Collection

Van Cleef & Arpels
Necklace, 1928
Platinum, diamonds
Van Cleef & Arpels Collection

Van Cleef & Arpels
Bracelet, 1928
Platinum, diamonds
Van Cleef & Arpels Collection

Van Cleef & Arpels
Egyptien brooch, 1924
Platinum, rock crystal, rubies,
emeralds, onyxes, diamonds
Van Cleef & Arpels Collection

Van Cleef & Arpels
Nécessaire, 1926
Gold, platinum, mother-of-
pearl, semi-precious stones,
enamel, diamonds
Private collection

Jean Fouquet
Sautoir with pendant, 1925
Gold, platinum, enamel, rock crystal, onyx
New York, private collection

Raymond Templier
Brooch, c. 1920
Gold, platinum, rock crystal, diamonds
Private collection

Georges Fouquet
Brooch, 1920–25
Platinum, enamel, onyx, jade, diamonds
Private collection

Jean Fouquet
Bracelet, 1940
Gold, chloromelanite
New York, private collection

Jean Fouquet
Bracelet and ring, 1931
Gold, amethysts, moonstone,
rock crystal
New York, Primavera Gallery

Jean Fouquet
Ring, c. 1938
Gold, diamonds
New York, Primavera Gallery

Jean Fouquet
Necklace and bracelet, c. 1931
Gold, chrome, ebony
Private collection

Georges Fouquet, designed
by Jean Lambert Rucki
Brooch, 1936–37
Gold
Paris, Musée des Arts
décoratifs

Jean Fouquet
Ring, 1937
Gold, topazes
Paris, Musée des Arts
décoratifs

Jean Fouquet
Brooch, 1925
Gold, rock crystal, onyx,
enamel, diamonds
Toledo, Ohio, Toledo Museum
of Art

Jean Fouquet
Brooch, 1937
Gold, platinum, lapis lazuli,
diamonds
Paris, Musée des Arts
décoratifs
Photo: Les Arts Décoratifs /
Laurent Sully Jaulmes

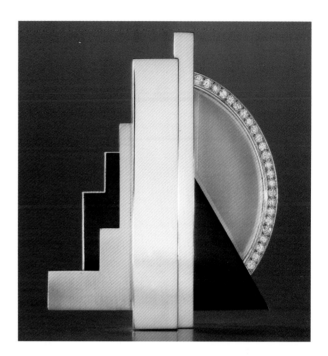

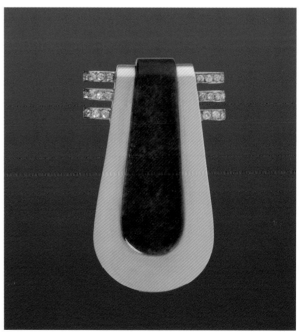

Jean Després
Brooch, c. 1930
Silver, gold
Private collection

Jean Després
Ring, c. 1928
Silver, gold, lacquer
New York, Primavera Gallery

Jean Després
Bracelet, 1937
Gold, onyx
Paris, Musée des Arts
décoratifs

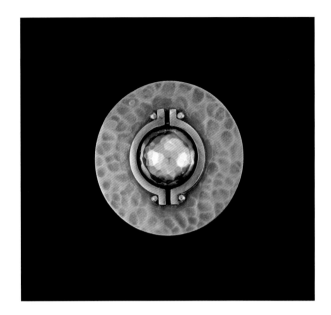

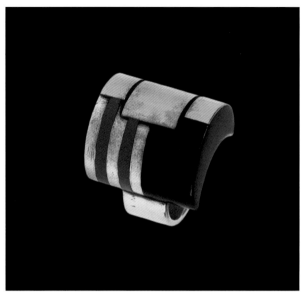

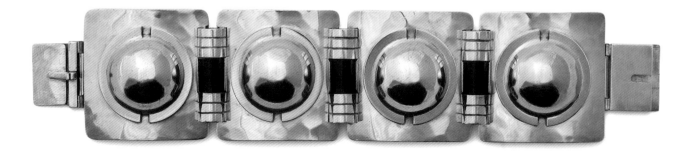

Jean Després
Necklace, c. 1928
Silver, gold
New York, Primavera Gallery

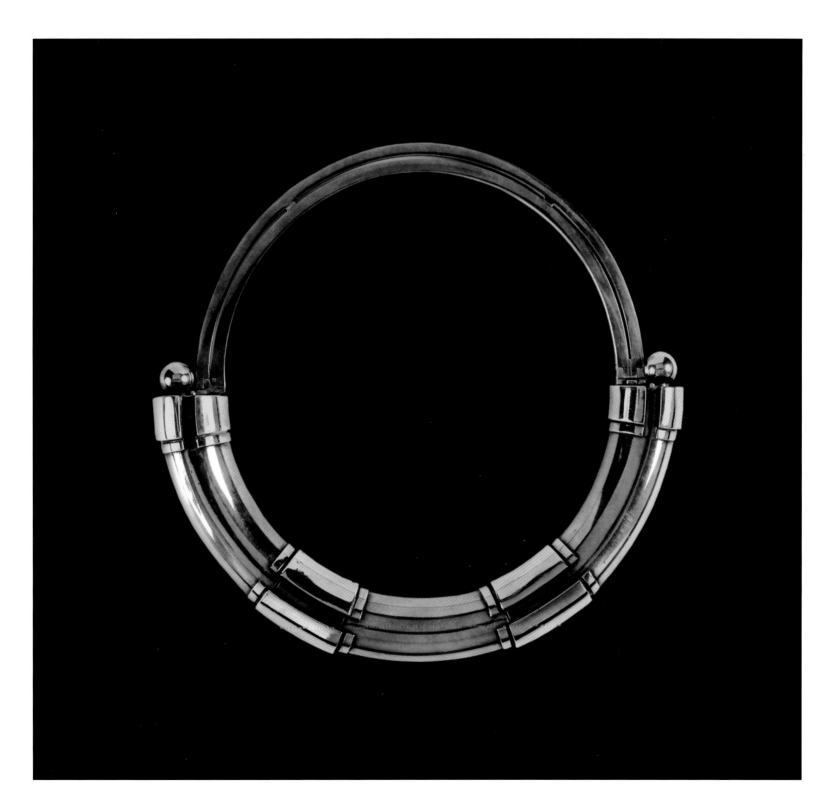

Raymond Templier
Ring, c. 1925
Gold, coral, onyx
New York, Primavera Gallery

Raymond Templier
Earrings, c. 1925
Gold, ivory, enamel
New York, Primavera Gallery

Raymond Templier
Bracelet, c. 1930
Silver, lacquer
New York, Primavera Gallery

Raymond Templier
Bracelet, 1930
Silver, lacquer
New York, Primavera Gallery

Raymond Templier
Pendant, c. 1925
Platinum, enamel, diamonds,
crystal
Paris, Musée Galliera

Raymond Templier
Brooch, 1933
Gold, diamonds, moonstone
New York, Primavera Gallery

Raymond Templier
Brooch, 1937
Platinum, onyx, rock crystal,
diamonds
Paris, Musée des Arts
décoratifs
Photo: Les Arts Décoratifs /
Laurent Sully Jaulmes

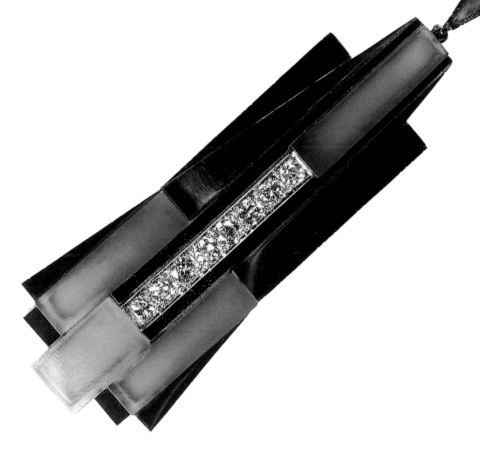

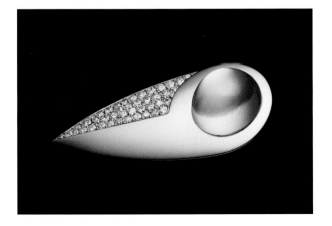

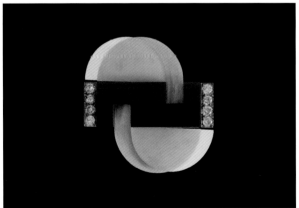

Maison René Boivin
Irradiante necklace, 1932–33
Silver, mirror mosaic
Private collection

Hélène Andrieux,
workmaster for Lacloche
Bracelet, c. 1930
Platinum, diamonds
Private collection

Suzanne Belperron
Bracelet, 1934
Platinum, rock crystal,
diamonds
Private collection

Henkel & Grosse, designed
by Heinrich Grosse
Bracelet, c. 1928
Bakelite, platinum
Pforzheim, Henkel & Große
Collection

Theodor Fahrner
Brooch, 1927
Silver, marcasite, amazonite,
chalcedony, quartz
New York, Primavera Gallery

Sibyl Dunlop
Bracelet, c. 1930
Silver, moonstone, opals,
amethysts, chalcedony, rubies
Private collection

Henry George Murphy
Brooch, 1934
Silver
London, Tadema Gallery

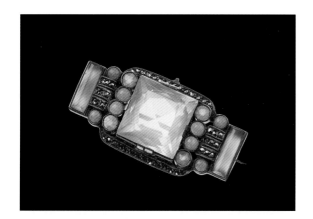

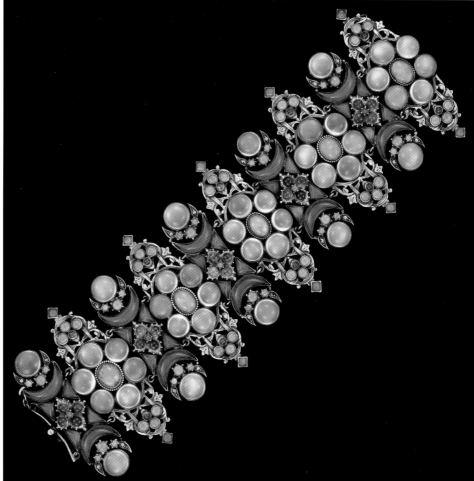

Janesich
Sautoir with watch, c. 1925
Gold, coral, onyx, diamonds
Private collection

Janesich
Earrings, 1925
Onyx, coral, gold, diamonds
Private collection

Janesich
Corsage ornament, c. 1930
Gold, natural pearls, diamonds
Private collection

Alfredo Ravasco
Pendant trousse, 1925
Gold, pearls, diamonds,
malachite
Private collection

Alfredo Ravasco
Sautoir with pendant, 1923
Silver, onyx, coral, freshwater
pearls, diamonds
Milan, Civiche Raccolte d'Arte
Applicata del Castello
Sforzesco

Alfredo Ravasco
Brooch, 1922
Platinum, freshwater pearls,
diamonds
Milan, Museo del
Risorgimento, De Marchi
Collection

Mario Buccellati,
commissioned by Gabriele
d'Annunzio
Necklace, 1923
Gold, rubies, beryl
Mario Buccellati Collection

Mario Buccellati
Bracelets, 1925
Silver, gold, diamonds
Mario Buccellati Collection

Mario Buccellati
Tiara, 1929
Gold, diamonds
Mario Buccellati Collection

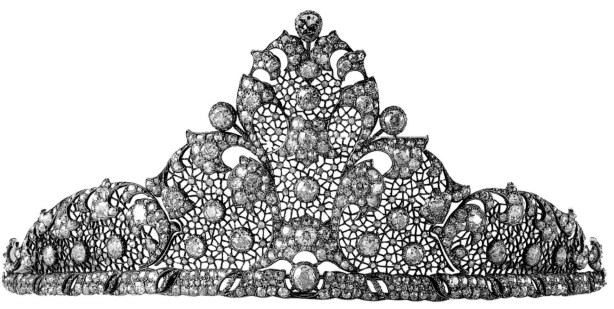

Bulgari
Watch-bracelet, c. 1925
Platinum, diamonds
Bulgari Vintage Collection

Bulgari
Bracelet, c. 1928
Platinum, diamonds
Bulgari Vintage Collection

Bulgari
Brooch, c. 1935
Platinum, diamonds
Bulgari Vintage Collection

Bulgari
Necklace, c. 1930
Platinum, diamonds
Bulgari Vintage Collection

Henry Blank & Co. for Tiffany
Set composed of cigarette-
case, lipstick-case, pillbox
and powder-compact, c. 1920
Gold, platinum, enamel, rubies,
diamonds
Tiffany Collection

J.E. Caldwell & Co.
Brooch, 1920
Gold, platinum, enamel,
diamonds, amethysts
Private collection

Henry Blank & Co. for Tiffany
Pocket watch, c. 1920
Platinum, brass, diamonds,
onyx, enamel, glass
Tiffany Collection

Tiffany & Co., designed by
Louis Comfort Tiffany
Brooch, 1920–33
Platinum, moonstone,
sapphires
Tiffany Collection

Tiffany & Co.
Bracelet, 1920–25
Platinum, gold, onyxes,
diamonds
Ralph Esmerian Collection

Tiffany & Co.
Bracelet, 1925–30
Platinum, sapphires, diamonds
Tiffany Collection

Tiffany & Co.
Brooch, 1925–30
Platinum, rock crystal, onyx,
diamonds
Ralph Esmerian Collection

Tiffany & Co.
Pocket watch, 1925–30
Platinum, enamel, diamonds
Ralph Esmerian Collection

Tiffany & Co.
Necklace, c. 1930–35
Platinum, diamonds
Tiffany Collection

Tiffany & Co.
Necklace, earrings and pair of
brooches, 1938–41
Gold, platinum, iridium,
emeralds, sapphires, diamonds
Tiffany Collection

Tiffany & Co., designed
by Jean Schlumberger
Brooch, 1941
Gold, platinum, enamel,
amethysts, rubies, diamonds
Tiffany Collection

Jakob Bengel
Necklace, c. 1931
Metal, galalith
Private collection

Dorrie Nossiter
Brooch, c. 1930
Silver, gold, yellow topazes,
opals, freshwater pearls
London, Tadema Gallery

Georg Jensen Company,
designed by Gundorph Albertus
Brooch no. 234A, c. 1935
Silver
London, private collection

Georg Jensen Company,
designed by Henning Koppel
Necklace no. 88A, 1946
Silver
London, private collection

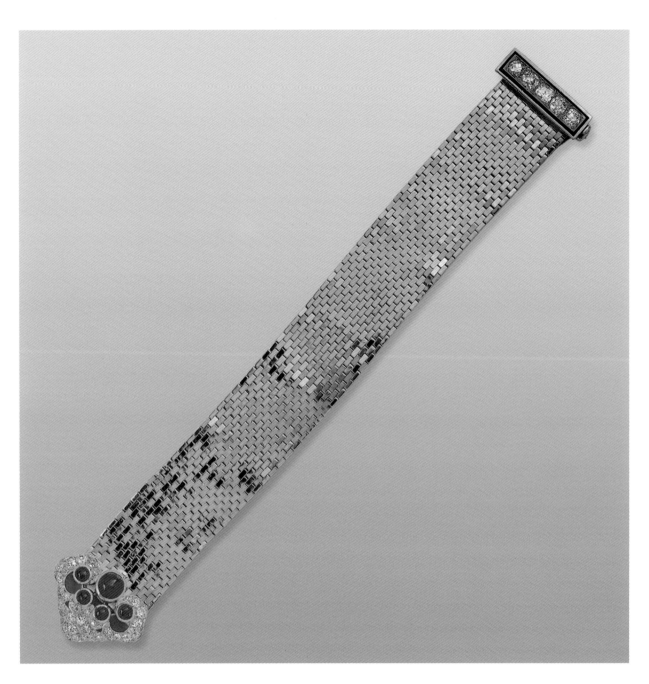

Van Cleef & Arpels
Ludo bracelet, c. 1935
Gold, rubies, diamonds
Private collection

Van Cleef & Arpels
Brooches, 1940
Rubies, diamonds, emeralds,
platinum
Van Cleef & Arpels Collection

Van Cleef & Arpels
Bouquet brooch, 1940
Gold, sapphires, rubies
Van Cleef & Arpels Collection

Van Cleef & Arpels
Ludo Hexagone bracelet, 1937
Platinum, sapphires, diamonds
Van Cleef & Arpels Collection

Van Cleef & Arpels
Brooch, 1931
Platinum, diamonds
Van Cleef & Arpels Collection

Van Cleef & Arpels
Pivoine brooch, 1937
Gold, platinum, rubies,
diamonds
Van Cleef & Arpels Collection

Van Cleef & Arpels
Rubans brooch, 1937
Platinum, diamonds
Van Cleef & Arpels Collection

139

Van Cleef & Arpels
Passe-Partout necklace,
1939–40
Gold "Tubogas", transformable
clips made of sapphires, rubies,
diamonds
Van Cleef & Arpels Collection

Van Cleef & Arpels
Soleil Rayonnant minaudière,
1934
Gold, rubies
Van Cleef & Arpels Collection

Van Cleef & Arpels
Cadenas watch-bracelet, 1937
Gold Omega twin band and
case
Van Cleef & Arpels Collection

Mauboussin
Necklace and bracelet, 1938
Gold Polonaise chain,
diamonds, sapphires, pearls
New York, Primavera Gallery

Mauboussin
Tassel necklace, c. 1954
Gold Polonaise chain, platinum,
diamonds
Fred Leighton Collection

Van Cleef & Arpels
Necklace, 1937
Gold and diamonds
Van Cleef & Arpels Collection

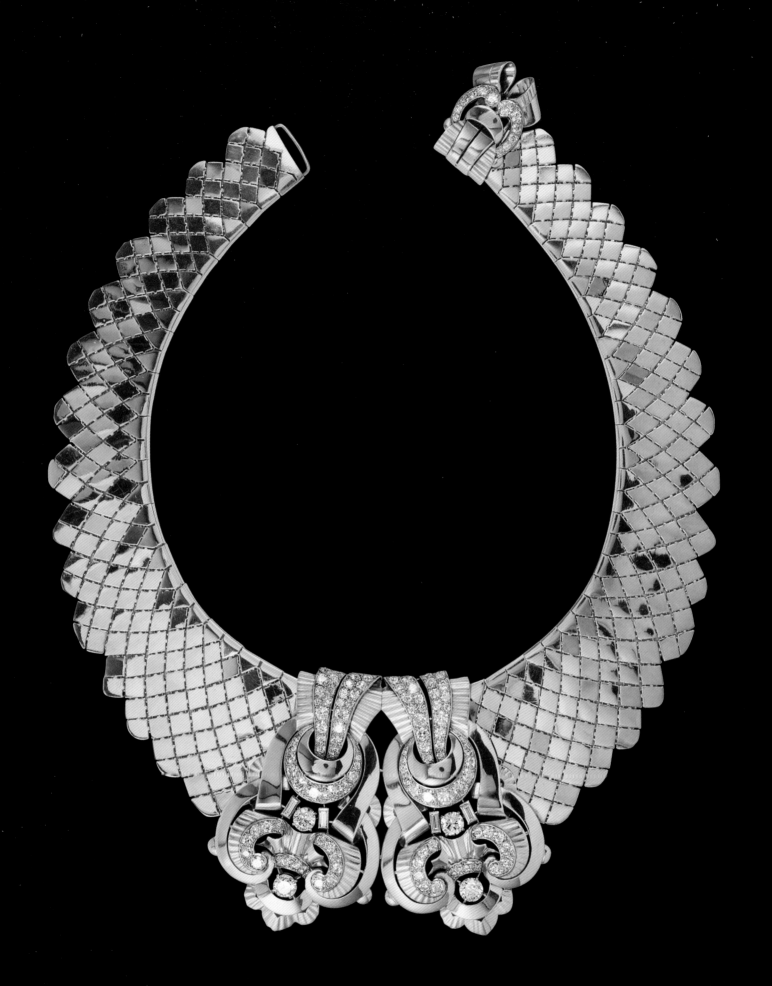

Boucheron
Watch-bracelet, 1942
Gold Polonaise chain and case,
platinum, sapphires, diamonds
Private collection

Boucheron
Bracelet, 1946
Gold, platinum, diamonds
Boucheron Collection

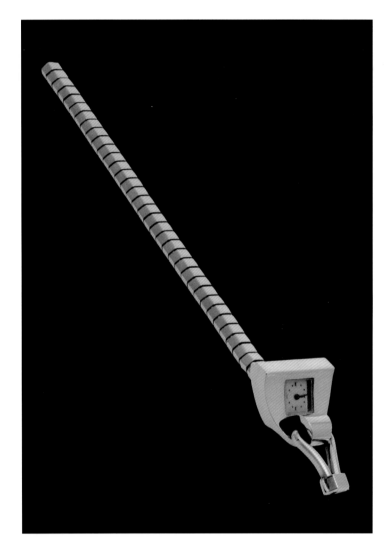

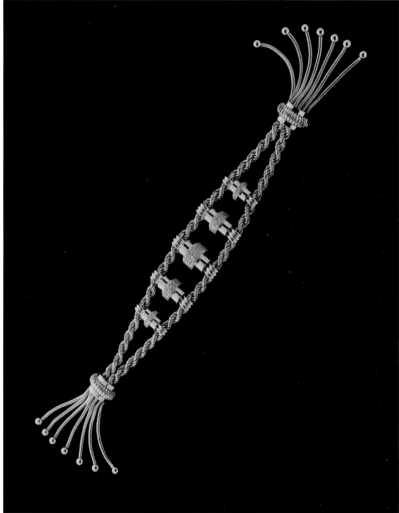

Cartier
Manette bracelet, 1939
Gold, amethyst, yellow topazes
Collection Cartier

Cartier
Orchid brooch, 1937
Gold, amethysts, aquamarines
Cartier Collection

Cartier
Watch-bracelet, 1938
Gold, yellow topazes
Cartier Collection

Marcus & Co.
Brooch and bracelet, c. 1935
Platinum, moonstone,
sapphires, diamonds
Private collection

Marcus & Co.
Birds in flight brooch, 1940
Gold, platinum, moonstone,
rubies, diamonds
Private collection

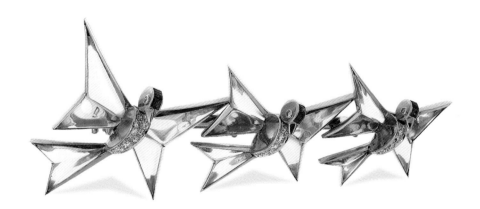

Paul Flato
Nuts and Bolts cufflinks, 1940
Gold
Private collection

Paul Flato
Miniature slippers, 1945
Gold, diamonds, rubies
Private collection

Paul Flato
Containers, 1940
Gold, enamel
Private collection

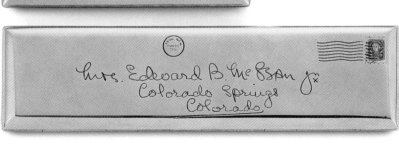

Paul Flato
Belt Buckle necklace, 1940
Platinum, aquamarines, rubies
Private collection

Seaman Shepps
Brooch, 1941
Platinum, gold, sapphires,
emeralds, diamonds
Seaman Schepps Collection

Paul Flato
Necklace and bracelet, c. 1960
Platinum, diamonds
Private collection

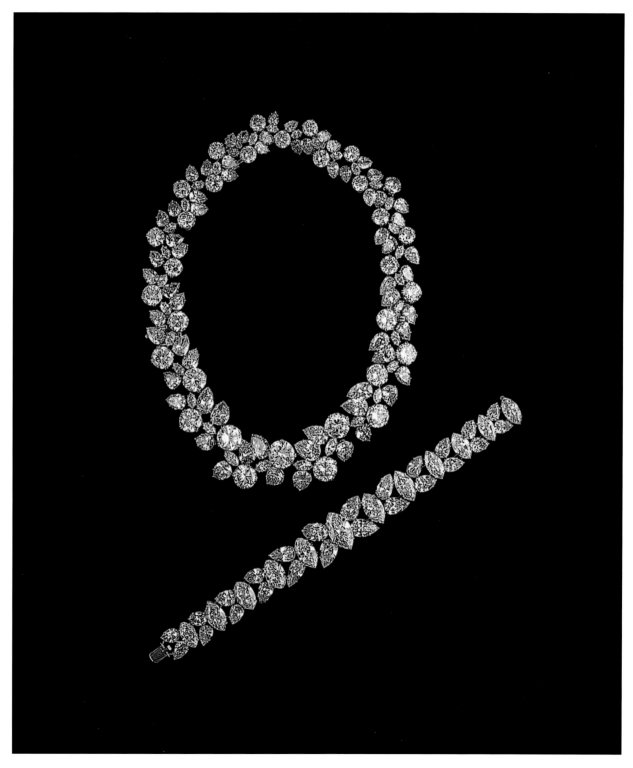

Chanel, designed by
Fulco di Verdura
Bracelet, 1935
Silver, gold, emeralds,
sapphires, rubies, enamel
New York, Primavera Gallery

Fulco di Verdura
Brooch, c. 1940
Lion's paw shell, gold,
diamonds
New York, Verdura Collection

Fulco di Verdura
Brooch, 1943
Gold, diamonds
New York, Verdura Collection

Fulco di Verdura
Brooch, 1943
Gold, sapphires, zircons
New York, Verdura Collection

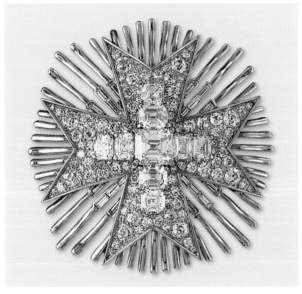

Van Cleef & Arpels
Dentelle brooch, 1949
Gold, platinum, diamonds
Van Cleef & Arpels Collection

Van Cleef & Arpels, designed
by René Sim Lacaze
Necklace, 1949
Platinum, rubies, diamonds
Private collection

Van Cleef & Arpels
Flower watch-bracelet, c. 1950
Gold, platinum, sapphires,
diamonds
Van Cleef & Arpels Collection

Van Cleef & Arpels
Zip necklace, 1950
Gold, rubies, diamonds
Van Cleef & Arpels Collection

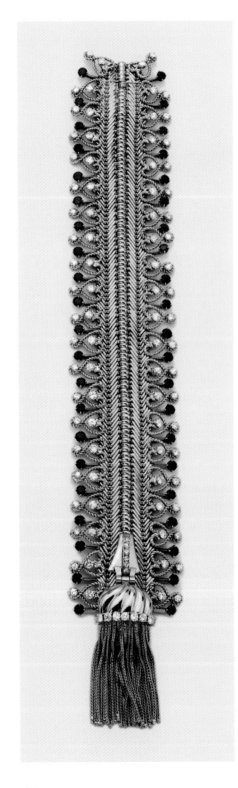

Cartier
Drapperie necklace, 1947
Gold, platinum, amethysts,
turquoises, diamonds
Cartier Collection

Cartier
Panther brooch, 1949
Platinum, gold, diamonds,
sapphires
Cartier Collection

Mauboussin
Jay brooch, c. 1959
Gold, platinum, diamonds,
rubies, sapphires, emeralds
Private collection

Jean Schlumberger
Brooch, 1956
Gold, aquamarines, amethysts,
rubies, lacquer
Paris, Musée des Arts
décoratifs

Jean Schlumberger
Hat brooch, 1958
Gilded metal, enamel, coral
Paris, Musée des Arts
décoratifs

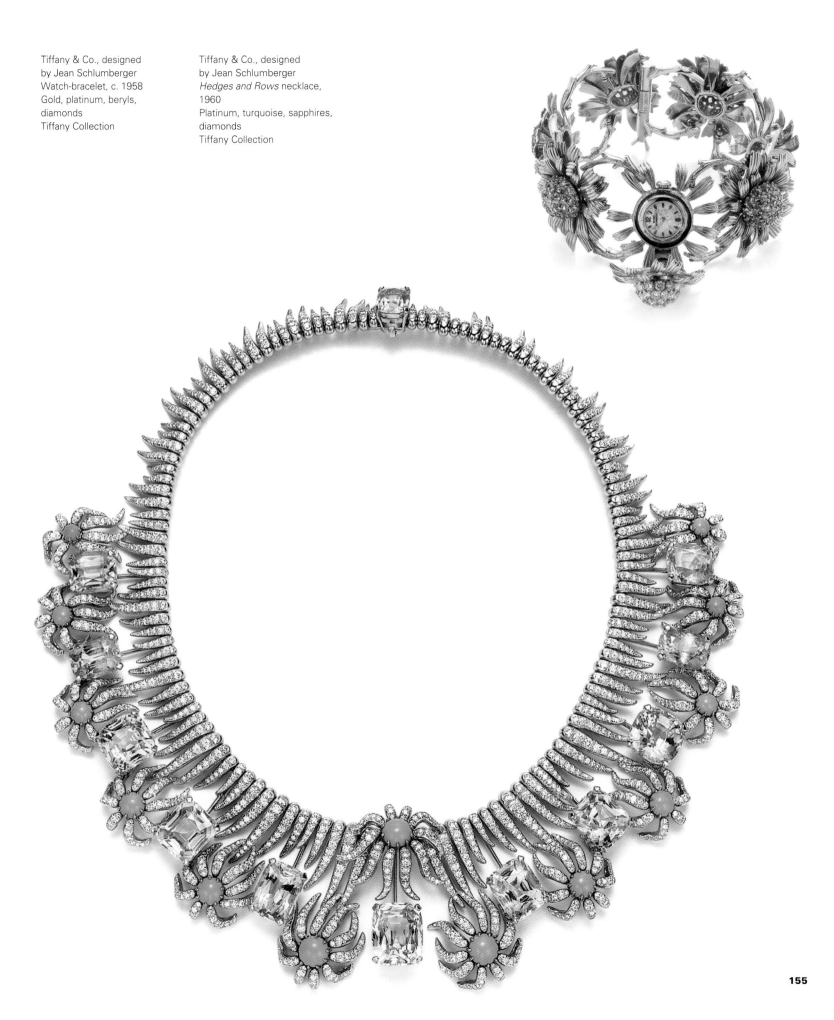

Tiffany & Co., designed
by Jean Schlumberger
Watch-bracelet, c. 1958
Gold, platinum, beryls,
diamonds
Tiffany Collection

Tiffany & Co., designed
by Jean Schlumberger
Hedges and Rows necklace,
1960
Platinum, turquoise, sapphires,
diamonds
Tiffany Collection

Tiffany & Co., designed
by Donald Claflin
Brooch, c. 1966
Gold, turquoise, emerald,
diamonds
Tiffany Collection

Tiffany & Co., designed
by Donald Claflin
Brooch, c. 1967
Gold, platinum, tourmaline,
coral, turquoise, diamonds
Tiffany Collection

Tiffany & Co., designed
by Donald Claflin
Brooch, c. 1967
Gold, platinum, corals, ivory,
enamel, diamonds
Tiffany Collection

Bulgari
Giardinetto brooch, c. 1962
Gold, platinum, sapphire,
rubies, emeralds, diamonds
Bulgari Vintage Collection

Bulgari
Necklace, 1967–68
Gold, platinum, sapphires,
rubies, emeralds, diamonds
Bulgari Vintage Collection

Bulgari
Sautoir, c. 1970
Gold, cornelian, turquoise,
diamonds
Bulgari Vintage Collection

Bulgari
Nummaria necklace, c. 1970
Gold Gourmette chain,
silver coin
Bulgari Vintage Collection

Miriam Haskell, designed
by Frank Hess
Necklace, c. 1945
Punched and glided metal,
vitreous paste, beads
Private collection

Miriam Haskell, designed
by Frank Hess
Necklace, 1957
Gilded metal, fake pearls,
vitreous paste, paste
Private collection

Chanel,
made by Maison Gripoix
Necklace, c. 1950
Silver, crystal, glass pearls,
paste
New York, Primavera Gallery

Chanel, designed by Goossens
Pendant, c. 1960
Gilded metal, enamel
Paris, Maison Goossens
Collection

Christian Dior,
made by Maison Gripoix
Lily of the Valley brooch,
c. 1950
Gilded metal, enamel
Paris, Maison Gripoix Collection

Paco Rabanne
Belt, c. 1965
Metal
London, David Gill Gallery
Collection

Lanvin
Necklace with pendant,
1968–72
Metal
London, David Gill Gallery
Collection

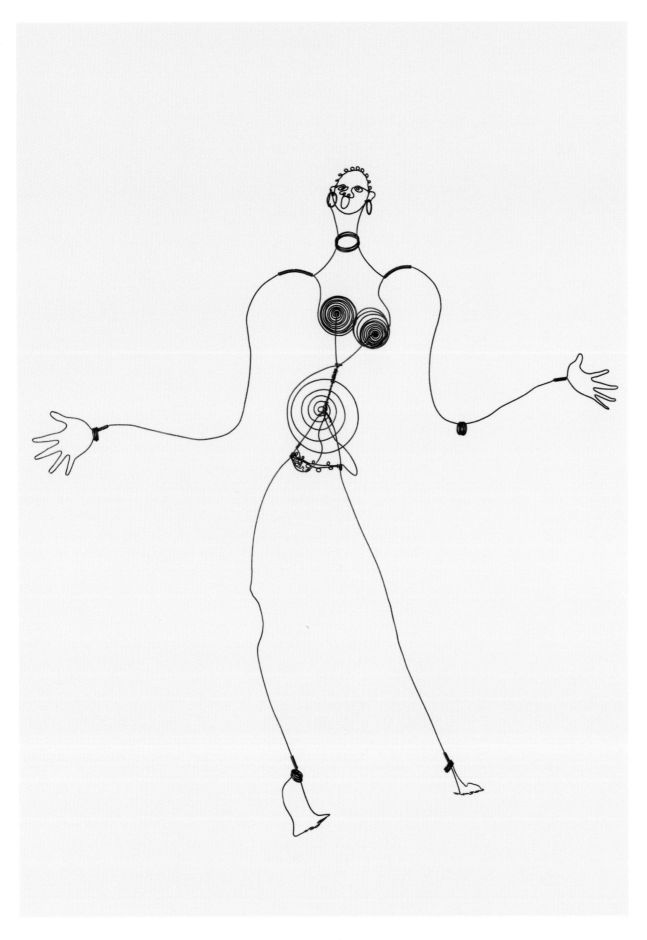

Alexander Calder
Joséphine Baker IV, 1926
Wire
Paris, Centre Georges
Pompidou, Musée national
d'Art moderne

Yves Tanguy,
made for Peggy Guggenheim
Earrings, 1938–39
Oil on plastic
New York, private collection

Alexander Calder
Brooch, c. 1940
Brass
The Montreal Museum of Fine
Arts, Liliane and David M.
Stewart Collection, donated by
Paul Leblanc
Photo: MMFA, Giles Rivest

Alexander Calder
Brooch, c. 1940
Silver
The Montreal Museum of Fine
Arts, Liliane and David M.
Stewart Collection, donated by
Paul Leblanc
Photo: MMFA, Christine Guest

Alexander Calder
Mobile shaped earrings,
c. 1946
Silver
New York, private collection

 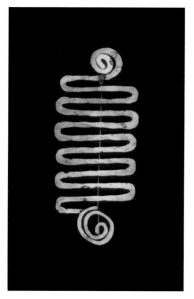 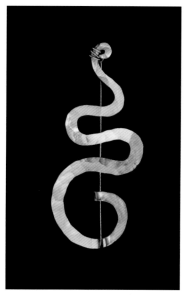

Harry Bertoia
Brooch, c. 1945
Silver
The Montreal Museum of Fine
Arts, Liliane and David
M. Stewart Collection,
donated by Paul Leblanc
Photo: MMFA, Christine Guest

Harry Bertoia
Ring, c. 1940
Aluminium
The Montreal Museum of Fine
Arts, Liliane and David
M. Stewart Collection,
donated by Paul Leblanc
Photo: MMFA, Giles Rivest

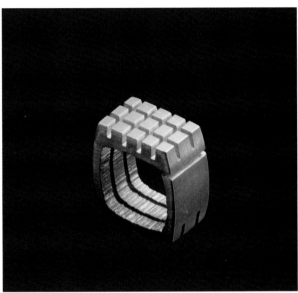

Salvador Dalí, made by Vaillant
& Devere
*Ruby Lips with Teeth like
Pearls* brooch, 1949
Gold, rubies, natural pearls
Fundació Gala-Salvador Dalí

Salvador Dalí
The Eye of Time brooch, 1949
Platinum, rubies, diamonds,
enamel; Movado watch
movement
Fundació Gala-Salvador Dalí

Georges Braque
Hera brooch, 1962
Gold, platinum, sapphires
Paris, Musée des Arts
décoratifs

Jean Lurçat
Soleil Lune pendant, 1959–60
Gold
Paris, Musée des Arts
décoratifs

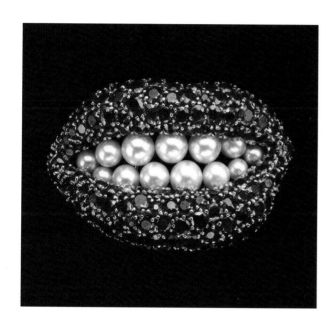

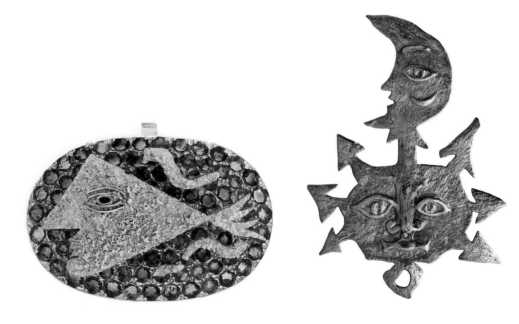

Line Vautrin
Saute-mouton necklace,
1950–55
Gilded bronze, enamel
Paris, Musée des Arts
décoratifs

Pol Bury
Bracelet, 1968
Gold
Paris, private collection

Max Ernst,
made by Pierre Hugo
Pendant, 1972
Gold
Paris, private collection

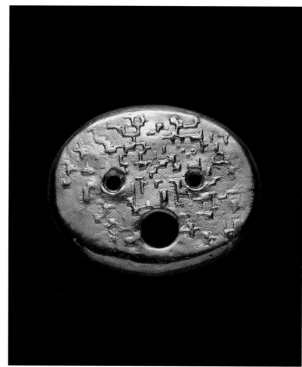

Sonia Delaunay,
made by Artcurial
Abstraction necklace, 1980
Silver, enamel
Rome, private collection

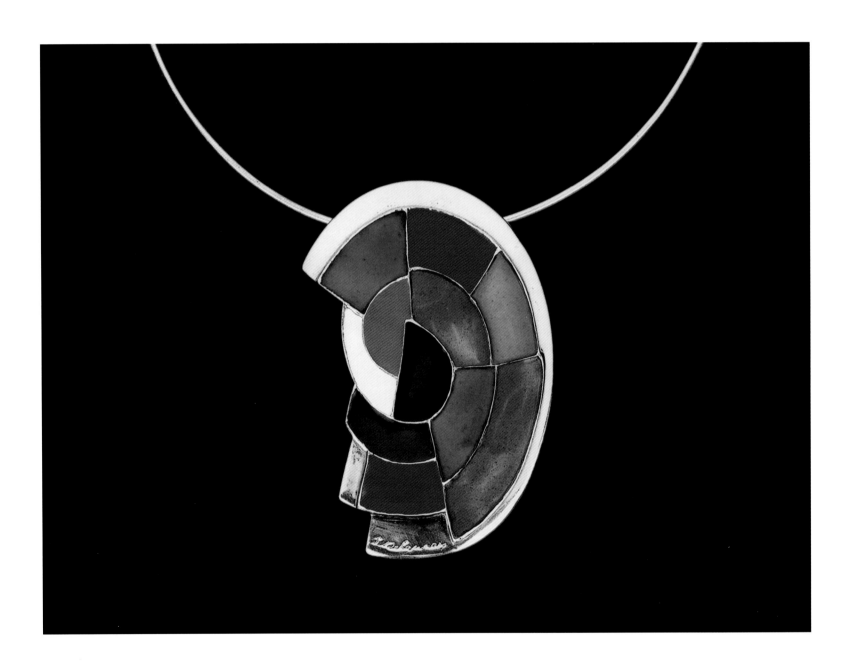

César
Pendant, 1970–71
Gold
Paris, private collection

Arman
Pendant, 1972
Gold and watch pieces
Paris, private collection

Fausto Melotti
Necklace, c. 1947
Terracotta, brass
Milan, Marta Melotti Collection

Mirko Basaldella
Abstract Motif bracelet, 1955
Gold
Rome, private collection

Getulio Alviani
Monorecchio earring, 1967
Aluminium
Milan, collection of the artist

Gabriele De Vecchi
Book brooch, 1963
Silver
Bassano del Grappa,
collection of the artist

Lucio Fontana,
made by GEM Montebello
Spatial Concept bracelet, 1964
Gold
Milan, Andrea Sirio Ortolan
Collection

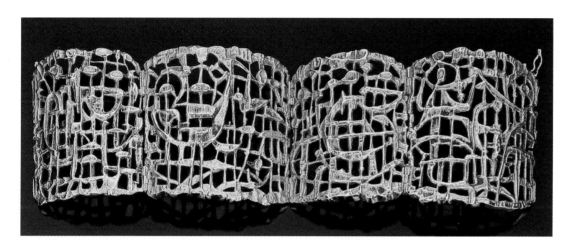

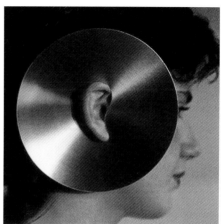

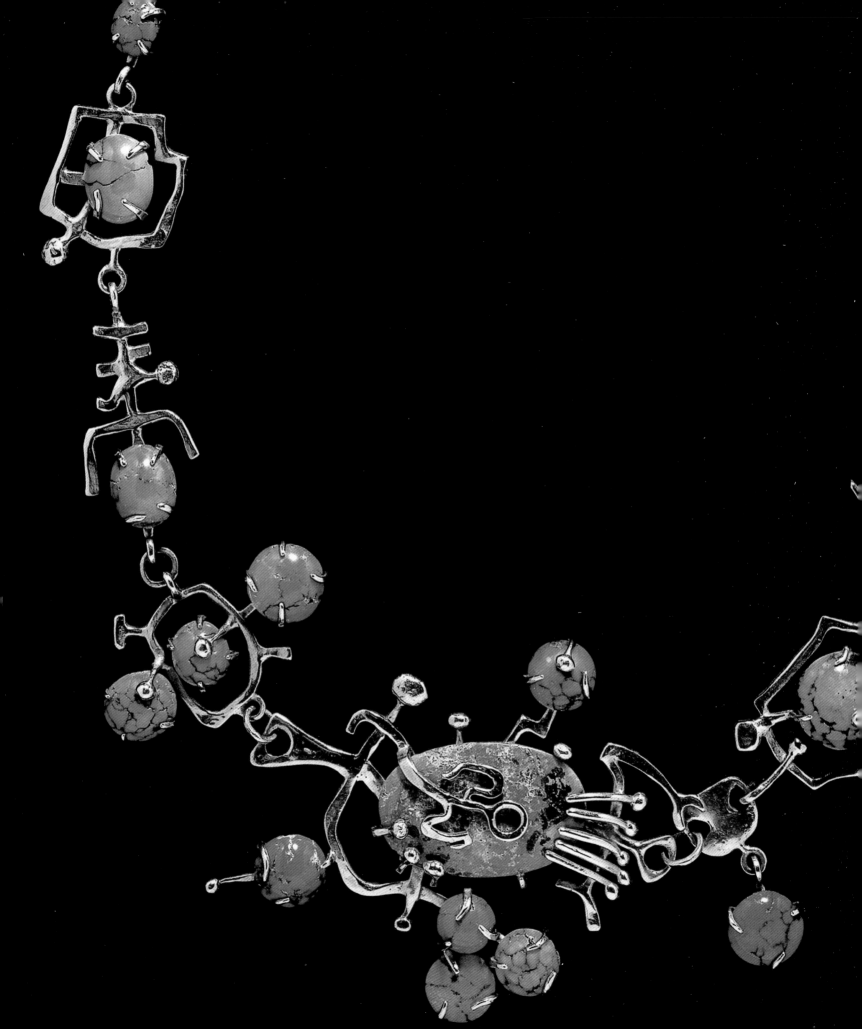

Arnaldo Pomodoro
Necklace, 1961
Gold, turquoises
Milan, private collection

Giò Pomodoro
Bracelet, 1967
Gold, rubies, diamonds
Milan, private collection

Gino Marotta,
made by Gioielleria Fumanti
Rose brooch, 1970
Gold, diamonds
Roma, Maria Camilla Pallavicini
Collection

Getulio Alviani,
made by Gioielleria Fumanti
Lozenge pendant, 1974
Gold, diamonds
Rome, Maria Camilla Pallavicini
Collection

Giuseppe Capogrossi,
made by Gioielleria Fumanti
Brooch, 1972
Gold, diamonds, onyx, coral
Rome, private collection

Arnaldo Pomodoro,
made by Uno A Erre, Arezzo
Micro-sculpture, 1992
Gold, coral
Orodautore Collection – Centro
Promozione e Servizi di Arezzo

Giò Pomodoro,
made by Centoundiciaerre,
Arezzo
Brooch, 1995
Gold, enamel, sapphires
Orodautore Collection – Centro
Promozione e Servizi di Arezzo

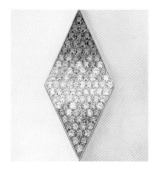

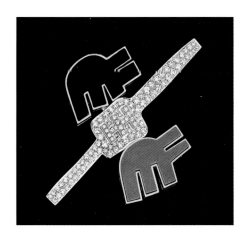

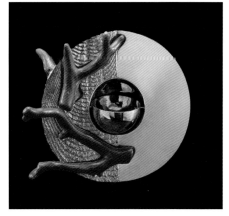

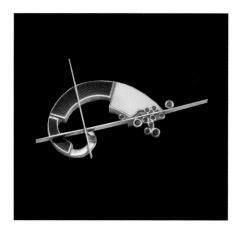

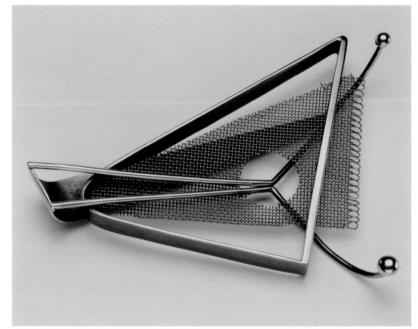

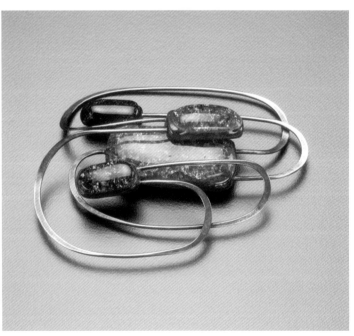

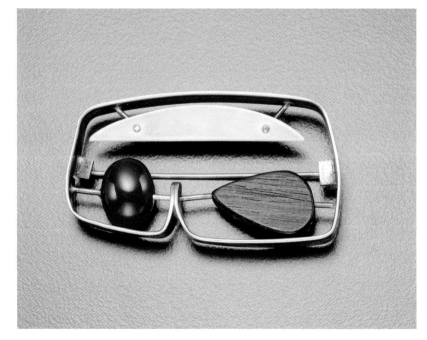

Henry Steig
Brooch, c. 1955
Silver
The Montreal Museum of Fine
Arts, Liliane and David
M. Stewart Collection
Photo: MMFA, Giles Rivest

Georg Jensen Company,
designed by Nanna
and Jørgen Ditzel
Brooch no. 328, c. 1956
Silver
London, private collection

Georg Jensen Company,
designed by Viviana Torun
Bülow-Hübe
Brooch no. 374, c. 1958
Silver
Copenhagen, Georg Jensen
Ltd.

Earl Pardon
Brooch, c. 1960
Silver, ebony, mahogany,
garnet
The Montreal Museum of Fine
Arts, Liliane and David
M. Stewart Collection, donated
by Paul Leblanc
Photo: MMFA, Giles Rivest

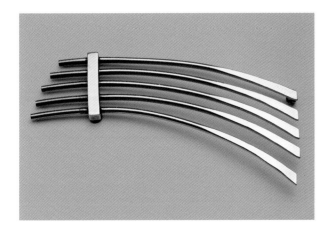

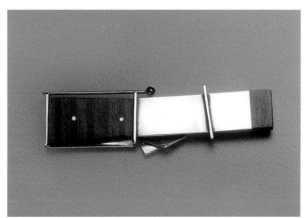

Gijs Bakker
Gouden Ui bracelet, 1965
Gold
Amsterdam, Gijs Bakker
Archive

Gijs Bakker
Tien Lussen bracelet, 1965
Gold
Amsterdam, Gijs Bakker
Archive

Gijs Bakker
Rings, 1962
Silver, rock crystal
Amsterdam, Gijs Bakker
Archive

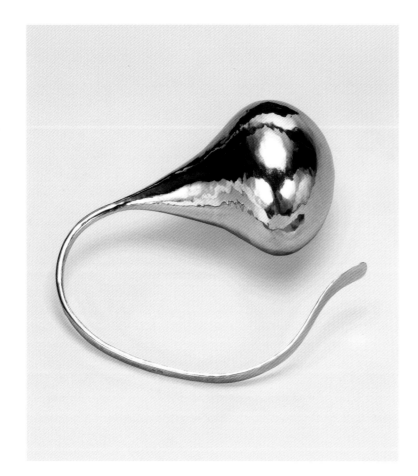

Emmy van Leersum
Bracelet, 1974
Stainless steel
Houston, The Museum of Fine
Arts, donated by Caroline
Weiss Law Foundation

Suzanne Esser
Bracelet, 1973
Aluminium
Amsterdam, Stedelijk
Museum, Françoise van den
Bosch collection

Gijs Bakker
Cirkel ring, 1967
Silver
Amsterdam, Gijs Bakker
Archive

Claus Bury
Brooch, 1972
Gold
Houston, The Museum of Fine
Arts, bought with funds from
the Mary Kathryn Lynch Kurtz
Charitable Lead Trust

Friedrich Becker
Emo brooch, 1987
Gold
Houston, The Museum of Fine
Arts, donated by Helen
Williams Drutt English in
honour of James S. Ackerman

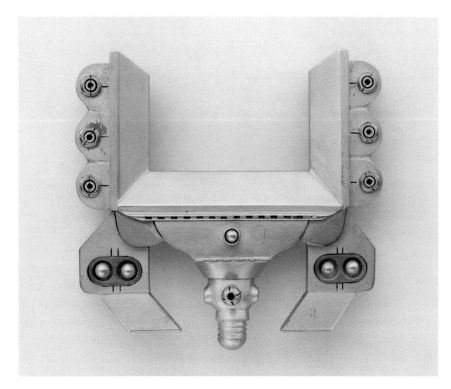

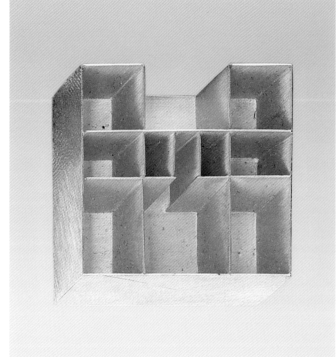

Ruudt Peters
Choker, 1972
Aluminium, rubber
Amsterdam, Stedelijk
Museum, Françoise van den
Bosch Collection

Otto Künzli
Bracelet, 1973
Gold, silver, hematite
Pforzheim, Schmuckmuseum

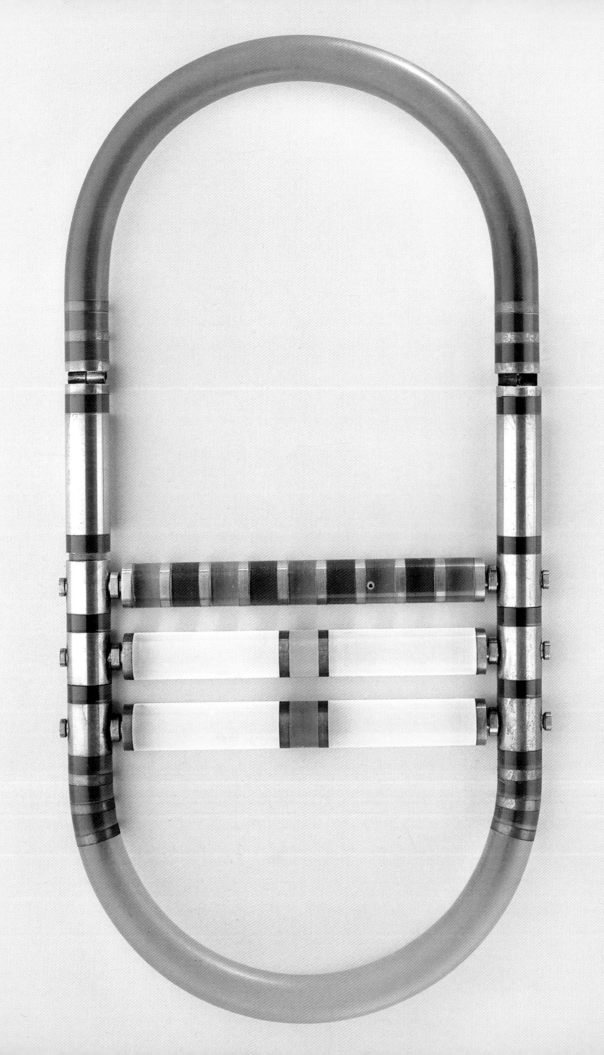

David Watkins
Necklace, 1974
Acrylic, silver
Houston, The Museum of Fine
Arts, donated by Caroline
Weiss Law Foundation

Robert Smit
Cwrt from Bryn-Dafydd
Necklace, 2004
Gold, pigment
Houston, The Museum of Fine
Arts, donated by Helen
Williams Drutt English

Tone Vigeland
Bracelet, 1989
Steel, silver
Tokyo, The National Museum
of Modern Art

Peter Chang
Bracelet, 1992
Acrylic resin, polyester
Houston, The Museum of Fine
Arts, donated by Morgan
Foundation

Onno Boekhoudt
Rings, 1990
Silver
Amsterdam, Stedelijk
Museum, Françoise van den
Bosch Collection
Photo: Tom Haartsen

Gijs Bakker
Waterman brooch, 1990
Gold, black and white
photograph, PVC, diamonds
Amsterdam, Gijs Bakker
Archive

Peter Skubic
Brooch, 2000
Stainless steel, photographic
paper, box, cardboard, ink
Houston, The Museum of Fine
Arts, donated by Helen
Williams Drutt English

Roger Morris
Laser brooch, 2007
Gold, laser cut acrylic print
Collection of the artist

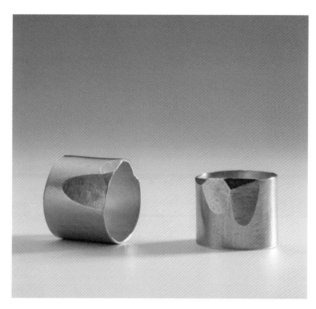

Francesco Pavan
Tribute to Raphael Soto brooch,
1982
Gold
Padua, collection of the artist

Mario Pinton,
made by Sa.Du.Sa, Arezzo
Brooch, 1988
Gold, ruby
Orodautore Collection – Centro
Promozione e Servizi di Arezzo

Bruno Martinazzi,
made by Treemme, Arezzo
Brooch, 1988
Gold
Orodautore Collection – Centro
Promozione e Servizi di Arezzo

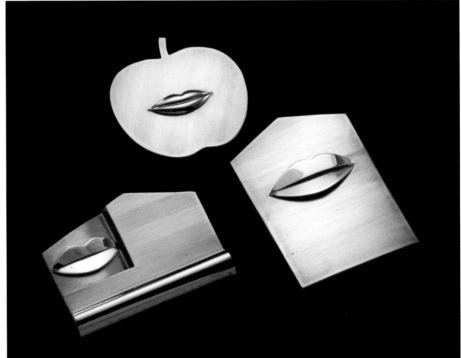

Giampaolo Babetto
Ring, 1970
Gold, niello
Arquà Petrarca, Giampaolo
Babetto Collection

Giampaolo Babetto
Necklace, 1975
Gold, niello
Arquà Petrarca, Giampaolo
Babetto Collection

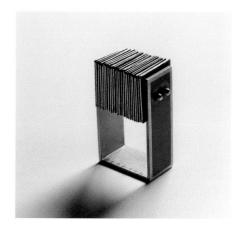

Alberto Zorzi,
made by Il Cerchio d'Oro,
Arezzo
Ring, 1992
Gold, rubellite
Orodautore Collection – Centro
Promozione e Servizi di Arezzo

Maria Rosa Franzin
Pendant, 1993
Silver, gold
Padua, collection of the artist

Graziano Visintin
Brooch, 1996
Gold, niello
Munich, Galerie Spektrum

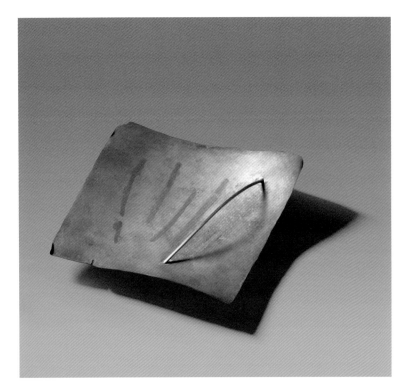

Annamaria Zanella
Fern brooch, 1993
Gold, silver, iron
Padua, collection of the artist

Stefano Marchetti
Brooch, 1992
Gold, silver, copper alloy
Padua, collection of the artist

Tiffany & Co., designed
by Jean Schlumberger
Purse, 1973
Woven gold wire, platinum,
diamonds
Tiffany Collection

194

Tiffany & Co., designed
by Elsa Peretti
Bra, c. 1974
Silver ring mesh
Tiffany Collection

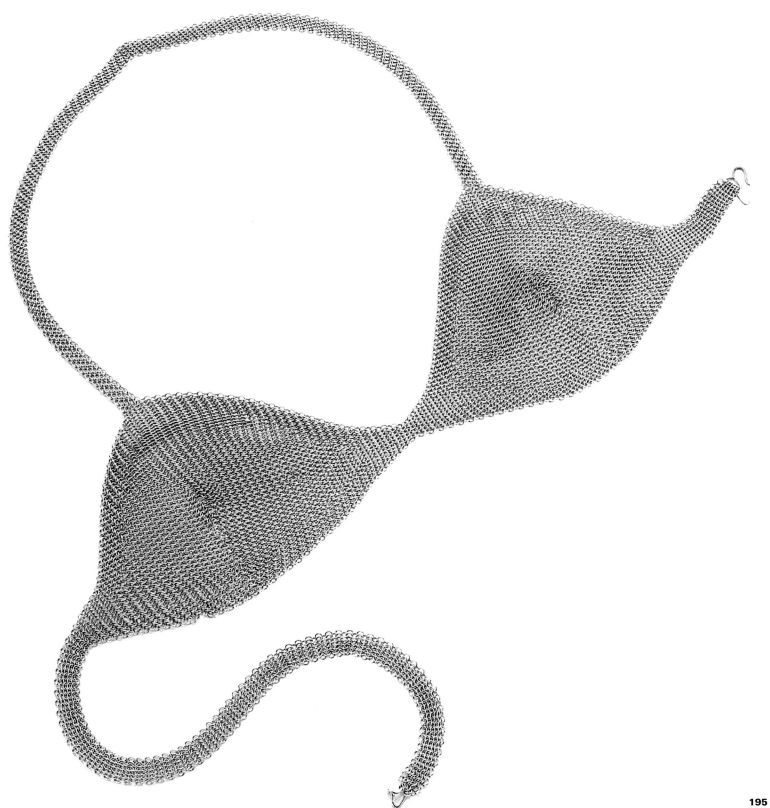

195

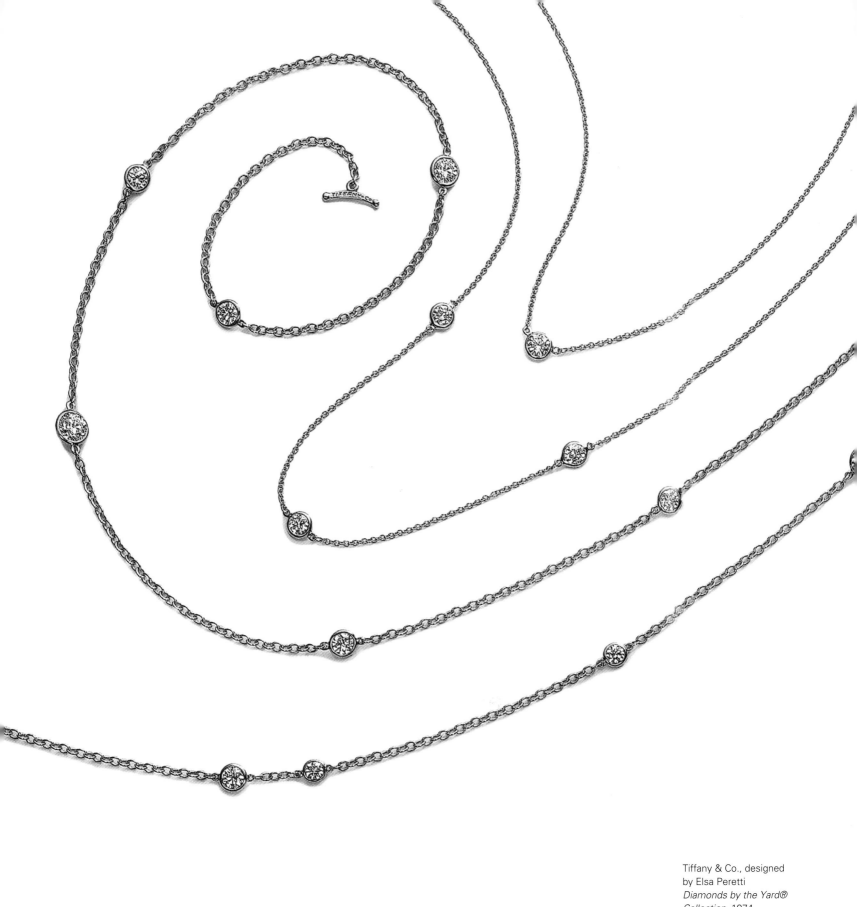

Tiffany & Co., designed
by Elsa Peretti
*Diamonds by the Yard®
Collection*, 1974
Gold, diamonds
Tiffany Collection

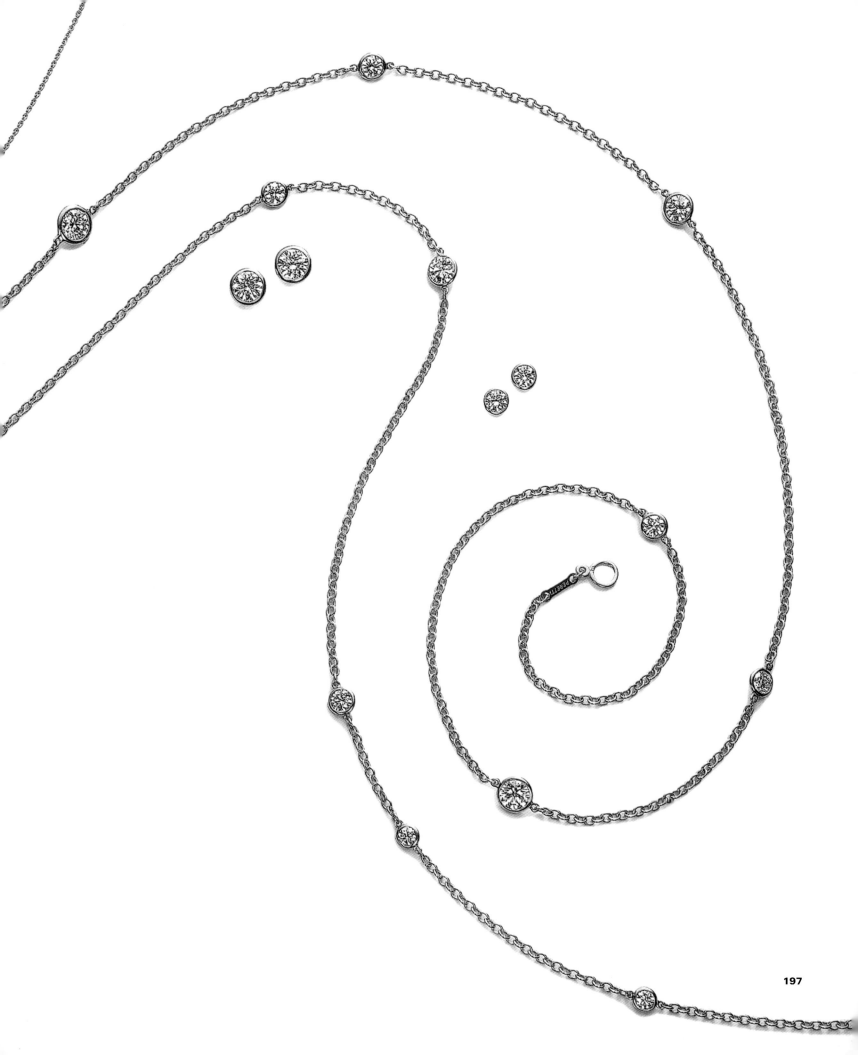

David Webb
Necklace and earrings c. 1970
Gold, platinum, diamonds, rock
crystal
Palermo, Serretta Fiorentino
Collection

Andrew Grima
Necklace and earrings, 1970
Gold, pearls, diamonds
Rome, private collection

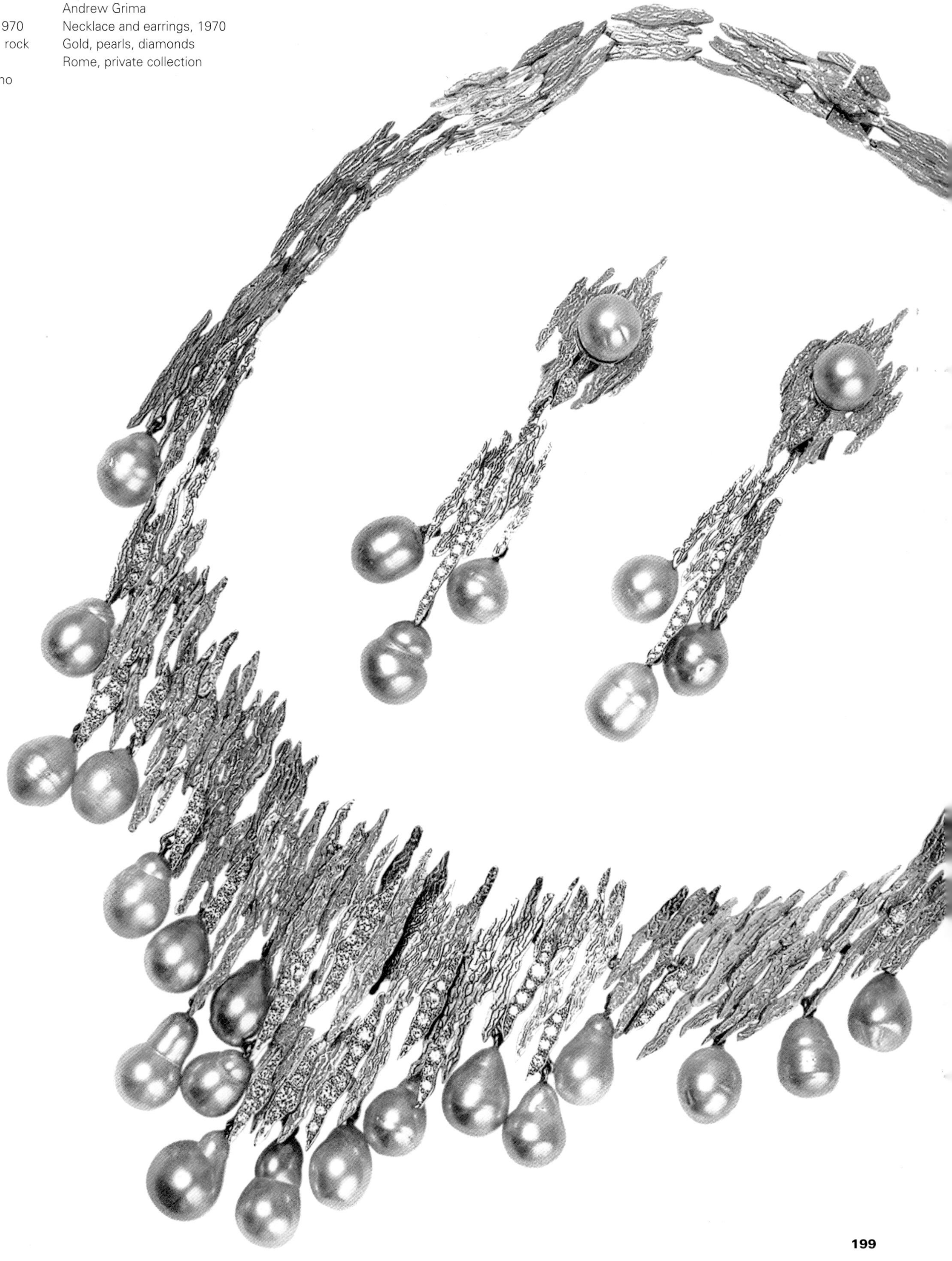

San Lorenzo,
designed by Franco Albini
and Franca Helg
Triangles necklace, 1973
Silver
Milan, San Lorenzo Collection

Tiffany & Co.,
designed by Elsa Peretti
Bracelets, 1976
Gold, ebony, lacquer
Tiffany Collection

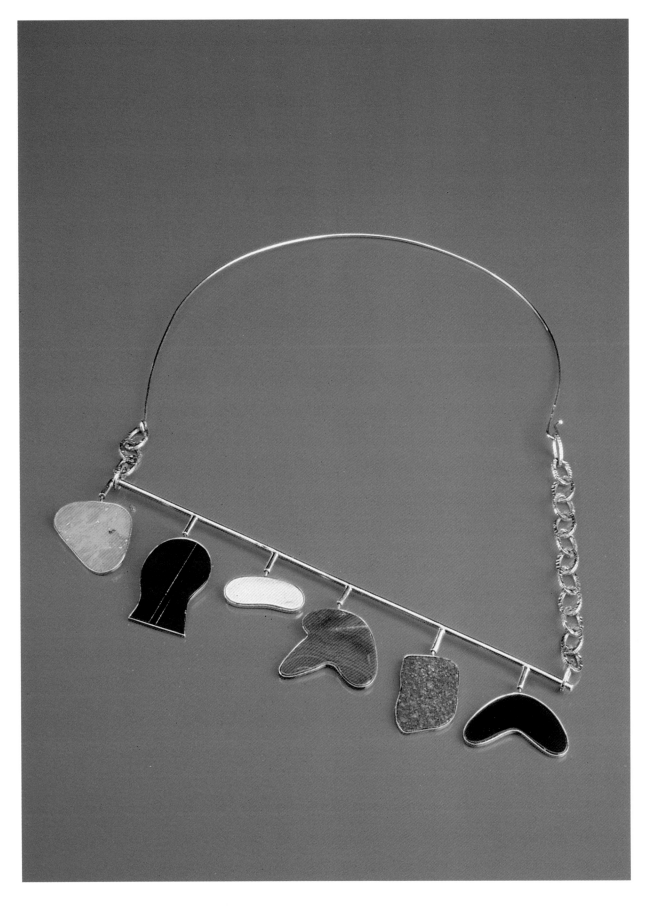

Meret Oppenheim, made by
Cleto Munari
Necklace, 1984–86
Gold, onyx, coral, chrysoprase
Private collection

Ettore Sottsass jr,
made by Cleto Munari
Seduction ring, no. 23, 2002
Gold, onyx
Milan, Cleto Munari Archive,
Galleria Colombari

Ettore Sottsass jr,
made by Cleto Munari
Seduction earrings, no. 25,
2002
Gold, coral
Milan, Cleto Munari Archive,
Galleria Colombari

Ettore Sottsass jr,
made by Cleto Munari
Seduction ring, no. 28, 2002
Gold, lapis lazuli
Milan, Cleto Munari Archive,
Galleria Colombari

Ettore Sottsass jr,
made by Cleto Munari
Seduction earrings, no. 32,
2002
Gold, onyx
Milan, Cleto Munari Archive,
Galleria Colombari

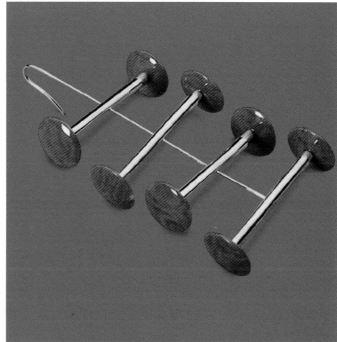

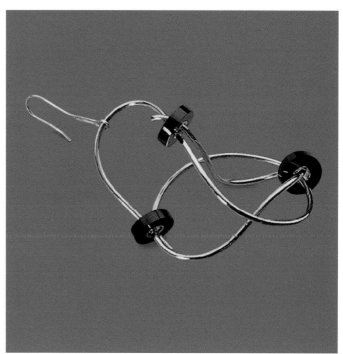

Ettore Sottsass,
made by Cleto Munari
Ring, 1984–86
Gold, coral, lapis lazuli
Milan, Cleto Munari Archive,
Galleria Colombari

Michele De Lucchi
Ring, 1984–86
Gold, coral, onyx, agate,
lapis lazuli
Private collection

Paolo Portoghesi,
made by Cleto Munari
Ring, 1984–86
Gold, sapphires
Missoni Collection

Peter Eisenman,
made by Cleto Munari
Ring, 1984–86
Gold, lapis lazuli, onyx,
turquoises
Milan, Cleto Munari Archive,
Galleria Colombari

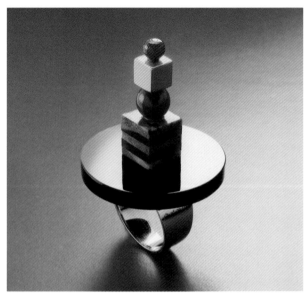

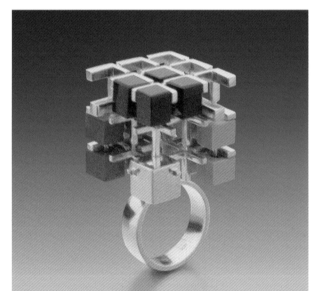

Bruno Munari,
made by Uno A Erre, Arezzo
Chain with pendant, 1995
Gold
Orodautore Collection – Centro
Promozione e Servizi di Arezzo

Mario Bellini,
made by Koala Preziosi, Arezzo
Slave bracelet, 1998
Gold
Orodautore Collection – Centro
Promozione e Servizi di Arezzo

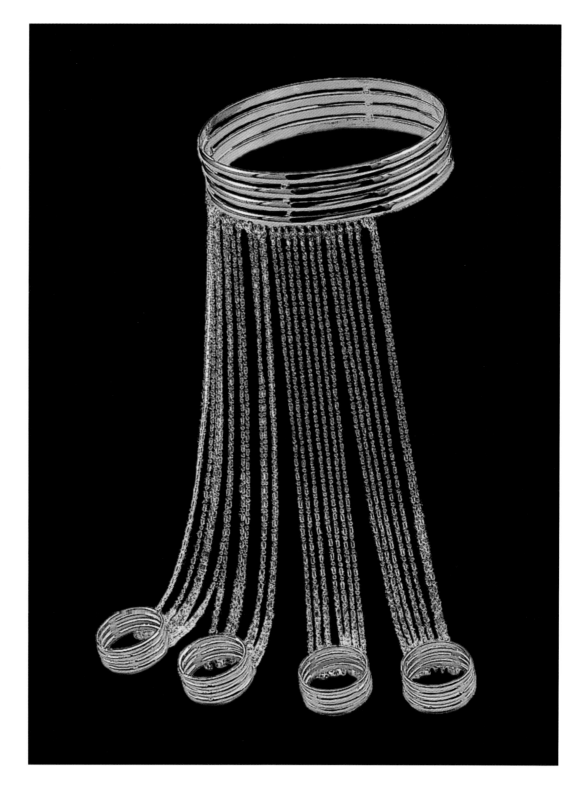

Angelo Mangiarotti
Vera Laica ring, 2000
Silver
Superego

Marc Newson
Orgone bracelet, 1994
Silver, synthetic enamel
Amsterdam, Who is afraid
of...? Foundation

Marco Romanelli
and Marta Laudani
Necklace with paper inserts,
2009
Private collection

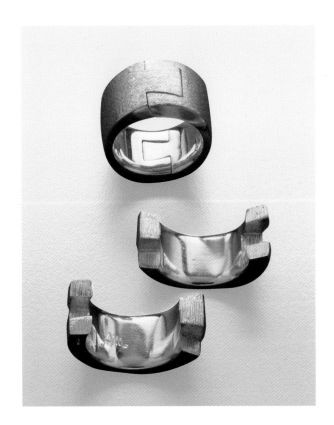

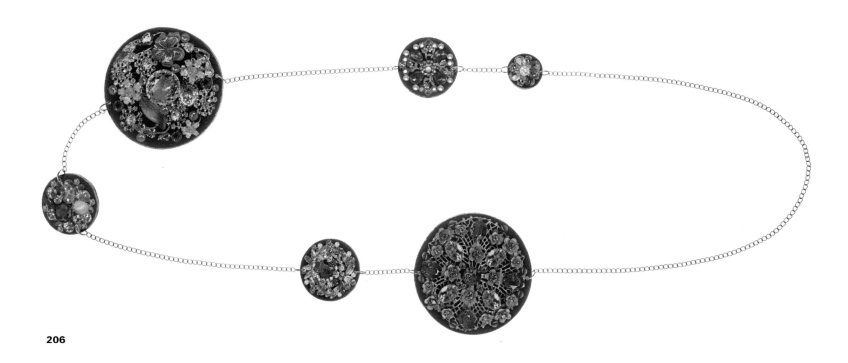

Bruno Munari
Constellation, 1975
Silver
Cantù, Galleria del Design
e dell'Arredamento

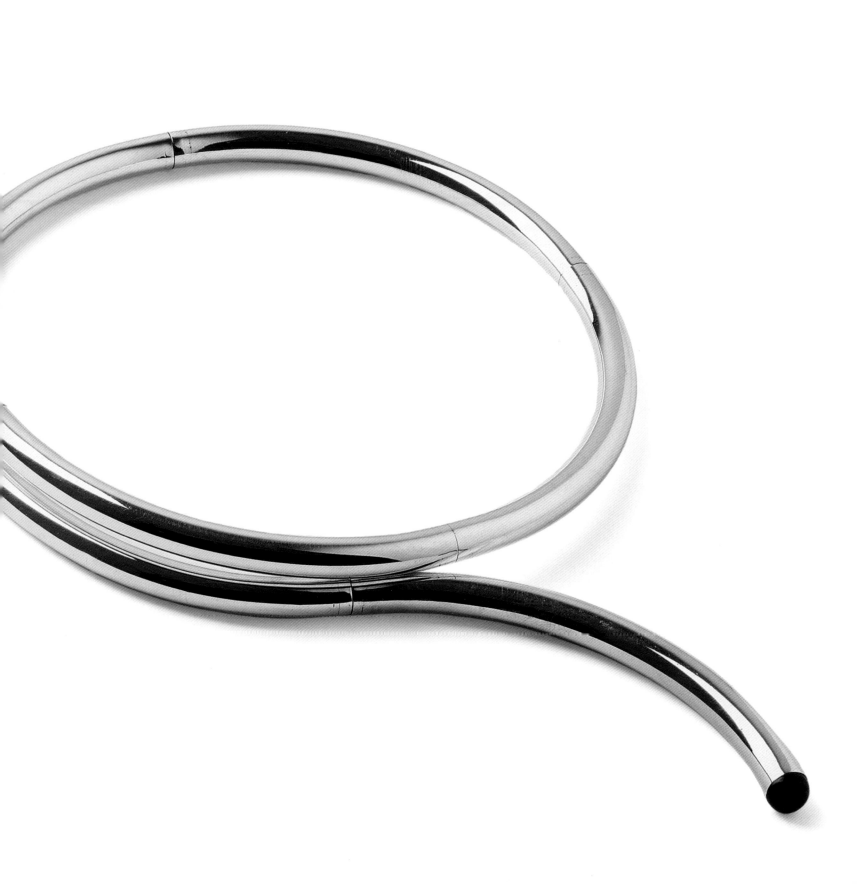

James Rivière
Bach Cupidoso necklace, 1979
Yellow gold, anodized titanium
Collection of the artist

Riccardo Dalisi
Enchanted Forest necklace,
1995
Silver, copper
Naples, collection of the artist

Gaetano Pesce
Spaghetti Ring rings, 1995
Resin
Milan, Fish Design

Carla Riccoboni
Alphabet chains, 1979–2000
Gold, silver
Bassano del Grappa,
collection of the artist

Karl Heinz Reister
Necklace, 1999
Gold, onyx, diamonds, steel
Reister Archive

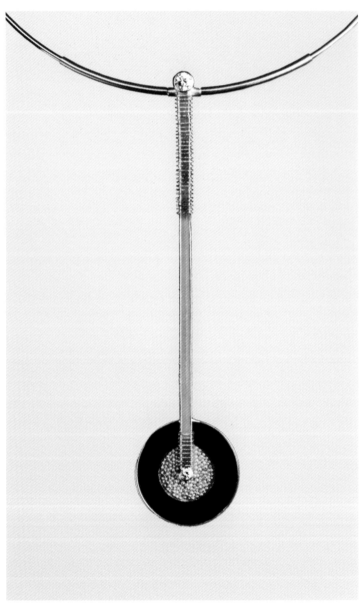

Alba Lisca Polenghi
Red copper brooch, 2000
Gold, silver, coral
Collection of the artist

Gabriele De Vecchi
Bloom ring, 2004
Gold, diamonds
Milan, De Vecchi Archive

Barbara Paganin
Brooch, 1996
Gold, silver, Venetian seed
beads
Collection of the artist

Giovanni Corvaja
Brooch, 2000
Gold, niello
Todi, Giovanni Corvaja
Collection

GianCarlo Montebello
Super-light spiral necklace,
2006
Stainless steel, gold
Milan, Montebello Collection

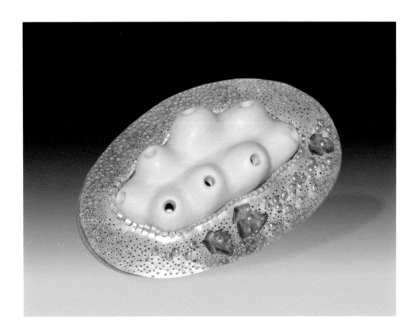

Giorgio Vigna
Water ring, 2009
Gold, rock crystal
Collection of the artist
Photo: Dea Gasparac

Giorgio Vigna
Gurgle ring, 2009
Gold, pearls
Collection of the artist
Photo: Dea Gasparac

Jacqueline Ryan
Chain with pendant, 1996
Gold, enamel
Todi, collection of the artist

Fabio Cammarata
Antithetic Opposite pendant,
2006
Gold, silver, gold leaf,
briarwood, polyester
Collection of the artist

Maurizio Stagni
Different Flower brooch, 2006
Silver, gold
Trieste, collection of the artist

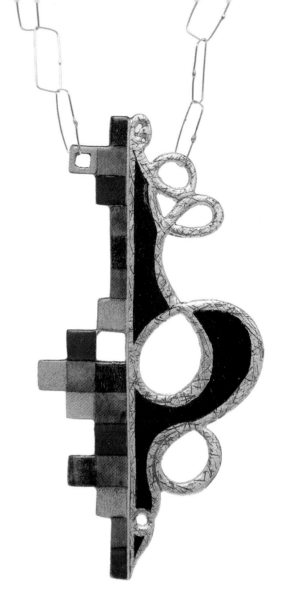

217

Rossella Tornquist
Necklace, 2007
Silver, gold
Collection of the artist

Chloé,
designed by Karl Lagerfeld
Necklace, 1979–80
Metal Tubogas, plastic, paste,
fake pearls
Milan, Ugo Correani Collection

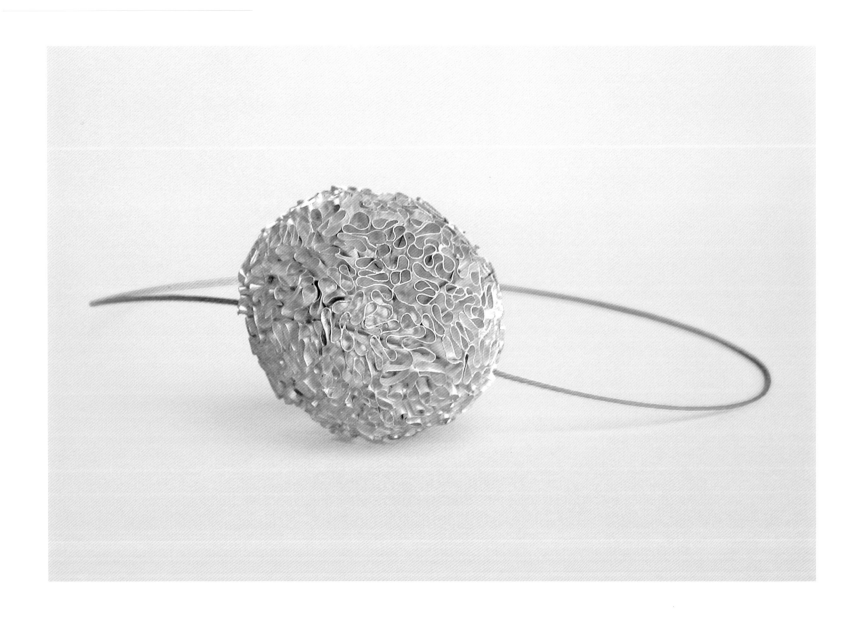

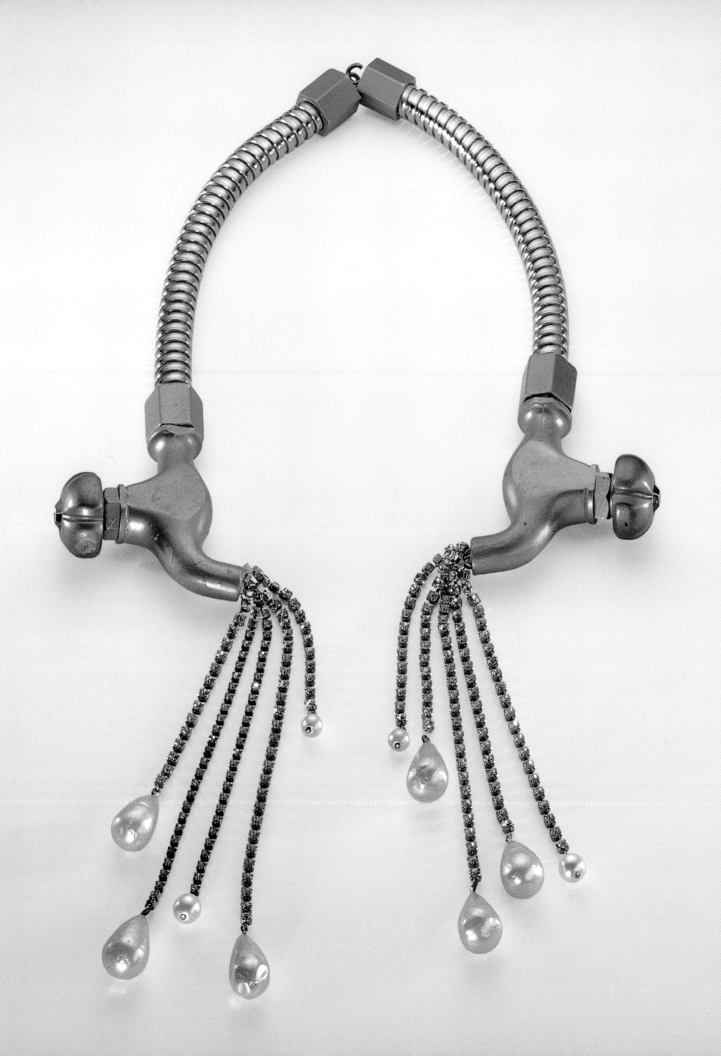

Gianfranco Ferré
Baroque necklace, 1985
Gold-plated brass
Milan, Fondazione Ferré

Sharra Pagano
Precious necklace, 2005–06
Onyx, amethyst
Milan, collection of the artist

Dior, designed
by Victoire de Castellane
Gwendoline ring, 2000
Gold, coral, diamonds
Paris, Dior Collection

Gucci
Horsebit Nail ring, c. 2005
Gold, diamonds
Gucci Collection

Donatella Pellini
Bracelets, 2006
Resin with inclusion of micro-
mosaic images mounted in
a metal frame
Private collection

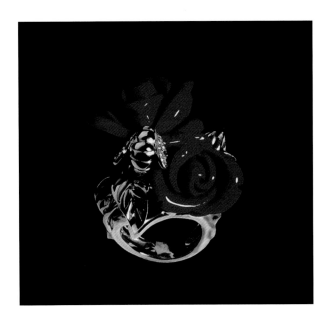

Vivienne Westwood,
made by Garzi, Arezzo
Tiara, 2005
Gold
Orodautore Collection – Centro
Promozione e Servizi di Arezzo

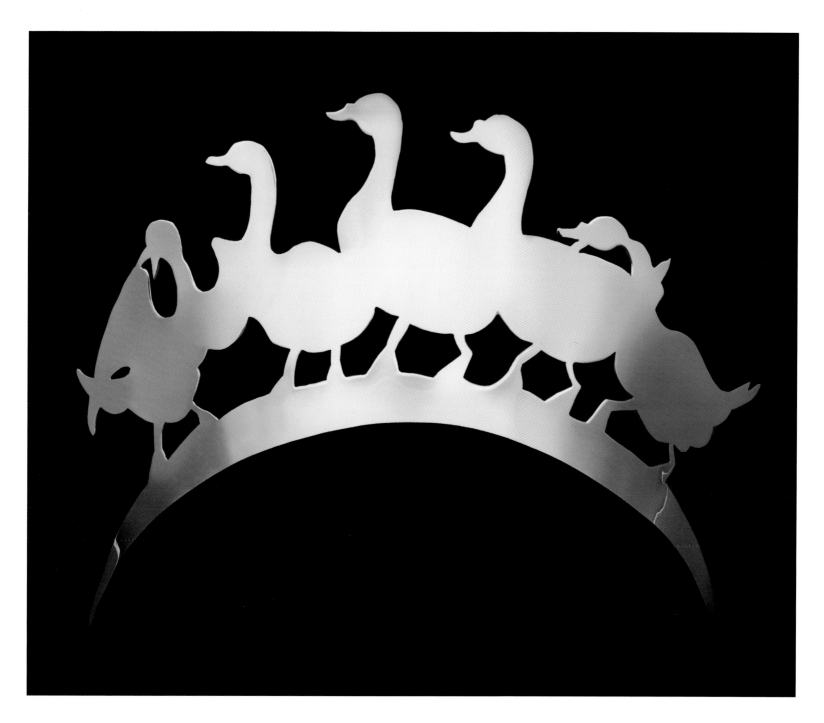

Tiffany & Co.,
designed by Paloma Picasso
Pendant, 1986
Gold, platinum, kunzite,
diamonds
Tiffany Collection
Courtesy of the Smithsonian
Institution, Washington, DC

Tiffany & Co., designed
by Paloma Picasso
Stiff bracelet, 1989
Gold, tourmaline
Tiffany Collection

JAR
Bracelet, c. 1987
Diamonds, coloured stones,
titanium
New York, private collection

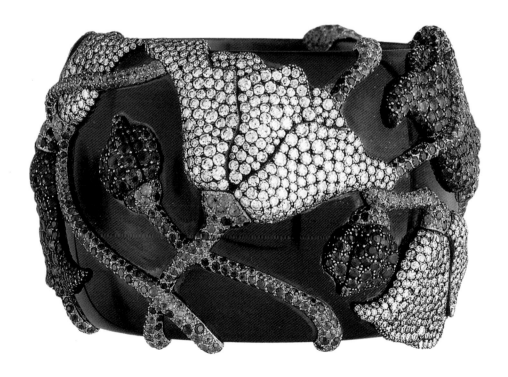

Vhernier
Callas necklace, 1997
Gold, ebony
Vhernier Collection

Bulgari
B.zero 1 ring, 1999
Gold
Bulgari Collection

Damiani
Damianissima ring, 2007
Gold, diamonds
Damiani Collection

Pomellato
Victoria rings, 2007
Gold, jet
Pomellato Collection

Pomellato
Victoria necklace, 2007
Gold, jet
Pomellato Collection

Breil
Mono earring, 2007
Brushed and polished stainless
steel with rose gold and brown
IP treatment
Steel Leaves IP Collection

Dodo
Dodo pendant, 2010
Gold, diamonds, leather string
Dodo Collection

Tiffany & Co.,
designed by Frank O. Gehry
Torque bracelet, 2004
Agate
Tiffany Collection

228

Mattioli
Necklace, 2009
Gold, titanium, grey diamonds
Piume Collection

Roberto Coin
Rings, 2009
Gold, diamonds
CapriPlus Collection

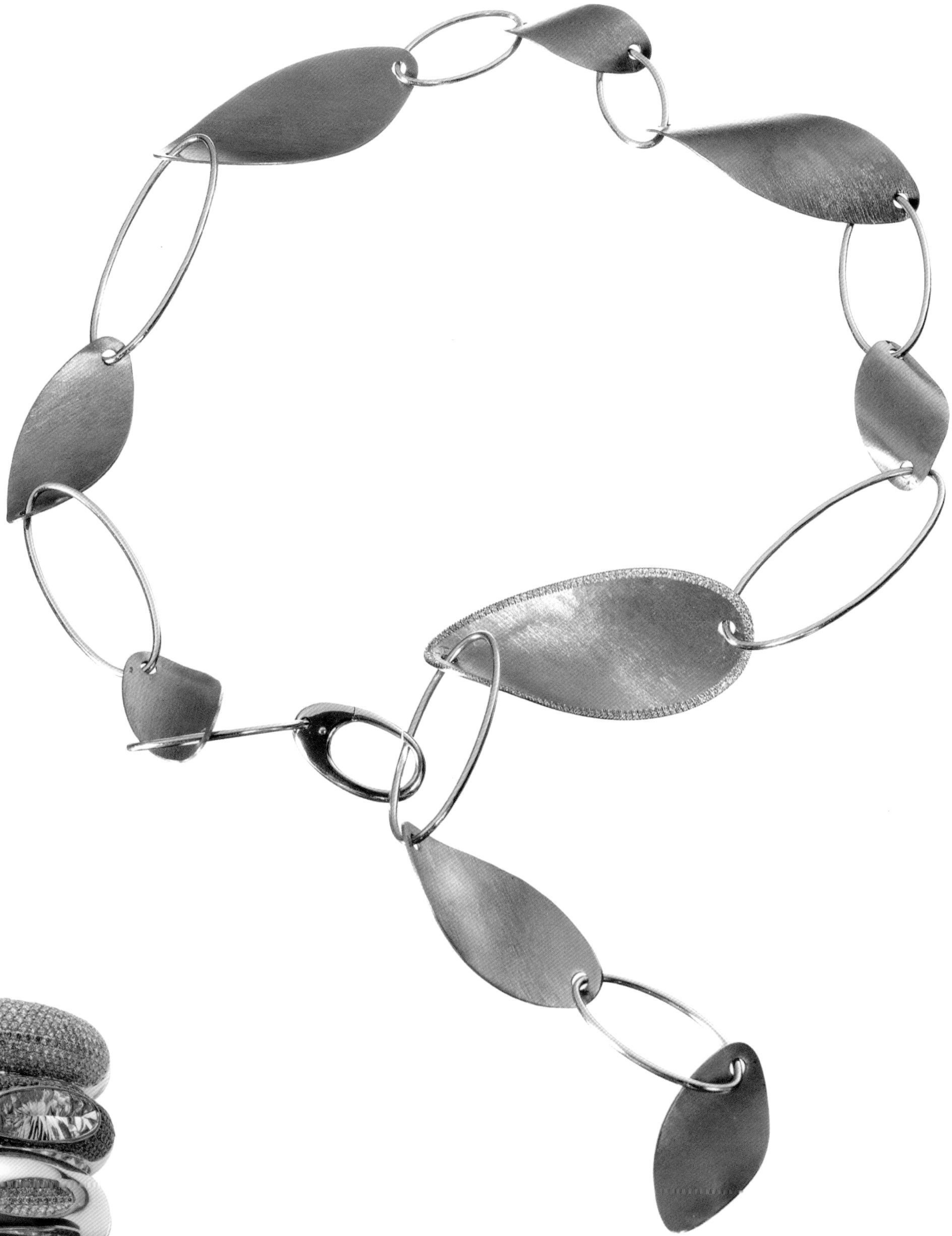

Glossary

Agate

This translucent chalcedony is found in many colours ranging from beige to brown and black. Its concentric bands and inclusions make it a valuable semi-precious stone and determine its miscellaneous varieties, such as floral and moss agates. This mineral's elevated degree of hardness and mix of colours, owing to the presence of stratification, mean it can be used for cameos and inlaid objects.

Aigrette

This refers to an ornament made from an egret plume (*aigrette* is French for egret), which is placed on turbans and in women's hair. In jewellery the aigrette is a decoration made from metal and precious stones, which is fixed to the head or hair to imitate feathers and plumes.

Alexandrite

The value of this rare and precious stone can sometimes exceed that of a diamond. The characteristic that makes this gem unique is its ability to change colour depending on the light source. Emerald green when exposed to natural light, it becomes dark red if lit artificially. It was discovered in 1831, on the birthday of Czar Alexander II of Russia. This is how it got its name.

Alloy

A metallic product obtained by the fusion and mixture of two or more different and pure metals. In jewellery almost all metals are used in alloys so as to increase their hardness, as in the case of gold and silver, or to make them easier to process, as in the case of platinum. The percentage of precious metal used establishes the degree of fineness which is stamped on the finished jewel. Adjusting the percentage of alloying metals can produce colour variations in the base metals.

Amber

A fossilised resin produced by the fossilisation of what, in prehistoric times, were organic vegetal compounds mostly produced by conifers. Found in knotty and asymmetrical lumps, it is transparent, with shades ranging from pale yellow to orange to brown or ruddy brown. Inclusions of vegetal fragments or small insects trapped in a prehistoric age, when the resin which had just oozed from the tree was still soft and sticky, are extremely rare and highly sought after.

Amethyst

A variety of quartz of a deep violet colour with patches and veins of a lighter shade, tending to white. Its degree of purity, absence of streaking and uniformity of colour determines its value. The colour can be made more intense by exposing the mineral to a moderate heat source. This produces what is known as burnt amethyst.

Anklet

A feminine ornament from the Orient, consisting of a chain that encircles the ankle. Tiny pendants are often fixed to the rings which form the links of the chain so that every movement of the foot is accompanied by a soft tinkling sound.

Aquamarine

Found in various colours ranging from blue-green to sky blue, it is judged to be just as precious as an emerald, while its physical properties and the way it refracts the light make it suitable for square cuts, such as the *baguette* shape, which exploit its brilliance and colour.

Armband

A jewel that comes in various sizes and is worn on the shoulder or forearm or, more often, on the wrist. In ancient times it was worn by men as a symbol of power or as a trophy. There are various types of armband, depending on the materials and techniques used to make them. They may be flexible if made with metal chains or links, rigid when made of a single circular piece or semi-rigid if composed of moving parts that are hinged together.

Asterism

An optical phenomenon produced by the reflection of light on inclusions in some gems such as *cabochon* rubies or sapphires. A reflection appears on the spherical surface of the stone, which is characterised by radial lines that form a star. Gems with these features are extremely rare and highly sought after and are known as "star stones".

Baciamano

A feminine ornament consisting of a bracelet worn around the wrist and one or more rings which are slipped onto the finger, linked by slender chains, often decorated with gems and rare stones. Originally from the Orient, it was considered to be a tool of seduction and a mark of female elegance.

Baguette

A method of cutting precious stones that gives the gem an elongated rectangular shape with a flat table. Technically tricky, it requires stones of an elevated degree of purity, as the flat table clearly reveals any inclusions.

Bandeau

A head ornament with a tight band that encircles the upper part of the forehead. It descends from the fabric ribbon that Italian ladies wore to hold their hair back in the Middle Ages. It underwent its transformation into a piece of jewellery around the mid-nineteenth century and became especially popular during the first three decades of the twentieth.

Brilliant

This is the name given to a round diamond cut into 58 facets divided as follows: 32 facets on the upper part which make up the crown and 24 facets on the lower part or pavilion, octagonal girdle and culet. This elaborate cut, refined in 1919 by Antwerp cutter Marcel Tolkowsky, is a particularly good cut for diamonds as it is able to invest the stone with the utmost splendour and beauty.

Briolette

A drop-cut gem whose entire surface is cut into triangular facets. Originally from India, the briolette cut entails a hole being drilled close to the pointed apex so it can be attached to a smaller bezel, increasing the surface exposed to the light.

Brooch

Brooches are used to adorn clothes or hats. They are equipped with a pin which pierces the fabric and is caught by a catch so as to guarantee fastening and safety. There are infinite types; circular, flower, pendant, single or series of three or five, in different sizes which sometimes make up a single large brooch or are transformed into decorations for necklaces or bracelets.

Cabochon

A polished, unfaceted stone with a shiny hemispherical surface. The *cabochon* cut is used on opaque or translucent semi-precious stones, including rubies and sapphires. Until the fifteenth century it was the only known method for exploiting the gem before faceted cuts were introduced from the Orient. There are various types of *cabochon* cut which act in different ways on the underside of the stone, producing convex or hollow gems, depending on the level of sparkle desired.

Calibré cut

The term refers to a number of faceted stones that are identical in shape, generally square or rectangular, and step-cut. *Calibré* cut stones are small in size and fit snugly together.

Cameo

This is a product of glyptography, consisting of an oval or round semi-precious stone, which is cut and engraved with small lapping wheels to produce a figure in relief. It is best to use stratified or variegated stones such as agate or chalcedony to highlight the figure in relief against the base of a different colour.

Carat
A standard unit of measurement that has been used since the beginning of the twentieth century to quantify the weight of precious stones. It is equivalent to 0.2 grams and expressed by two decimal numbers.

Casting and *cire perdue*
This produces infinite copies of an object or component starting from a mould made by modelling a synthetic wax using small scalpels and files. Once the model has been produced a rubber mould is made of it. Subsequent castings of molten wax inside the mould can generate series of replicas which are then neatly arranged on a wax base to create a cluster structure. The composition is then immersed in a cylinder containing liquid plaster which solidifies around it to bear its negative print. The next step is to heat the mixture to allow the wax contained in the mould to liquefy and pour out of a series of holes prepared when the plaster is still liquid. The cast metal is poured into the mould at a high temperature and controlled pressures. Once the metal has been cooled the structure obtained is released and the individual replicas are separated. A subsequent polishing of the surfaces finishes the object.

Cat's-Eye
An optical phenomenon produced by some gems, such as tourmaline or tiger's eye, cut *en cabochon*. Struck by the light, the particles or inclusions found in the gem emanate a reflection which has an elongated shape that recalls the pupils of felines.

Chain
An item of jewellery consisting of a series of ring-shaped parts linked together to produce a supple strand. The sizes and shapes of the elements placed in succession are variable and, in some cases, determine the type of chain: rollo in the case where links have identical circular shapes; marina, when the links alternate with oval elements with two holes; byzantine, torchon, etc. Making chains requires cylindrical instruments around which the goldsmith winds the metal wire in order to produce the shape of the link desired. Enormous skill is required when soldering the rings to avoid soldering them to each other, and thus compromising the suppleness of the whole.

Chalcedony
An aggregate of microscopic quartz crystals, whose colour ranges from blue to pale yellow to grey. The presence of other chemical elements or compounds gives the mineral different hues and shades, generating an equal number of varieties with different names: onyx if the semi-precious stone is black or white, cornelian if it is red-orange, chrysoprase if it is bright green. The aggregation of particles sometimes generates irregular stratifications, such as in agate and jasper. The porosity of the mineral means the colours can be exploited in different ways, making it one of the most popular stones.

Chasing
This means engraving and embossing the surface of precious metals using a chisel, consisting of a metal blade whose end is flat and rounded. Chasing allows metal to be shaped without damaging the surface and without removing any material. During the procedure the chisel is beaten on the metal with a special little hammer and the flat point of the instrument buckles the surface, producing hollows and indentations. Chasing is generally used for decorating the surfaces of an article with motifs in bas relief or for finishing three-dimensional objects produced with the microfusion technique. The end result is tiny details that appear to be sculpted and moulded into the metal.

Chatelaine
This jewel combines the practical and the purely ornamental. Popular in the eighteenth century, it is worn by day, on one hip, at waist height. It consists of a clip to which various small chains are attached from which small objects hang: scent bottles and knives, watches and other objects used for household chores.

Citrine
This is a variety of quartz consisting of large yellow-orange crystals. Natural citrine is a rather rare and precious stone. The artificial equivalent, obtained by heating amethyst, a variety with identical properties, is often used. This produces large, flawless stones.

Clip
An ornament for clothes or hats, which, unlike brooches, has no pin but serrated pincers on a spring that trap the edges of the fabric without making holes. It is used singly or in pairs to decorate the collars of jackets and the brims or edges of hats.

Collier de chien
A band that tightly hugs the neck at throat height. Very much in vogue during the Victorian and Art Nouveau age, it consists of a black velvet or grosgrain ribbon to which a curved ornamental plaque made of precious metals and stones is attached. In more opulent versions the fabric is replaced by bands made of slender strings of pearls spaced by variously decorated strips of precious metals.

Coral
A solid material of organic origin, produced by colonies of miniscule marine polyps that live in shallow water on the rocky beds of sheltered bays. In its natural state it is grouped in complex branching formations in the shape of shrubs. Colours vary from red to deep or pale pink to white. Coral branches are rather small and, given that they are hard to procure, this material has been considered rare and precious since ancient times. Used in jewellery from time immemorial, it is enormously versatile, complying with various tastes that either prefer it in its natural state in the form of branching shrubs or instead made into round beads or carved into plaques and cameos and veritable works of sculpture.

Cornelian
Also known as cairngorm, it is a translucent variety of red-orange chalcedony which, due to the hardness and compactness of the grain, becomes shiny with polishing. It is cut *en cabochon*, or used for inlays.

Corundum
This is the name of the mineral which identifies a family of precious stones that includes rubies and sapphires.

Cuff-links
Men's jewellery used to fasten shirtcuffs. Made of gold or silver with enamel or small precious stones, a cuff-link consists of two flat, circular elements, like buttons, joined by a very short chain.

Damascening
A technique of decorating metal or wooden surfaces by inlaying gold or silver thread or leaf. Grooves are cut on the surface that is to be decorated, thereby creating a pattern. The grooves are undercut and beaten metal leaves are inserted. The decorated surface is then treated with abrasives that polish and smooth the metal flaws and residue. The finished work creates a play of contrasts between the colours of the various metals used whilst the thin leaves produce texture and graphic effects that increase the preciousness of the jewel.

Demantoid
A rare garnet whose colour varies from bright to dark green. It owes its name to its diamond-like sparkle when faceted, a quality it shares with emeralds. Its softness, which makes it easy to scratch, restricts it to being used as an ornamental setting for pendants or brooches.

Diadem
An ornament worn around the forehead. In the past it was a badge of sovereignty and made of precious metals and fabulous gems. The most elaborate models have ornamental chains which fall across the temples or drape the back.

Diamond
The ultimate precious stone. The hardest, rarest and most immutable in time. It reflects the light beautifully, so much so that its sparkle is unmatched by any other stone. In nature it is found in various colours, ranging from white to straw yellow and, in very rare cases, pink, light blue, green and dark blue. It is extremely precious, to the point that it has been deemed necessary to establish parameters to determine its value and international laws to regularise its purchase and sale.

Doublet
This article is produced by cementing or sometimes fusing two layers of different stones together. It may involve the use of natural or synthetic stones or even glass. This practice is carried out to imitate natural, rare and precious stones.

Earrings
Often equipped with a pin that passes through a hole in the earlobe, there are also clip-on versions which do not require the flesh to be pierced but attach to the lobe thanks to a spring mechanism or screw-on clip. Whether they are hoops, drop earrings, clusters or studs, the practise of decorating one's ears is an ancient one, though there have been periods when this type of jewellery was temporarily forgotten, due to constantly evolving fashions and tastes.

Electroforming
An electrochemical process for producing large finished or semi-finished pieces, keeping the quantity of precious metal used to a minimum. It produces three-dimensional hollow elements with complex shapes, which are hard to produce by other methods. By means of a galvanic process of electrolysis a layer of precious alloy is placed on a die produced using low-cost materials, metallic waxes or metal alloys with a low point of fusion. These materials are then eliminated by a process of chemical-physical corrosion that does not alter the precious metal but hollows it out internally. The pieces and parts produced are then subjected to a thermal treatment of annealing and tempering that guarantees the mechanical resistance of the finished jewel. Electroforming means formal details of the die can be reproduced, guaranteeing exact replicas.

Emerald
A rare and precious stone, particularly

sought after for its deep green colour. If struck with force it tends to crumble. It lends itself to being cut into the classic rectangular shape which takes its name from this gem. The variegated inclusions often found in the stone, which make up the so-called "garden", are highly prized. In this case the gem's splendour and the three-dimensional effect of the sparkle is enhanced by a *cabochon* cut or by smoothing the jaggedness of the raw stone.

Enamelling

This allows metal surfaces to be decorated with a vitreous, polychrome layer, which is baked onto the artefact. The base material consists of a mixture of vitreous substances and silicon sand, enriched by metallic oxides that act as colourings, and other chemical substances which increase the hardness and resistance of the finished decoration. The mixture produced is spread, while still damp, on the metal surface of the object to be decorated. This is then placed in a small oven where the mixture is fired. As it melts it generates the enamel. The firing has to be done at a controlled temperature since, depending on the compound mixture used, there may be variations that will modify the melting point. Indeed, different colourings of the enamel on the same object mean it is necessary to fire it repeatedly, at gradually lower temperatures. Subsequent lapping and polishing, using lapping wheels and rotating brushes, give the enamels their sheen.

Basse-taille enamelling

This involves the application of a translucent enamel onto an embossed metal plate. The transparency of the enamel highlights the graphic effect of the underlying engraved and chased relief.

Champlevé enamelling

This is carried out on a metal base which is engraved and chased to create grooves and cells depending on the decoration required. The depressions in the metal are filled with opaque enamel and, after firing, the surface of the object is polished to even out irregularities.

Cloisonné enamelling

This is carried out on gold or silver plate onto which a lattice of bent metal wires is soldered so as to produce a series of separate cells which make up the decoration. The enamel is poured into each cavity. Fused at a high temperature, it generates a flat, uniform decoration delimited by the metallic lattice.

Flinqué enamelling

A layer of translucent coloured enamel is applied to protect and highlight the contrasts of a decoration engraved on a metal plate, as in the case of guilloché

decorations. This type of technique was mostly used to decorate sophisticated accessories such as cigarette boxes or nécessaires.

Plique-à-jour enamelling

This procedure is similar to the technique of cloisonné enamelling and is carried out on delicate decorations traced with flat strips of metal. These are soldered together to produce a lacy pattern of separate cells. Subsequently the cells are filled with translucent enamel which, after firing, sticks to the metal so as to create a transparent and coloured decoration delimited by a thin strip of gold or silver recalling the effect of the stained glass windows in gothic cathedrals.

En ronde-bosse enamelling

Like basse-taille enamelling this technique involves the application of generally translucent, sometimes opaque, enamel, on a chased metal base in full or high relief. This treatment produces a greater chiaroscuro contrast between the indentations in which the vitreous material accumulates and the protrusions which remain covered by a thin layer of colour. It means the finished work acquires greater character and definition.

Engraving

A scorper or cutting instrument is beaten on metal to remove shavings. Engraving produces tiny decorations hollowed from flat and curved surfaces or finishes three-dimensional objects produced by the microfusion technique. Although in the past this method produced finished pieces of jewellery of excellent workmanship, it has often been associated with extra, additional work or finishing touches: niello, or inlaying, to create a marked contrast between the background and the decoration, or enamelling, to protect the engraved patterns with a shiny, transparent and coloured patina.

Epaulette

An ornament worn on the shoulder of military uniforms. It ends with a fringe made of thin metal chains. Originally it was used to decorate army uniforms and indicated the rank and position of the wearer.

Fancy colour

This term identifies precious stones, such as diamonds and coloured pearls, which have unusual and rare colours in nature. These are exceptional pieces worth far more than stones with ordinary colouring.

Fibula

Extremely common in the Classical age, the function of this ornament is to join

two strips of fabric and hold them together by means of a large pin. It is curved with a long catch-plate which guards the pin and prevents the person wearing it from being pricked.

Filigree

It generates light, lacy patterns composed of slender threads of silver or gold which, twisted into fine decorations, create three-dimensional elements. The metal threads, previously drawn into extremely slender sections are joined and braided. Woven together in this way, they are then worked to create small decorative elements known as scrolls or volutes. Subsequently, these parts are soldered together and placed on thin frames where they create more complex and flowing motifs.

Florentine mosaic

A technique of working marble and semi-precious stones, which are arranged to compose geometrical elements and other figurative subjects. The process exploits the different veins and colourings of the stone materials used, so as to produce the effect of a painting. Unlike stone marquetry and tarsia, the underlying surface is completely covered and not part of the decoration.

Fretwork

Carried out on metal plates to produce complex lacy patterns that generate arabesques, geometrical motifs and ornamental figures. The decorative plate is first engraved with scorpers to produce the design, which is divided into zones and sectors and delimited by an engraved edge. An awl or punch is used to pierce holes in the plate at specific points, indicating the zones to be cut. The thin blade of a small arcsaw cuts into the plate starting from the hole and then proceeds to carefully trace the engraved edges of the ornamental motif. When the work is finished the edges of the decoration are polished and made uniform to eliminate any swarf and eventual flaws produced by the blade. The final result is enhanced by polishing the fretted surface.

Garnet

An extended family of minerals that all share the same composition and structure which, contrary to popular opinion, is not distinguished by the same red colour. The dark red colour is specific to the pyrope. Other coloured varieties have different names: alamandine is purple red, rhodolite is pink, while demantoid is a rare and valuable emerald-green garnet.

Gem

This is the name of all those minerals used to adorn jewels. These rare and highly prized stones are selected on the

basis of their purity or colour and are polished or faceted to enhance their shine and brilliance. As well as minerals, the term is also used to refer to pearls, coral, amber and other organic substances.

Glass

The use of glass in the world of jewellery has been an established feature since ancient times. This material has been used from time immemorial to imitate or fake precious stones, gems or pearls by varying the chemical composition of the mixture and altering its colours. Enamels, also consisting of glass paste, are more highly prized from the artistic point of view. In this case tradition attributes the material with a higher value, making the artefact more precious. Nowadays, many experiments are linked to the use of glass, suggesting new uses and new values.

Glyptography

This is the art of engraving semi-precious stones, gems and other materials, such as coral or shells, to create illustrations and motifs, using small grindstones of varying hardness. Two types of product are generated depending on which procedure is used. The first produces cameos. Here the gems are carved in relief, exploiting the different colours created by veins and layers of colour. The upper part is carved to produce a figure while a different coloured layer underneath acts as the background to the composition. The second procedure produces carved and engraved gems where the image is hollowed from the table of the stone. Unlike cameos this is generally monotone.

Godron

An ornamental engraved pattern arranged in a sheaf of rounded parallel grooves.

Gold

The ultimate precious metal. Adored and worked by man since ancient times. Ductile and malleable, its glitter and deep yellow colour remains unaltered in time, resisting almost any type of chemical or physical aggression. It is common for goldsmiths to combine gold in alloys with other metals, such as copper, silver or palladium, to increase the hardness of the finished jewel and to change the colour. The percentage of gold found in the alloy is variable and regulated by international laws that guarantee its quality. This value is expressed by a number hallmarked on metal which is known as its fineness.

Grain

The unit of weight for pearls, equivalent to a quarter of a carat (0.05 grams). It is also the name used to signify the three or four metal shavings which are bent to hold gems in place. This type of setting is known as grain setting or millegrain setting.

Grano

A *grano* is also an uneven fragment of a gem, generally made from stone-cutters' scraps. These are salvaged, polished and bored with holes so that they can be strung together.

Granulation

This decoration, dating from the time of the Etruscans, affixes microscopic spheres of gold to the surface of the jewel to create patterns of lines which then arrange themselves into figurative or abstract subjects. A blend of fine gold powder and charcoal is compounded in a crucible. The mixture is then heated with a flame to fuse the gold particles which, thanks to the charcoal, remain separate and become spherical. Later these are arranged in curvilinear patterns, often alternating with small filigree elements. The decoration produced is soldered to the jewel using a fluid compound containing copper which, due to the heat of the oven, solders the parts colloidally.

Griffes

These are from three to six metal prongs that keep a stone from wobbling inside its setting. In some cases they may be decorated with one or more gems, enhancing the splendour of the jewel.

Guilloché

A decoration engraved on gold or silver which has a pattern of concentric whorls. It is produced by an engine-turning lathe that can engrave infinite combinations and radial motifs. The final effect is a sort of damascening produced by the reflection of the light, which strikes the engravings in different ways. It is mainly carried out on flat surfaces and is therefore suitable for decorating small objects and accessories.

Horn

An organic substance of animal origin and a material that has been used from time immemorial to create jewels and ornaments. Its fibrous structure softens if immersed in hot water, making it malleable and suitable for carving.

Inclusions

Foreign bodies of gas, liquids or solids that remain trapped in the gem when it is formed. Anomalies in the crystal lattice or in the composition of the mineral which leads to colour mutation or tarnishing are also called inclusions. There are various types of inclusion: polyhedral crystals, crystalline needles, (rutilated quartz, for instance), crystalline tufts (in emeralds or in moss agate), and so on.

Inclusions may lower the value of a stone when they dull its sheen but may also increase it in the case of asterism, cat's-eye or the ornamental branching that characterises some semi-precious stones.

Intaglio

A technique used on softer materials, using cutting tools and small blades. It is used to engrave and carve horn, amber, coral and ivory in bas relief. As for the engraving of gems, small laps are used followed by treatment with abrasive powders to polish the finished work and make it shine.

Ivory

A material of animal origin formed from dentine, which makes up the bulk of the tusks of elephants and other mammals. It is used to produce decorative inlaid parts and elements. Ivory has a hard and uniform grain of a straw white colour. Its surface can be polished to make it bright and glossy. The fact that it is so hard to procure, as it comes from protected species, makes it rare and precious.

Jade

This term identifies two types of mineral which have different compositions but a rather similar structure. Jade and nephrite are traditionally used in the Orient to produce precious ornaments and objects. Both extremely hard, their colour ranges from white to dark green, producing unusual variegated effects. Used in carving and engraving, jade gleams when polished.

Jasper

An opaque quartz that comes in an enormous variety of colours combined in unusual ways. Often the colour indicates the variety: floral, musky, striped, Egyptian. One of the most prized varieties is the bloody jasper, bright green in colour with red spots that resemble drops of blood.

Lacquer

A vegetal resin which is secreted by numerous varieties of a tree of Asian origin found in China or Japan. The Chinese and Japanese are traditionally masters of lacquering, a technique which is also used in jewellery. The resin is collected, filtered, dyed and then applied in a series of layers onto small objects and surfaces made of wood or metal. Once it has dried, the lacquer is polished until it is astonishingly glossy. The possibility to modify its colour and transparency has led to the discovery of infinite techniques, which sometimes lend their name to the finished decoration.

Lapidary

The art of cutting and faceting gems and precious stones. It is a complex operation which has to take into account the optical and geometrical properties that characterise the crystalline structures of the minerals. Lapidary gives the stones symmetrical shapes that exploit the way they refract the light and their colours. In an initial phase of the process the raw stone is worked on to eliminate flaws and impurities and to hint at the form which will subsequently be defined in the cutting phase. This is followed by many phases that involve grinding the gem from controlled angles. Facets are generated by special metal laps with diamond surfaces. The final grinding phase polishes the cut gem and makes the surfaces gleam.

Lapis lazuli

A semi-precious stone of a dark blue colour crisscrossed by pyrite veins that create an extraordinary pattern of spangles on the blue background of the gem. It is used to produce carved and engraved decorative elements.

Laser engraving, laser cutting and laser fretwork

These terms represent the modern forms of the traditional techniques of the same names, which today make use of laser technology and numerical control systems. The processes are carried out on flat surfaces as the laser beam is only efficient if projected perpendicularly onto the surfaces to be treated. The laser removes a thin layer of material to produce the engraving. The movement of the beam on the surface to be engraved is regulated by an optical system which translates the mathematical coordinates from a two-dimensional model designed by software. These technologies significantly reduce working times and the use of specialised labour.

Lava stone

The name did not originally refer to the typical minerals of volcanic origin but to a family of sedimentary stones that are easy to fashion and which, above all in the past, were engraved and carved to decorate jewels and ornaments. Its dark hue and the location of centres of production near Naples contributed to perpetrating the misunderstanding and associating this stone with the eruptions of Vesuvius. Currently the term "lava stone" more accurately describes those materials of volcanic origin that are characterised by an elevated coefficient of hardness. This makes it just as complex as semi-precious stones to process.

Lavallière

A necklace consisting of a long chain or string of mounted pearls or stones and a locket-clasp which is worn, like a tie, leaving the ends of the chain free. The locket can be positioned as one pleas-es so that the lengths of the loose ends can be regulated. They may be positioned asymmetrically, one longer than the other.

Lorgnette

A pair of eye-glasses equipped with a handle. This often ends in a ring that is slipped onto the finger to steady the grip. It has been used since the Twenties when in high society it was considered improper for women to be seen in public wearing spectacles. The larger French jewellery *maisons* used to produce precious versions destined for an elite clientele.

Malachite

A bright green semi-precious stone which has bands of concentric rings. Its relatively low degree of hardness makes it easy to carve and engrave so that it is suitable for producing inlaid ornaments and decorating precious accessories.

Marquetry and intarsia of semi-precious stones

These techniques cover a flat wooden, stone or metal base with patterns of differently shaped and coloured tiles which are fixed by cementing. This produces decorations on coloured backgrounds. The skill lies in keeping the spaces between tiles minimal and uniform. Subsequent polishing makes the finished work consistent and compact. Marquetry involves the use of wooden tiles and exploits the veins and shades of the various woods to create decorative panels and plaques. Often the base of the work acts as a background for the decoration. Stone intarsia exploits the intense colours of semi-precious stones and the wealth of patterns produced by veins and stratifications.

Marquise

An oval, faceted cut which is pointed at both ends. It is also known as the "navette" or shuttle, cut in reference to the shape of the ancient tool used by weavers. The latter name is specifically used to indicate this shape of cut on coloured stones, while the term "marquise" usually only indicates diamonds.

Medallion

A flat, oval or round jewel worn as a pendant or brooch. It has a central, illustrated motif, often a portrait, which is enamelled, engraved or carved.

Micromosaic

This technique, which derives from traditional mosaic, comes from Italy. Towards the end of the eighteenth century a method of manufacturing mosaic tiles was devised, reducing their size to produce a mosaic composition in miniature. The tiles were then fixed to a wooden base in order to produce small decorative mosaic plaques used to decorate snuff-boxes, buttons and jewels.

Minaudière

An evening bag launched by Van Cleef & Arpels in 1934, whose name means "simperer". It has several compartments for beauty accessories: powder compacts, lipstick holders, cigarette boxes, scent bottles, mirrors and watches. The more sophisticated versions were modular and had ingenious mechanisms. They were made of platinum and decorated with elaborate motifs of diamonds and other precious stones.

Moonstone

A precious variety of feldspar which is milky white or translucent. Its silvery and pearly sheen, known as adularescence, is enhanced by the frequently used *cabochon* cut. Like the opal it was highly sought-after during the Art Nouveau period.

Mother-of-pearl

An organic substance deriving from the secretion of numerous molluscs, including pearl oysters. Characterised by elaborate iridescent reflections, it is dissected and polished to produce inlaid decorations, carved and engraved plaques and small decorative objects.

Navette

See Marquise.

Nécessaire

A metallic bag containing the principal female beauty accessories. Made of gold or silver, it was often decorated with stones and enamels. Until the Fifties the larger jewellery *maisons* used to combine their production of jewellery with small ranges of precious versions of sophisticated accessories such as cigarette boxes and nécessaires.

Necklace

First seen in ancient times, it consists of a series of decorative elements that are laced together and worn around the neck. Originally it consisted of a string of shells, teeth or bone fragments, whose function was apotropaic, protective and auspicious. As time passed and tastes and fashions changed, infinite varieties and forms were introduced, using both precious and non-precious metals. From the belly chain to the pearl choker, the necklace has been a constant presence in the stock of ornaments of every culture, unlike other types of jewel, such as earrings, which are missing from certain periods of history.

Niello

Used to decorate gold and, more frequently, silver objects. A compound of copper, silver, lead, sulphur and borax powder is spread on a metallic surface that has previously been decoratively engraved with a scorper, filling the indented portions. The black colour this mixture (nigellum) acquires gave the technique its name. The final step entails exposing the engraved part, which has been blackened by the mixture, to the heat of a flame. The decoration is thus fused in the grooves while subsequent scraping and polishing highlights the characteristic graphic play of contrasts that evoke ancient engravings on parchment.

Non-precious metals

Steel, copper, brass, titanium, superalloys and many others are increasingly used instead of gold or silver in jewellery production. Many of these derive from the world of applied arts, others from sectors of the mechanical industry, whilst, for others still, their application appears to be still in the experimental stages and not as yet fully codified. The different and specific characteristics of these materials allow new solutions to be explored, introducing new techniques and producing hybrids of traditional branches of jewellery.

Onyx

A name for chalcedony when slightly translucent black, or striped black and white. The vast majority of onyx on the market is opaque as it is dyed using a simple and ancient process. It is one of the most popular semi-precious stones in jewellery due to its blackness, providing an efficient contrast to the purity of diamonds and platinum. The black-and-white striped variety is also extremely popular in the production of carved cameos and lockets.

Opal

There are different varieties that all share the same reflective qualities, something that few other semi-precious stones can claim. The most well-known opals are: white opal, which is milky white with small, multicolour, iridescent inclusions; fire opal, translucent and red-orange with red glints; and black opal, extremely rare and precious, a blue-black colour with extraordinary polychrome iridescences.

Orient

The iridescent lustre of pearls. It has been given this name as it recalls the colour of the sky at sunrise. Its intensity, expressed by a numerical scale, helps to establish the commercial value of pearls.

Palladium

It belongs to the platinum family and, as such, is a precious metal which is both malleable and pure white. In its natural state it is found in alloys with gold and platinum, producing a white alloy in the former case and making the metal easier to work in the latter.

Pavé

This indicates a very close setting, in which the precious stones, which may even be of different carats, are set so close to each other that they cover entire surfaces or some sectors of a jewel. To prepare this type of setting an infinite number of holes are bored into the metal, equivalent to the number of stones to be mounted. Due to the lack of room, owing to the narrow spacing between the stones, burrs are used to hold the stones in place.

Pavé secret

Also known as invisible serti or *serti mysterieux*, it represents the technical excellence of the art of setting precious stones in a jewel. It was refined in Paris in the Thirties and contributed to revolutionising tastes in high-class jewellery. This setting eliminates *griffes*, apparently freeing the stone from its setting. The stones are prepared by making angular and calibrated cuts and V-shaped grooves on the pavilion. They are then inserted in special metal tracks, placed by the jeweller on the jewel which is being made. The stones are inserted into the tracks and placed close together. The setting is thus moved underneath the stone so that is invisible.

Pearl

A spherical organic concretion composed of thin layers of mother of pearl produced by a secretion of the mollusc of marine or freshwater pearl oysters. In natural pearls this secretion is produced spontaneously, and is the mollusc's reaction to a foreign body aggressively penetrating the shell. In cultured pearls this process is stimulated by introducing grains of mother-of-pearl or other materials that are then covered with pearly secretions. The quality of a pearl is determined by specific parameters: the intensity of the "orient", or the iridescent reflection produced by the light on layers of mother of pearl; the shades of white, grey and yellow and, in rare cases, other colours. Finally, there is its shape, which may be perfectly spherical in the most precious specimens or asymmetrical and uneven.

Pendant

A decorated plaque, locket or tassel, generally an ornament equipped with a ring hook which is hung from a chain worn around the neck. Pendant is also the name used for all those ornaments hooked to jewels which swing loosely as the body changes position. These include drop earrings, brooches with pendants and terminal pendants for tiaras, diadems, *sautoirs*, bracelets and anklets. Often made of large gems or pearls to seal the preciousness of the ornament.

Peridot

Lime green, sometimes olive and therefore also known as olivine. This semi-precious stone is generally found in large crystalline agglomerates. Its transparency and purity make it suitable for lapping whilst the best cuts for exploiting its colour and sheen are, as in the case of the aquamarine, the square cut and the *briolette*.

Plaque de cou

This is a plaque made of metal or other precious materials worn as a neck ornament. It has a curved rectangular shape to fit the contour of the neck and two loops on the back so it can be strung onto a fabric ribbon. In most cases the fabric is made of silk, velvet or grosgrain.

Platinum

The most expensive metal used by jewellers. Of a pure white colour, like palladium, it is as immutable and stainless as gold, but harder. This malleable metal has an extremely high melting point of over 1700°C. This is why it was little used until the invention of the jeweller's torch. Mistaken for an inferior alloy of silver, hence its name, its true value was finally recognised towards the end of the nineteenth century when Louis-Françoise Cartier began to use it instead of silver as a setting for diamonds. Today platinum continues to be recommended as the ideal setting for diamonds.

Polish chain

A type of chain that was especially popular in the 1940s. It is composed of tubular elements in variable sections. These are usually round, although they may also be square or hexagonal, and are attached to one another by hollow tubular hinges so that the chain maintains a certain suppleness. The Polish chain is extremely lightweight despite being large in volume.

Polishing

This is performed on a surface to make it smooth, uniform to the touch and shiny. It involves various steps, using increasingly fine abrasive powders and, finally, adding special fluids.

Polsiera

A broad, stiff or supple bracelet. It is worn tightly on the wrist or the forearm, like a shirt cuff.

Precious stones

Diamonds, rubies, emeralds or sapphires are precious stones that are rare and difficult to extract. Their elevated value is established by international parameters and their sale is regulated by laws that protect their value and guarantee their quality. From time immemorial they have been venerated and used to decorate and embellish jewels.

Punch

A small metal stamp which, beaten onto precious metal, guarantees its quality and source. Currently international laws regulating the sale of precious objects and jewels demand a dual stamp. One indicates the fineness of the metal, the other the maker's hallmark and the city of origin. There may be further stamps on a jewel to indicate the serial number or the year in which it was made.

Quartz

A large family of minerals found in vast quantities on Earth. Transparent or translucent, they are found in large aggregates of crystals and have various names depending on their different colours: rock crystal if they are colourless with opaque white inclusions, pink, citrine or smoky quartz. Inclusions are common as in rutilated quartz, which has dark needle-shaped filaments, or in jasper, where multicolour inclusions render the gem almost completely opaque.

Repoussé

This means hammering and punching on a metal plate using large rounded bits. It produces relief motifs working in negative, on the reverse of the plate, so as to produce a sunken decoration which, to the observer, appears to emerge from the surface. The piece is finished on the obverse, using scorpers to engrave outlines and shading, in order to highlight the contrasts and bring out the volumes.

Ring

One of the oldest types of ornament, already common in primitive civilisations. Its simple shape is produced by strips or bands of gold or other metals which are curved to make a circle that is slipped onto the finger. Over the centuries the ring has evolved formally and symbolically, from the imperial seal of the classical age, a symbol of temporal and spiritual power, to the magnificent creations encrusted with large stones, which are evidence of wealth and opulence, to the wedding ring, a symbol of conjugal devotion and fidelity.

Rock crystal

A variety of colourless crystal that often appears transparent and devoid of inclusions or veins. In some cases the white veining found in impure samples gives the material the appearance of a block of ice. It is extremely hard and carved with a lapping wheel and polished to produce bas relief plates, carved beads, etc.

Ruby

Second only to the diamond in terms of rarity and hardness, the ruby is a precious stone whose shades range from fuchsia to blood-red, like the garnet. The spectacular, deep red glints are seen at their best when the gem has no inclusions and is oval cut. Due to rampant mining in the past it is now rare to find pure gems, which, very often, contain opaque inclusions. In these cases the splendour of the stone is revealed by the *cabochon* cut or by elaborate engravings and carvings.

Sapphire

It belongs, like the ruby, to the corundum family, and has an intense blue colour which varies from lighter shades to blue violet and ultramarine. If pure and transparent this extremely hard precious stone is lapped with oval and round cuts that increase its sparkle. More frequently, if opaque or sprinkled with branching inclusions, it is cut *en cabochon* or used in its raw state to produce polished beads or engraved plaques.

Sautoir

A long necklace which, in some cases, falls to the belly button. It is a string of small beads or a long chain made of large links although there are also versions embellished with diamonds and other precious stones. It often ends with a tassel or an ornamental locket decorated with a fringe and small chains. It may be worn in a traditional fashion, like a necklace, or draped across one shoulder.

Semi-precious stones

These belong to a large variety of crystalline structure semi-precious minerals characterised by their compactness and elevated hardness. Used for jewellery from time immemorial, they are both prized and sought after due to the intensity of their colours, which are usually bright with spots, veins, stratifications and other patterns generating decorative effects. Their rarity and the difficulty of working them, due to their hardness, establishes their value and makes them worthy of being used to decorate jewels or other luxury items. Engraved, incised, carved or lapped, they are then set in gold or silver. This category of stones includes all those rare gems used in jewellery due to their aesthetic characteristics, linked to their colour, brilliance, lastingness and, consequently, their value. They may be transparent and reflect light and, once faceted, create a sparkle, as in the case of aquamarine, demantoid and citrine. Vice versa, we find opaque gems, such as opals or garnets, which contain extraordinary colour mixes or inclusions that create curious optical effects.

Serpent chain

After being soldered together, the links that compose this type of chain are compacted. In fact, the chain is run through a wire-drawing machine, which compacts the narrow spaces between one module and the next several times, rendering the shape of the section uniform. This may vary from round to square to oval. The ensuing finished product is highly uniform but not terribly supple.

Setting

The art of mounting precious stones in a jewel. Generally speaking there are two methods of setting gems; closed setting, or *serti clos*, is the most ancient and solid method as it consists of soldering a thin plate around the entire circumference of the stone. This means its edge is rimmed all round by metal. The griffes setting bends the prongs over the crown of the stone. These may have different shapes: hooks (griffes), nails (clous) or shavings raised in the metal by means of a scorper (grains). This latter method allows more light to shine on the stone, enhancing its splendour.

Shell

Composed of generally calcareous organic materials, it is produced by the secretions of some marine animals such as molluscs, which grow protective layers. Thanks to their bright colours, their miscellaneous shapes and the fact that they are easy to procure, shells have been used from time immemorial for the purpose of decoration. They can be simply drilled with a hole and strung together to create jewellery in which the shape of the shell is left unaltered, or they can be carved and engraved to produce buttons and beads, decorative cameos and plaques.

Silver

A rare metal, though much less precious than gold since it is available in larger quantities. Straw white in colour, it is highly ductile and malleable. In its natural state it is found in alloys with other metals such as gold or copper, or with other alloys. Exposure to the elements leads to rapid oxidation which makes its surface dull and gives it dark stains. To increase its hardness and to curb rapid oxidation, silver is amalgamated in alloys with other metals such as gold or copper.

Soldering

The junction of two metal parts by means of heating the point of contact and melting a special metallic mixture, which becomes liquid at lower temperatures than the metal to be soldered. The two parts are thus joined. Subsequent filing and grinding hides the join, making the whole appear to be made from a single piece.

Stamping

A mechanical process that uses mechanical presses to obtain three-dimensional shapes or decorations starting with metal plates or rods of different thicknesses. Two "dies" reproduce the shape of the object or element to be stamped, one in positive and the other in negative. The plates are pressed between the dies by special machinery which distributes the pressure uniformly so as to emboss the plate and produce a three-dimensional form. Stamping can also be an intermediate phase in the production of semi-finished products such as chain links or other parts.

Tiara

This adorns the head of queens, emulating the bright halo of saints and angels. It has a circular shape, almost like a crescent moon, and is worn high on the forehead. It has points like a crown, which are highest in the centre, and is made of precious metals and fabulous gems.

Topaz

This semi-precious gem is a deep yellow colour, though it is also found in different shades, pink being the most precious. In nature it comes in macrocrystalline blocks making it easy to obtain large crystals without any inclusions that are lapped into various cuts.

Tortoiseshell

Extremely popular in the past, the practice of exploiting the shells of sea turtles in order to make jewels and ornaments came to an abrupt end when the animals were declared a species threatened with extinction. Of a fibrous texture, like horn, it has a translucent and variegated colouring that ranges from amber to burnt orange. It was used for bracelets, necklaces and accessories and could be polished until it was shiny. Different varieties have different names depending on their colour.

Tourmaline

This gem is also found in large crystalline agglomerates. It has opaque inclusions that make it resemble a block of ice in its raw state. It is one of the several semi-precious stones found in a wide range of colours and shades. Generally green, there are also red tourmalines and the so-called "watermelon" varieties, whose red centre is ringed with green. Deep blue tourmalines are highly sought after.

Turquoise

It owes its name to Turkey, a country where large quantities of this semi-precious stone, extracted in Middle-Eastern countries and destined for European markets, regularly transited. Opaque, and of a deep colour ranging from sky blue to aquamarine, it may contain dark veins. It is used to create engraved plaques and decorated medallions or made into polished or *cabochon* beads to embellish jewels.

Tuyau à gaz
A flexible tubular strip used to produce bracelets and necklaces which became fashionable in the 1940s and 1950s. It is made by fixing together in a coil two sections of gold or other metals which are U-shaped in cross-section. This produces a double coil that, when firmly secured, allows the whole to maintain a measure of flexibility and elasticity. It is possible to work on the shape of the section, which may be flat, round or oval, while in more elaborate cases the measurement of the coil may be gradually adjusted.

Vermeil
A silver of varying degrees of fineness covered with a thin layer of gold. It may be gilded by different methods, such as electrolysis.

Wedding ring
A ring consisting of a thin band of various sections, generally oval or semi-circle, usually made of gold or platinum. It symbolises the reciprocal love and fidelity of husband and wife.

Bibliography

1923

Prima Esposizione Internazionale delle Arti Decorative, exhibition catalogue, edited by Consorzio Milano-Monza-Umanitaria, Monza, Villa Reale, May–October 1923 (Milan: Bestetti e Tumminelli, 1923).

1925

Encyclopédie des arts décoratifs et industriels modernes au XXème siècle en douze volumes (Paris: Office central d'éditions et de librairie, 1925).

W. George, "L'Exposition des Arts Décoratifs et industriels de 1925 – les tendances générales", *L'Amour de l'art*, 1925, p. 283.

G. Marangoni (ed.), *La seconda mostra Internazionale delle Arti Decorative nella Villa Reale di Monza, 1925: notizie, rilievi, risultati* (Milan: Alpes, 1925).

Seconda Esposizione Internazionale delle Arti Decorative, exhibition catalogue, edited by Consorzio Milano-Monza-Umanitaria, Monza, Villa Reale, May–October 1925 (Monza: Alpes e F. De Rio, 1925).

1927

Catalogo ufficiale della III Esposizione Internazionale delle Arti Decorative di Monza, exhibition catalogue, Monza, Villa Reale, May–October 1927 (Milan: Casa Editrice Ceschina, 1927).

1929

M. Deloche, *La Bague en France à travers l'histoire* (Paris: Didot, 1929).

1930

Catalogo Ufficiale della IV Esposizione Triennale Internazionale delle arti decorative ed industriali moderne, exhibition catalogue, Monza, Villa Reale, May–October 1930 (Milano: Casa Editrice Ceschina, 1930).

1931

J. Fouquet, *Bijoux et orfèvrerie*, Art International d'aujourd'hui, no. 16 (Paris: Éditions d'art Charles Moreau, 1931).

1933

Esposizione Triennale Internazionale delle arti decorative ed industriali moderne, exhibition catalogue, Monza, Villa Reale, May–October 1933 (Milan: Casa Editrice Ceschina, 1933).

1936

6. Triennale di Milano 1936: esposizione internazionale delle arti decorative e industriali moderne e dell'architettura moderna, regolamento della sezione italiana, exhibition catalogue, Milano, Palazzo dell'Arte al Parco, May – October 1936 (Milan: S.A.M.E., 1936).

1941

G. Pack, *Jewellery and Enameling* (New York: D. Van Nostrand, 1941).

1949

W. Blum and G. Hogaboom, *Principles of Electroplating and Electroforming* (New York: McGraw-Hill, 1949).

A. Invernizzi, entry "Oreficeria-industria", in *Enciclopedia Italiana Treccani*, XXV (Rome: Istituto dell'Enciclopedia Italiana Treccani, 1949).

U. Nebbia, entry "Oreficeria dal secolo XIX in poi", in *Enciclopedia Italiana Treccani*, XXV (Rome: Istituto dell'Enciclopedia Italiana Treccani, 1949).

1950

W. T. Baxter, *Jewelry, Gem Cutting and Metalcraft* (New York: McGraw-Hill, 1950).

1951

K. F. Bates, *Enameling: Principles and Practice* (Cleveland, OH: World Publishing, 1951).

M. Flower, *Victorian Jewelry* (New York: Duell, Sloane and Pearce, 1951).

M. Leloir, *Dictionnaire du Costume et de ses Accessoires* (Paris: Gründ, 1951).

A. and L. Sanger, *Cabochon Jewelry Making* (Peoria, IL: Bennett, 1951).

L. Vitiello, *Oreficeria moderna tecnica pratica* (Milan: Hoepli, 1951).

1953

E. D. S. Bradford, *Four Centuries of European Jewelry* (New York: Philosophical Library, 1953).

J. Evans, *A History of Jewelry, 1100–1870* (New York: Pitman, 1953).

R. Jessup, *Anglo-Saxon Jewely* (New York: Praeger, 1953).

1954

10. Triennale di Milano, Milan, Triennale di Milano, 1954 (Milano: Triennale di Milano, 1954).

R. Aloi, *Esempi di decorazione moderna di tutto il mondo. Gioielli, sbalzi, argenti* (Milan: Hoepli, 1954).

1955

A. R. Emerson, *Handmade Jewellery* (Leicester: Dryad, 1955).

K. D. Winebrenner, *Jewelry Making as an Art Expression*, International Textbook (Scranton, PA, 1955).

1956

P. Lyon, *Design in Jewellery* (London: Owen, 1956).

G. Speenburgh, *The Arts of the Tiffanys* (Chicago, IL: Lightner Publishing Corporation, 1956).

1957

11. Triennale di Milano, Milan, Triennale di Milano, 1957 (Milan: Triennale di Milano, 1957).

XX Biennale nazionale di Milano, exhibition catalogue, edited by R. Taccani, Milan, Palazzo della Permanente, November–December 1957 (Milan: Permanente, 1957).

A. Pica, *Storia della Triennale 1918–1957* (Milan: Il Milione, 1957).

E. Steingräber, *Antique Jewelry* (New York: Preager, 1957).

1958

M. Weinstein, *The World of Jewel Stones* (New York: Sheridan, 1958).

E. Winter, *Enamel Art on Metals* (New York: Watson-Guptill, 1958).

1959

P. Lyon, *Salvador Dalí: A Study of His Art in Jewels* (Greenwich, CT: New York Graphic, 1959).

L. Quick and H. Leiper, *Gemcraft: How to Cut and Polish Gemstones* (Radnor, PA: Chilton Book Company, 1959).

H. Zarchy, *Jewelry Making and Enameling* (New York: Knopf, 1959).

1960

12. Triennale di Milano, Milan, Palazzo dell'Arte, 1960 (Milan: Arti Grafiche Crespi, 1960).

M. Bearwald and T. Mahoney, *Story of Jewelry* (New York: Abelard-Schuman, 1960).

1961

J. Francis, *The Art of the Lapidary* (Milwaukee, WI: Bruce Publishing, 1961).

1962

G. Ballo, *Dalla poetica del segno alla presenza continua. Arnaldo e Giò Pomodoro* (Milan: Luigi Maestri, 1962).

E. Frank Lois, *Handwrought Jewelry* (Bloomington. IL: McKnight & McKnight, 1962).

R. A. Higgins, *Greek and Roman Jewelry* (New York: Mathuen-Barnes & Noble, 1962).

A. Sinkankas, *Gem Cutting: A Lapidary's Manual* (Princeton: NJ: Van Nostrand, 1962).

1963

C. Carducci, *Gold and Silver of Ancient Italy Jewels* (Greenwich, CT: New York Graphic, 1963).

G. Hughes, *Modern Jewelry: An International Survey, 1890–1963* (New York: Crown, 1963).

A. J. and A. F. Shirley, *Handcraft in Metal: A Textbook for the Use of Teachers, Students, and Craftsmen* (Philadelphia, PA: Lippincott, 1963).

1964

A. Smith, *The Art of Personal Adornment* (New York: Museum of Contemporary Crafts, 1964).

1965

E. Steingraber, *L'arte del gioiello in Europa dal Medioevo al Liberty* (Milan: Edam, 1965).

1966

K. Neville, *The Craft of Enameling* (New York: Tapilinger, 1966).

1967

L. Gaudenzio, *L'Istituto d'Arte Pietro Selvatico* (Padua: Grafiche Erreci, 1967).

1968

14. Triennale di Milano, Milan, Palazzo dell'Arte al Parco, 30 May – 28 July 1968 (Milan: Casa Editrice Crespi & Occhipinti, 1968).

S. Abbey, *The Goldsmith's and Silversmith's Handbook* (New York: Heinman, 1968).

I. Brynner, *Modern Jewerly, Design and Technique* (New York: Van Nostrand Reinhold, 1968).

C. Hornung, *A Source Book of Antiques and Jewelry Designs* (New York: Braziller, 1968).

F. Pivano, "Gioielli come sculture", *Vogue Italia*, III, 200, 1968, pp. 74 and 104.

E. Sottsass, "Sono mille volte meglio gli ornamenti dei nomadi del sole", *Domus*, 464, 1968, pp. 39–43.

1969

I. Barsali Belli, *Medieval Goldsmith's Work* (London: Hamlyn, 1969).

A. W. Bealer, *The Art of Blacksmithing* (New York: Funk and Wagnalls, 1969).

G. Gregorietti, *Il gioiello nei secoli* (Milan: Mondadori, 1969).

M. Seeler, *The Art of Enameling* (New York: Van Nostrand Reinhold, 1969).

1970

S. Choate, *Creative Gold and Silversmithing* (New York: Crown, 1970).

A. M. Di Nola, entry "Amuleti e talismani", in *Enciclopedia delle religioni*, I (Florence: Vallecchi, 1970), pp. 310–22.

M. Guidetti, *Viaggio nel pianeta dell'arte orafa* (Arezzo: Gori & Zucchi, 1970).

L. Taubes, *Basic Enameling* (New York: Pitman, 1970).

1971

C. Aldred, *Jewels of the Pharaohs: Egyptian jewelry of the Dynastic Period* (New York: Praeger, 1971).

J. Boardman, *Greek Gems and Finger Rings: Early Bronze Age to Late Classical* (London, 1971).

A. Clifford, *Cut-Steel and Berlin Iron Jewelry* (Cranbury: Barnes, 1971)

G. Franklin, *Simple Enameling* (New York: Watson-Guptill, 1971).

G. Hood, *American Silver: A History of Style 1650–1900* (New York: Praeger, 1971).

J. Purtell, *The Tiffany Touch* (New York: Random House, 1971).

P. Spiro, *Electroforming* (New York: International Publications, 1971).

1972

W. E. Garrison and E. Merle Dowde, *Handcrafting Jewelry: Designs and Techniques* (Chicago, IL: Regnery, 1972).

M. Hayes, *Jewelry Book* (New York: Van Nostrand Reinhold, 1972).

H. B. Hollader, *Plastics for Artists and Craftsmen* (New York: Watson-Guptill, 1972).

G. Hughes, *The Arts of Jewelry*, Viking, New York.

P. Muller, *Jewelry in Spain, 1500–1800* (New York: Hispanic Society of America, 1972).

R. von Neumann, *The Design and Creation of Jewelry* (Radnor, PA: Chilton Book Company, 1972).

N. Ponente, *Gioielli come opere d'arte* (Florence, 1972).

1973

15. Triennale di Milano, Milan, Palazzo dell'Arte al Parco, 20 September – 20 November 1973 (Milan: Casa Editrice Crespi & Occhipinti, 1973).

M. Bovin, *Jewelry Making for Schools, Tradesmen, Craftsmen* (Forest Hills, NY: Bovin, 1973).

P. Bucarelli, *La Galleria Nazionale d'Arte Moderna* (Rome: Istituto Poligrafico dello Stato, 1973).

C. Gere, "Il disegno dei gioielli neoclassici", *Arte illustrata*, VI, 52, 1973, pp. 47–55.

J. Marcadé, *Bijoux* (Geneva: Nagel & Hachette, 1973).

D. J. Willcox, *Body Jewelry: International Perspectives* (Chicago, IL: Regnery, 1973).

1974

Aurea 74. Biennale dell'arte orafa, exhibition catalogue, Florence, Palazzo Strozzi, 21 September – 7 October 1974 (Florence: Grafiche Senatori, 1974).

J. Black Anderson, *The Story of Jewelry* (New York: Morrow, 1974).

A. Ernst and J. Einiger, *Le Grand Livre des Bijoux* (Lausanne, 1974).

H. B. Hollader, *Plastics for Jewelry* (New York: Watson-Guptill, 1974).

L. Lenti and G. Pugnetti, *Arte orafa valenzana*, edited by Cassa di Risparmio di Alessandria (Cinisello Balsamo: Arti Grafiche Amilcare Pizzi, 1974).

C. Oman, *British Rings 800–1914* (London: B.T. Batsford, 1974).

J. Schoenfelt, *Seven Golden Years* (London: Worshipful Company of Goldsmiths, 1974).

J. Schoenfelt, *The Goldsmith* (Saint Paul, MN: Minnesota Museum of Art, 1974).

A. K. Snowman, *The Art of Carl Fabergé* (Greenwich, CN: New York Graphic, 1974).

A. Weygers, *The Modern Blacksmithing* (New York: Van Nostrand Reinhold, 1974).

D. Willcox, *Evolution du Bijou* (Paris: Dessain et Tolra, 1974).

1975

L. L. Anderson, *The Art of the Silversmith in Mexico: 1519–1936* (New York: Hacker, 1975).

C. Gere, *American & European Jewelry 1830–1914* (New York: Crown Publishers, 1975).

K. Scollamayer, *Art contemporain du Bijou* (Paris: Dessain et Tolra, 1975).

1976

Aurea 76. Biennale dell'arte orafa, exhibition catalogue, Florence, Palazzo Strozzi, 25 September – 11 October 1976 (Florence: Grafiche Senatori, 1976).

J. Lipman, *Calder's Universe* (New York: Harrison House, 1976).

1977

S. Barten, *René Lalique* (Munich: Prestel Verlag, 1977).

1978

C. H. Carpenter Jr and M. Grace, *Tiffany Silver* (New York: Alan Wofsy Fine Art, 1978).

G. Gregorietti, *I gioielli. Storia e tecnica dagli Egizi ai contemporanei* (Milan: Mondadori, 1978).

1979

I. Brynner, *Jewelry As An Art Form* (New York: Van Nostrand Reinhold, 1979).

A. Garside, *Jewelry: Ancient to Modern* (Baltimore, MD: Xs Books, 1979).

A. Habsbourg-Solodkoff, *Fabergé* (Fribourg: Office du Livre, 1979).

J. Lenfant, *Bijouterie-Joaillerie* (Paris: Chêne, 1979).

R. Maillard, *Le diamant. Mithe, Magie et Réalité* (Paris: Flammarion, 1979).

A. Trotto, "Luci ed ombre dell'artigianato orafo", in *Storia dell'artigianato italiano* (Milan: Etas Libri, 1979).

1980

D. Vallier, *L'Art Abstrait* (Paris: Librairie Générale Française, Le Livre de Poche, 1980).

D. Bourdon, *Calder: Mobilist / Ringmaster / Innovator* (New York: Macmillan, 1980).

H. F. McKean, *The "Lost" Treasures of Louis Comfort Tiffany* (New York: Doubleday, 1980).

Progettare con l'Oro, exhibition catalogue, edited by P. C. Santini, Milan, Castello Sforzesco, Sala della Balla, February–March 1980 (Florence: Nuova Vallecchi, 1980).

1981

A. Ward, J. Cherry, C. Gere and B. Cartlidge, *La Bague. De l'Antiquité à Nos Jours* (Paris: Office du Livre, Bibliothèque des arts, 1981).

1982

M. Gabardi, *Gioielli anni '40* (Milan: Giorgio Mondadori, 1982).

K. Harlow, "A Pioneer Master of Art Nouveau", *Apollo*, CXVI, no. 245, July 1982.

O. Untracht, *Jewelry Concepts and Technology* (New York: Doubleday, 1982).

E. Pressmar, *Indian Rings* (Frankfurt am Main: Insel Verlag, 1982).

Wendy Ramshaw, exhibition catalogue (London: Victoria & Albert Museum, 1982).

1983

10 orafi padovani – Moderne Goldschmiedekunst aus Italien, exhibition catalogue, edited by F. Falk, Pforzheim, Schmuckmuseum, 22 January – 4 April 1983 (Pforzheim: Schmuckmuseum Pforzheim, 1983).

Art du Bijou (Paris: Société d'Encouragement aux Métiers d'Art, 1983).

Les Fouquet, bijoutiers et joailliers à Paris 1860–1960, exhibition catalogue (Paris: Musée des arts décoratifs, 1983).

Pariser Schmück (Munich: Himer Verlag, 1983).

A. J. Pulos, "Metalsmithing in the 1940s and 1950s: A Personal Recollection", *Metalsmith*, no. 3, 1983.

1984

D. Mascetti, *Gioielli dell'Ottocento* (Novara: Istituto geografico De Agostini, 1984).

Modern Artists' Jewels, exhibition catalogue (London: Victoria and Albert Museum, 1984).

H. Nadelhoffer, *Cartier* (Milan: Longanesi, 1984).

M. Renk and C. Adell, "The San Francisco Metal Arts Guild: Yesterday and Today", *Metalsmith*, 1984.

J. Sataloff, *Art Nouveau Jewelry* (Bryn Mawr, PA: Dorrance & Company, 1984).

D. Scarisbrick, *Il valore dei gioielli e degli orologi da collezione* (Turin: Allemandi, 1984).

H. Tait, *The Art of the Jeweller, a Catalogue of the Hull Grundy Gift to the British Museum*, 2 vols. (London: British Museum Publications, 1984).

1985

V. Becker, *Gioielli art nouveau* (Milan: Frassinelli, 1985).

Coates Kevin, exhibition catalogue (London: Victoria and Albert Museum, 1985).

C. Broadhead, *New tradition. The evolution of jewellery 1966–1985* (London: British Crafts Centre, 1985).

S. Bury, *The Use of Hair in Jewellery in an Introduction to Sentimental Jewellery* (London: Victoria and Albert Museum, 1985).

1986

XIV Biennale Internazionale del Bronzetto e Piccola Scultura. Nove artisti di scuola padovana, exhibition catalogue, Padua, Palazzo della Ragione, 8 November – 15 January 1987 (Padua: Commune of Padua, 1986).

L'arte del corallo in Sicilia, exhibition catalogue, edited by C. Maltese and M. C. Di Natale, Trapani, Museo Regionale Pepoli, 1 March – 1 June 1986 (Palermo: Novecento, 1986).

B. Cartlidge, *Les Bijoux au XXème Siècle* (Paris: Payot, 1986).

Créateurs de Bijoux Contemporains (Paris: Sociète d'Encouragement aux Mètiers d'Art, 1986).

Flockinger Gerda, exhibition catalogue (London: Victoria and Albert Museum, 1986).

M. Gabardi, *Gioielli anni '50* (Milan: Giorgio Mondadori, 1986).

Gioielli. Moda, magia, sentimento, exhibition catalogue, Milan, 1986 (Milan: Mazzotta, 1986).

I gioielli degli anni '20-'40. Cartier e i grandi del Déco, exhibition catalogue, Venice, Palazzo Fortuny, 7 September – 2 November 1986 (Milan: Electa, 1986).

J. A. Goldberg, "Earl Pardon Master American Jeweller", *Ornament*, no. 10, 1986.

G. Segato, "Un'oreficeria di ricerca", in *XIV Biennale Internazionale del Bronzetto e Piccola Scultura. Nove artisti orafi di scuola padovana*, exhibition catalogue, Padua, Palazzo della Ragione, 8 November – 15 January 1987 (Padua: Commune of Padua, 1986).

M. E. Tittoni, "La collezione dei gioielli del Museo Napoleonico di Roma", in *Gioielli. Moda, magia, sentimento*, exhibition catalogue, Milan, 1986 (Milan: Mazzotta, 1986).

1987

Artisti e disegno nell'oreficeria moderna, exhibition catalogue, Arezzo, 1987 (Florence: Il Torchio, 1987).

Biennale Svizzera del gioiello d'arte contemporaneo, exhibition catalogue, edited by R. and P. Hildebrand, Lugano, 1987 (Amriswil: Scheiwiler Druck AG, 1987).

A. Bulgari Calissoni, *Maestri, argentieri, gemmari, orafi di Roma* (Rome: Fratelli Palombi Editori, 1987).

C. H. Carpenter Jr and J. Zapata, *The Silver of Tiffany & Co. 1850–1987* (Boston: Museum of Fine Arts, 1987).

C. Ciavolino, *La scuola del corallo a Torre del Greco* (Naples: Marimar, 1987).

J. Culme and N. Rayner, *The Jewels of the Duchess of Windsor* (New York: Press, 1987).

Disegni e diamanti: cento anni di Cusi di via Clerici, exhibition catalogue, edited by M. Gabardi (Milan: 1987).

P. Dormer and R. Turner, *Le Nouveau Bijou* (Paris: Flammarion, 1987) .

Europea Contemporaria Joeria (Barcelona: Fundació Caixa de Pensions, 1987).

D. Healy and P. Proddow, *American Jewelry* (New York: Rizzoli, 1987).

Landschaft und Garten, Schmuck, exhibition catalogue, edited by A. Heindl, Vienna, Galerie Krinzinger, 25 November – 23 December 1987 (Vienna: Galerie Krinzinger, 1987).

J. Loring, *Tiffany's 150 Years* (New York: Doubleday, 1987).

S. J. Montgomery, "The Sound and the Surface: The Metalwork and Jewelry of Harry Bertoia", *Metalsmith*, no. 7, 1987.

G. Néret, *Boucheron* (Fribourg: Office du Livre, 1987).

Première Triennale du Bijou Contemporain, exhibition catalogue, Paris, Hôtel de Sens, 8 September – 12 November 1987 (Paris, 1987)..

P. Proddow and D. Healy, *Tiffany e i gioiellieri americani* (Milan: Mondadori, 1987).

B. Radice, *Gioielli di architetti* (Milan: Electa, 1987).

S. Raulet, *Bijoux des Années 1940–1950* (Paris: Editions du Regard, 1987).

S. Raulet, *Van Cleef&Arpels New York* (New York: Rizzoli International Publications, 1987).

G. Sambonet, *Gli argentieri milanesi: maestri, botteghe, punzoni dal XIV al XIX secolo* (Milan: Longanesi, 1987).

A. K. Snowman, *Tiffany et les joailliers américains* (Fribourg: Office du Livre, 1987).

H. J. Schubrel, *Pierres de Lumière et Objets* (Paris: Arthaud, 1987).

A. de Tugny, *Guide des Pierres de Rêve* (Paris: Flammarion, 1987).

O. Untracht, *Enameling on Metal* (Radnor, PA: Chilton Book, 1987).

1988

P. Anderson, *Contemporary Jewellery in Australia and New Zealand* (Sydney: Craftsman House, 1988).

J. Arax, *Le Guide Pratique des Bijoux et des Pierres Prècieuses* (Paris: Sand, 1988).

D. Alcouffe, *Le arti decorative alle grandi esposizioni universali: 1851–1900* (Milan: Idealibri, 1988).

Frits Maierhofer, exhibition catalogue (London: Victoria and Albert Museum, 1988).

M. Jodice, *Capolavori di Cartier: joailliers depuis 1847* (Naples: Electa, 1988).

L. V. Masini and G. Centrodi, *Oro d'autore. Materiali e progetti per una nuova collezione orafa* (Arezzo: Centro Affari e Promozioni, 1988).

S. Rauet, *Jewelry of the 1940s and 1950s* (New York: Rizzoli International Publications, 1988).

T. Andrighetto (ed.), *Progettisti d'oro* (Vicenza, 1988).

J. Zapata, "Authenticating Tiffany Jewelry, Heritage", *Jewelers' Circular Keystone*, August 1988, pp. 226–30.

B. Zucker, *Gemmes et joyaux* (Geneva: Saphir, 1988).

1989

F. Cailles, *Le prix des bijoux 1986–1987–1988* (Paris: A.C.R., 1989).

G. Folchini Grassetto (ed.), *Antologia di arte orafa contemporanea* (Rome, 1989).

William Harper. Artist as alchemist, exhibition catalogue, edited by T. Manhart (Orlando, FL: Orlando Museum of Art, 1989).

Ornamenta 1, exhibition catalogue (Pforzheim: Schmuckmuseum, 1989).

1990

I capolavori di Louis Comfort Tiffany (Milan: Longanesi, 1990).

G. Chazal, *L'Art de Cartier*, exhibition catalogue Rome, Accademia del Valentino, May–August 1990 (Bologna: Mise, 1990).

Deuxième Triennale du Bijou Contemporain, exhibition catalogue, Paris, Musée du Luxembourg, 18 September – 18 October 1990 (Paris, 1990).

T. Faravelli Giacobone, *'900: arti decorative e applicate del XX Secolo* (Milan: Lybra immagine, 1990).

Th. Farner, *Schmück zwischen Avant-Garde et Tradition* (Stuttgart: Forum, 1990).

G. Folchini Grassetto (ed.), *Gioielli e legature. Artisti del XX secolo* (Padua: L'Orafo Italiano Editore, 1990).

J. Houston, *Caroline Broadhead: Jewellery in Studio* (London: Bellew Publishing, 1990).

R. Joppien, *Elisabeth Treshow*, exhibition catalogue (Cologne: Museum für Angewandte Kunst, 1990).

D. Marchesseau, *The Intimate World of Alexander Calder* (New York: Harry N. Abrams, 1990).

G. Néret, *Ces Bijoux qui font Rêver* (Paris: Solar, 1990).

Arthur Smith, A Jeweler's Retrospective, exhibition catalogue (New York: Jamaica Art Center, 1990).

S. Smith Bedell, *In All His Glory: The Life of William S. Paley* (New York: Simon & Schuster, 1990).

A. K. Snowman, *The Master Jewelers* (New York: Harry N. Abrams, 1990).

1991

B. Ettagale, *Contemporary American Jewelry Design* (New York: Van Nostrand Reinhold, 1991).

F. Cailles, *Le prix de bijoux 1985–1988* (Paris: A.C.R., 1991).

O. Cavalcanti, *Ori antichi di Calabria: segni simboli funzioni* (Palermo: Sellerio, 1991).

Design Orafo & Designers: Design Gold, (Milan: ADOR–Edizioni Gold, 1991).

A. du Bois, *Elsa Freund: American Studio Jeweler* (Little Rock: The Arkansas Arts Center Decorative Arts Museum, 1991).

D. Farneti Cera, *I gioielli della fantasia, Ornamenti del XX secolo nell'arte, nel costume e nella moda* (Milan: Idea Books, 1991).

Florence Lehmann Bijoux (Bourg-lès-Valence: Société Bellon, 1991).

D. Mascetti and A. Triossi, *Gli orecchini dall'antichità a oggi* (Milan: Longanesi, 1991).

A. T. Nencioni, *Giampaolo Babetto* (uürich: Aurum, 1991).

G. Redington Dawes and C. Davidov, *Victorian Jewelry, Unexplored Treasures* (New York: Abbeville Press, 1991).

Rarefazioni, exhibition catalogue (Padua: Commune of Padua, 1991).

N. U. Russel, "Modern Jewelry Pioneer: Elsa Freund", *Ornament*, no. 15, 1991.

1992

L'Art du Bijou (Paris: Flammarion, 1992).

L'arte della Filigrana in Liguria e nel mondo, exhibition catalogue, edited by G. Roccatagliata, Genoa, 1992 (Genoa: Tormena, 1992).

F. Barletta and C. Ascione, *I gioielli del Mare* (Naples: G. Sbarra, 1992).

Ori e tesori d'Europa. Mille anni di oreficeria nel Friuli Venezia Giulia, exhibition catalogue, edited by G. Bergamini, Passariano, 1992 (Milan: Electa, 1992).

P. Cabanes, *Introduction à l'Histoire de l'Antiquité* (Paris: Armand Colin, 1992).

G. Dorflcs, G. Ccntrodi and C. Rooolgni, *Oro d'autore. "Omaggio a Piero"*, (Arezzo, 1992).

D. Farneti Cera, *L'Art du Bijou* (Paris: Flammarion, 1992).

C. Ferraro, "Cento anni di preziosi: gli Janesich di Trieste e Parigi", in *Ori e tesori d'Europa*, edited by P. Goi and G. Bergamini, conference papers (Udine: Arti Grafiche Friulane, 1992), pp. 549–62.

C. Joannis, *Les Bijoux des Régions de France* (Paris: Flammarion, 1992).

C. and S. Levitt, "Henry Steig: Jazz Man, Writer, Jeweler", *Metalsmith*, no. 12, 1992.

M. Malni Pascoletti, "I capelli nella gioielleria sentimentale dell'Ottocento", in *Ori e tesori d'Europa*, edited by P. Goi and G. Bergamini, conference papers (Udine: Arti Grafiche Friulane, 1992), pp. 543–48.

M. Malni Pascoletti, "I gioielli borghesi dell'Ottocento", in *Ori e tesori d'Europa. Mille anni di oreficeria nel Friuli Venezia Giulia*, exhibition catalogue, edited by G. Bergamini, Passariano, 1992 (Milan: Electa, 1992), pp. 350–53.

M. Nofil de Gary, *Anneauxet Bagues. Dessins* (Paris: Musèe des Arts Dècoratifs, Rèunion des Musées de France, 1992).

Orafi del Friuli Venezia Giulia, exhibition catalogue (Udine: Arti Grafiche Friulane, 1992).

M. Pietribiasi, *Robert Smith* (Zurich: Aurum, 1992).

Troisièmc Triennale du Bijou Contemporain, exhibition catalogue, Paris, Musée des arts décoratifs, 20 October – 20 December 1992 (Paris: Musée des arts décoratifs, 1992).

J. Valke, *Bijoux Belges Contemporains – Contemporary Belgian Jewellery* (Wavre, Mardaga, 1992).

1993

C. Cattaneo, E. Sabbadin and R. Virtuani *Il settore orafo: strategie di prodotto, di marketing e di area* (Milan: Giuffrè, 1993).

M. De Ceval, *Mauboussin* (Paris: Editions du Regard, 1993).

G. Folchini Grassetto, "La Scuola di Padova", *Gioielli Collezione*, Milan, 1993.

"Il significato simbolico degli ornamenti", in *A onor del falso. Umori e tendenze del bijou dagli anni '20 agli anni '80*, exhibition catalogue, edited by E. Morini (Rome: De Luca, 1993).

D. Scarisbrick, *Les Bagues: Symboles de Richesse, de Pouvoir et d'Amour* (Paris: Celiv, 1993).

Today's Jewels. From Paper to Gold, exhibition catalogue (London: Lesley Craze Gallery, 1993).

1994

R. Aguiari, *Il marketing nel settore orafo* (Rome: Edalo, 1994).

Torino 1902. Le arti decorative internazionali del nuovo secolo, exhibition catalogue, edited by R. Bossaglia, E. Godoli and M. Rosci, Turin, 1994–95 (Milan: Fabbri, 1994).

Design Orafo & Designers: Design Gold 2 (Milano: ADOR-Edizioni Gold, 1994).

W. Dyfri and O. Jack, *Greek Gold Jewellery of the Classical World* (London; British Museum Press, 1994).

L. Eleuteri Rizzoli, *Twentieth Century Jewelry* (Milan: Electa, 1994).

Gioielleria europea 1850–1920. Collezione Schmuckmuseum di Pforzheim, exhibition catalogue, edited by F. Falk and L. Mattarella, Vicenza, 1994 (Milan: Electa, 1994).

A. Galli, "Musy padre e figli", in *Torino 1902. Le arti decorative internazionali del nuovo secolo*, exhibition catalogue, Turin, 1994–95 (Milan: Fabbri, 1994).

T. Greenbaum, "Bizarre Bijoux: Surrealism in Jewelry", *Journal of Decorative and Propaganda Arts*, no. 20, 1994.

L. Lenti, *Gioielli e gioiellieri di Valenza. Arte e storia orafa 1825–1975* (Turin: Allemandi, 1994).

G. Nestler and E. Formigli, *Granulazione etrusca. Un'antica arte orafa* (Siena: Nuova Immagine, 1994).

N. Pietravalle, *Ori e Argenti di Agnone* (Rome: De Luca, 1994).

The Italian Metamorphosis, 1943–1968, exhibition catalogue, New York, Guggenheim Museum (Milan: Progetti museali editori, 1994).

J. Traina, *Extraordinary Jewels* (New York: Doubleday, 1994).

D. Watkins, *The Best of Contemporary Jewellery* (Hove: Rotovision, 1994).

1995

G. Altea, *Il progetto e l'ornamento* (Sassari: Delfino, 1995).

G. Altea, *I gioielli d'arte in Sardegna* (Sassari: Delfino, 1995).

M. T. Balboni Brizza and A. Zanni (eds.), *Gioielli. Museo Poldi Pezzoli* (Turin: Allemandi, 1995).

S. Barraja, *I marchi degli argentieri e orafi di Palermo dal XVII secolo ad oggi* (Milan: Publieditor, 1995).

E. and C. Catello, *I marchi dell'argenteria napoletana: dal XV al XIX secolo* (Sorrento: Di Mauro, 1995).

G. Celant, *Giampaolo Babetto* (Milan: Skira, 1995).

F. Cologni and E. Nussbaum, *Cartier, l'arte del Platino* (Milan: Mondadori, 1995).

E. Crispolti, *L'oro della ricerca plastica* (Milan: Mazzotta, 1995).

C. Cumo and C. Mazloum, *Gemme e gioielli. Materiali e artisti* (Rome: Gremese, 1995).

Design Orafo & Designers: Design Gold 3 (Milan: ADOR-Edizioni Gold, 1995).

H. Drutt, *Jewelry of Our Time* (New York: Rizzoli, 1995).

D. Farneti Cera, *Bijoux* (Milan: Mondadori, 1995).

E. Formigli (ed.), *Preziosi in oro, avorio, osso e corno* (Siena: Nuova Immagine, 1995).

M. Gabardi, *Gioielli anni '40 e '50* (Milan: Editoriale Giorgio Mondadori, 1995).

Gabriele de Vecchi, exhibition catalogue, L'archivolto, Milano.

A. M. Gaibisso (ed.), *L'industria orafa italiana: struttura e strategie di settore* (Milan: Franco Angeli, 1995).

A. Giusti, *Opificio delle Pietre Dure. Guida al Museo* (Venice: Marsilio, 1995).

Mario Pinton, L'oreficeria, exhibition catalogue (Padua: Opificio dell'immagine, 1995).

J. McGrath, *The Encyclopedia of Jewelry-Making Techniques* (Philadelphia, PA: Running Press Book Publishers, 1995).

Shining Through, exhibition catalogue (London: Crafts Council, 1995).

L. Somaini and C. Cerritelli (eds.), *Gioielli d'artista in Italia 1945–1995* (Milan: Electa, 1995).

H. Tait, *Seven Thousand Years of Jewellery* (London: British Museum Press, 1995).

A. Vezzosi, *Cleto Munari: gioielli, argenti, vetri, orologi* (Florence: Edifir, 1995).

1996

A. Barré-Despond, *Dictionnaire International des Arts Appliquès et du Design* (Paris: Edition du Regard, 1996).

E. Biffi Gentili, "Arte ceramica e design auratico", *Grafica e oggetti d'arte*, no. 24, 1996.

G. Bucco, "Le tecniche orafe in Italia nel XIX secolo fra tradizione e progresso tecnologico", in *Gioielli in Italia. Temi e problemi del gioiello italiano dal XIX al XX secolo*, edited by L. Lenti and D. Liscia Bemporad, conference papers, Valenza, 1996, edited by L. Lenti and D. Liscia Bemporad (Venice: Associazione Orafa Valenzana-Marsilio, 1996), pp. 25–44.

G. Centrodi, *Giò Pomodoro. Ornamenti 1954–1996* (Florence: Artificio, 1996).

G. Folchini Grassetto, "Il gioiello italiano contemporaneo tra progettualità e sperimentazione tecnica", in G. Folchini Grassetto (ed.), *Gioielli. Arte programmata e cinetica* (Padua, 1996).

Grafica e oggetti d'arte. Catalogo dell'arte moltiplicata in Italia, no. 24, 1996.

Gioielli in Italia. Temi e problemi del gioiello italiano dal XIX al XX secolo, conference papers, Valenza, 1996, edited by L. Lenti and D. Liscia Bemporad (Venice: Associazione Orafa Valenzana-Marsilio, 1996).

T. Greenbaum, *Les Messagers du Modernisme, Bijoux Artistiques aux États-Unis de 1940 à 1960* (Paris: Flammarion, 1996).

L. Lenti, "Il Liberty. Rinnovamento dello stile e dei modelli nella gioielleria italiana del primo Novecento", in *Gioielli in Italia. Temi e problemi del gioiello italiano dal XIX al XX secolo*, conference papers, Valenza, 1996, edited by L. Lenti and D. Liscia Bemporad (Venice: Associazione Orafa Valenzana-Marsilio, 1996), pp. 103–14.

Magie des Plastiques, exhibition catalogue, Paris, École Nationale Supérieure des Beaux-Arts, 20 September – 10 November 1996 (Paris: École Nationale Supérieure des Beaux-Arts, 1996).

E. Possémé, *Bijouterie. Joaillerie* (Paris: Massin, 1996).

J.-M. Schaeffer, *Les célibataires da l'art. Pour une esthétique sans mythes* (Paris: Gallimard Essais, 1996).

R. Turner, *Jewelry in Europe and America. New Times, New Thinking* (London: Thames and Hudson, 1996).

1997

1930: nuove tendenze nell'arte del gioiello, exhibition catalogue, edited by M. Gabardi (Milan, 1997).

C. Ascione (ed.), *Rosso corallo. Due secoli di coralli e cammei di Torre del Greco* (Torre del Greco: Paolo Pepe, 1997).

V. Becker, *Fabulous Costume Jewelry: History of Fantasy and Fashion in Jewels* (Atglen, PA: Schiffer Publishing, 1997).

D. Farneti Cera, *I gioielli di Miriam Haskell* (Milan: Idea Books, 1997).

L. Field, *The Queen's Jewels: The Personal Collection of Elizabeth II* (New York: Harry N. Abrams, 1997).

G. Folchini Grassetto, "Testimonianza del risveglio di interesse in Italia per l'oreficeria contemporanea", *Grafica e oggetti d'arte. Catalogo dell'arte moltiplicata in Italia*, no. 25, 1997.

S. Grassi Damiani, *I gioielli: istruzioni per l'uso* (Milan: Mondadori, 1997).

P. Venturelli, *Gioielli e gioiellieri milanesi. Storia, arte, moda (1450–1630)* (Cinisello Balsamo: Silvana Editoriale, 1997).

L. Vinca Masini and G. Centrodi (eds.), *Artisti e disegno nell'oreficeria italiana* (Arezzo, 1997).

1998

Y. Brunhammer, *The Jewels of Lalique* (Paris: Flammarion, 1998).

M. De Cerval, *Dictionnaire International du Bijou* (Paris: Editions du Regard, 1998).

M. Corgnati, *Mario Buccellati: storie di uomini e gioielli* (Milan: Leonardo Arte, 1998).

G. Folchini Grassetto (ed.), *British Gold – Italian Gold, Oro Italiano – Oro Britannico* (Edinburgh, 1998).

S. Grassi Damiani, *I gioielli* (Milan: Mondadori, *1998*).

A. M. Massinelli, *Pomellato* (Milan: Leonardo Arte, 1998).

V. Montali, *James Riviere, Gioielli verso il futuro. Jewels for the Future* (Milan: L'agrifoglio, 1998).

D. Scarisbrick, *Jewelry Design Source Book* (New York: Knickerbocker Press, 1998).

1999

Alberto Zorzi (Mantua: Corraini, 1999).

D. Alessi (ed.), *Fulco Di Verdura. Gioielli*, exhibition catalogue (Palermo: Novecento, 1999).

F. Falk, *Schmuck Der Moderne: 1960–1998, Modern Jewellery* (Stuttgart: Arnoldsche, 1999).

G. Folchini Grassetto (ed.), *Gioielli contemporanei. L'alternativa al prezioso* (Padua, 1999).

L. Lenti and D. Bemporad, *Gioielli in Italia. Tradizione e novità nel gioiello italiano dal XVI al XX secolo* (Venice: Marsilio, 1999).

J. Loring, *Louis Comfort Tiffany at Tiffany & Co.* (New York: Harry N. Abrams, 1999).

C. Mazloum, *I gioielli del XXI secolo* (Rome: Gremese, 1999).

S. Papi and A. Rhodes, *Famous Jewelry Collectors* (New York: Harry N. Abrams, 1999).

D. Pinton, *Tecnologia orafa. Processi produttivi, mezzi, strumenti* (Milan: Gold, 1999).

G. Segato, *Annamaria Zanella. Il senso della gioia* (Padua: La Matita, 1999).

V. Terraroli (ed.), *Le arti decorative in Lombardia nell'età moderna 1780–1940* (Milan: Skira, 1999).

2000

C. Ascione, *La Real Fabbrica de' coralli della Torre del Greco* (Naples: Albano, 2000).

Babetto 1996–2000. Geometrie di gioielli, exhibition catalogue (Venice: Cicero, 2000).

M. C. Bergesio and L. Lenti, *Dizionario del gioiello italiano dal XIX secolo al XX secolo* (Turin: Umberto Allemandi & co., 2000).

G. Folchini Grassetto (ed.), *Gioielleria contemporanea in Europa* (Padua, 2000).

S. Lambert, *La Bague, parcours historique et symbolique* (Paris: Editions du Collectionneur, 2000).

T. Serretta Fiorentino, *Gioielli: simbologie, miti e suggestioni* (Milan: Giorgio Mondadori, 2000).

P. Venturelli, "La collezione di arte applicata", in *Luigi Malaspina di Sannazzaro 1754–1835. Cultura e collezionismo in Lombardia tra Sette e Ottocento*, conference papers, Pavia, 1999 (Pavia: Musei Civici, 2000), pp. 567–91.

2001

F. Alfano Miglietti, "Giorgio Vigna. Materie di luce", *Virus Mutations*, September–October 2001.

L'arte del gioiello e il gioiello d'artista dal '900 ad oggi, exhibition catalogue, Florence, Museo degli Argenti, March–June 2001 (Florence: Giunti, 2001).

P. L. Bernstein, *The Power of Gold: The History of an Obsession* (New York: Wiley, 2001).

E. Crispolti, *Immaginazione aurea* (Cinisello Balsamo: Silvana Editoriale, 2001).

G. Folchini Grassetto, *Francesco Pavan. Oreficerie 1998–2001* (Padua, 2001).

O. Künzli (ed.), *Mikromegas* (Munich, 2001).

L. Lenti, "Vecchi e nuovi simboli", in *Gioielli in Italia. Sacro e profano dall'antichità ai giorni nostri*, conference papers, Valenza, 2000, edited by L. Lenti and D. Liscia Bemporad (Venice: Associazione Orafa Valenzana-Marsilio, 2001), pp. 175–82.

M. Mosco, *L'arte del gioiello e il gioiello d'artista* (Florence: Giunti, 2001).

A. Pansera, *1923–1930. Monza verso l'unità delle arti* (Cinisello Balsamo: Silvana Editoriale, 2001).

L. Silander, *A View by Two: Contemporary Jewelry* (Rhode Island School of Design, 2001).

S. Tennenbaum and J. Zapata, *Jeweled Menagerie* (New York: Thames and Hudson, 2001).

V. Terraroli, *Dizionario delle arti decorative moderne 1851–1942* (Milan: Skira, 2001).

H. Vever, *La Bijouterie française au XIXème Siècle*, 3 vols. (New York: Thames and Hudson, 2001).

2002

The Art of Cartier (Paris: Cartier & Structures, 2002).

P. Corbett, *Fulco di Verdura* (Palermo: Novecento, 2002).

L. De Sanctis, "Il gioiello virtuale di Giorgio Vigna", *Valenza Gioielli*, February 2002.

Ettore Sottsass più Cleto Munari: la seduzione, exhibition catalogue, Verona, 2002 (Trento: Arca, Lavis, 2002).

S. Everitt and D. Lancaster, *Christie's Twentieth Century Jewelry* (New York: Watson-Guptile Publication, 2002).

S. Fraser and T. Hida, *Contemporary, Japanese Jewelry* (London: Merrell Publishers, 2002).

M. Gabardi, "Lei per lei: gioielli creati dalle donne nella prima metà del xx secolo", in *Gioielli in Italia. Donne e ori: storia, arte e passione*, conference papers, Valenza, 2002, edited by L. Lenti (Venice: Associazione Orafa Valenzana-Marsilio, 2002), pp. 93–100.

A. Gandolfi, *Amuleti. Ornamenti magici d'Abruzzo* (Pescara: Edizioni "Trace", 2002).

Masterpieces/Capolavori. L'artista artigiano tra Picasso e Sottsass, exhibition catalogue, edited by E. Biffi Gentili and A. Leclerque, Turin, 2002–03 (Turin: Fondazione per il Libro, la Musica, la Cultura, 2002).

Il modo orafo tra tradizione e innovazione (Milan: Etas, 2002).

M. G. di Savoia and S. Papi, *I gioielli di Casa Savoia* (Milan: Electa, 2002).

S. Rauet, *Art Deco Jewelry* (New York: Thames and Hudson, 2002).

E. Silvestrini, O. Ori and R. Pagnozzato, *Donne Madonne Dee. Abito sacro e riti di vestizione, gioiello votivo, "vestitrici". Un itinerario antropologico in area lagunare veneta* (Padua: Il Poligrafo, 2002).

P. Venturelli, *Alfredo Ravasco* (Milan: Skira, 2002).

2003

D. Bennet and D. Mascerti, *Understanding Jewellery* (Massachusetts: England Antique Collectors' Club, 2003).

M. C. Bergesio, *Maria Rosa Franzin. Gioiello, pensiero indossabile* (Padua: Limena, 2003).

M. C. Bergesio and L. Davanzo, *Sul filo del gioiello* (Padua: Limena, 2003).

G. Garofoli (ed.), *Il distretto orafo di Valenza. Tendenze evolutive e prospettive future* (Milano: Franco Angeli, 2003).

F. M. Messina, *Fabergé* (Rome: Artemide, 2003).

C. Philips, *Gioielli, Breve storia dall'antichità a oggi* (Milan: Rizzoli–Skira, 2003).

A. Poli, "Il gioiello come scrittura preziosa per la pagina corpo", in *Gioielli in Italia. Donne e ori: storia, arte e passione*, conference papers, Valenza, 2002, edited by L. Lenti (Venice: Associazione Orafa Valenzana-Marsilio, 2003), pp. 101–07.

F. Sborgi and A. K. Snowman, *Capolavori dei grandi gioiellieri* (Milan: Rizzoli, 2003).

2004

Il Déco in Italia, exhibition catalogue, edited by F. Benzi, Rome, 2004 (Milan: Mondadori Electa, 2004).

F. R. Morelli, *Ori d'artista: il gioiello nell'arte italiana, 1900–2004* (Cinisello Balsamo: Silvana Editoriale, 2004).

M. Mosco and O. Casazza, *Il Museo degli Argenti. Collezioni e collezionisti* (Florence: Giunti, 2004).

P. Venturelli, "Orafi e oreficerie in Italia durante il Ventennio", in *Il Déco in Italia*, exhibition catalogue, edited by F. Benzi, Rome, 2004 (Milan: Mondadori-Electa, 2004).

2005

J. Astfalck, C. Broadhead and P. Derrez, *New Directions in Jewellery* (London: Black Dog Publishing, 2005).

A. Cappellieri and M. Romanelli, *Il design della gioia, Il gioiello tra progetto e ornamento* (Milan: Charta, 2005).

G. Folchini Grassetto, *Contemporary Jewellery: The Padua School – Gioielleria Contemporanea* (Stuttgart: Arnoldsche, 2005).

2006

Contemporary Jewellery from Italy, exhibition catalogue, edited by the Associazione Gioiello Contemporaneo (travelling).

L. Carcano, A. Catalani and P. Varacca Capello, *Il gioiello italiano ad una svolta. Dalla crisi alla costruzione di nuove opportunità* (Milan: Franco Angeli, 2006).

V. Finlay, *Jewels: A Secret History* (New York: Ballantine Books, 2006).

A. Fisch, *Crocheted Wire Jewelry – Innovative Designs & Projects by Leading Artists* (New York: Lark Books, 2006).

L. Mouillefarine and V. Ristelhueber, *Raymond Templier: le bijou modern* (Paris: Norma Editions, 2006).

D. A. Taylor, *Geog Jensen Jewelry* (New Haven–London: Yale University Press, 2006).

2007

A. Sackville, *New Directions in Jewellery II* (London: Black Dog Publishing, 2007).

I. Van Zijl and J. Yvýnne, *Gijs Bakker and Jewelry* (Stuttgart: Arnoldsche, 2007).

2008

Gioiello italiano contemporaneo. Tecniche e materiali tra arte e design, exhibition catalogue, edited by A. Cappellieri, Vicenza and Milan, 2008 (Milan: Skira, 2008).

Index of Artists, Designers and Manufactures

A

Accardi Carla 48
Ackerly Peggy *178*
Acouc 23
Adams Jane 55
Agam 49
Albert Gilbert 47
Albini Franco 52, *201*
Albini Walter 45
Alemany & Ertman 43
Alviani Getulio 48, *175, 177*
Andrieux Hélène *121*
Angeli Franco 48
Ansaldi Alessia 57
Anteloh 26
Antonini 57
AOL Associazione Orafa Lombarda 27
Aragon Louis 36
Arman 37, *173*
Armani Giorgio 50, 57
Arp Jean 37
Ascione Giovanni 17, 57
Ashbee Charles Robert 15, 26, *86*
Asprey 55
Assetto Francesco 43

B

Babetto Giampaolo 49, 50, *191*
Baj Enrico 43
Bakeland Leo 31
Bakker Gijs 46, 47, 53, 55, *182–183, 189*
Bakker Ralph 55
Baretti Lina 40
Barney Arthur 32
Basaldella Afro 48
Basaldella Dino 48
Basaldella Mirko 48, *175*
Bauhaus 10, 20, 21, 30
Becker Friedrich 48, 56, *184*
Beckerm Michael 56
Belkina Tatjana 54
Bellini Mario 45, *205*
Belperron Suzanne *122*
Bengel Jacob *136*
Bennet Jamie 54
Bérard Christian 36
Bergolli Aldo 43
Bernabei Roberta 57
Bertoia Harry 36, *168*
Biasi Alberto 49
Bicego Marco 57
Biegel Marc-Jens 56

Bing Marcel 12, *76*
Bing Samuel 10, 12, 15
Bjorg Toril 48
Black Starr & Frost 27, 33
Boekhoudt Onno 56, *189*
Boivin Germaine 41
Boivin Jeanne 54
Boivin René 41, 42, *120*
Bonati Patrizia 57
Bonaz Auguste 31
Bonoli Massimiliano 57
Borelli and Vitelli 27
Borghesi Marco 57
Borshchevsky Mikhail 54
Bott Rudolf 56
Boucher 32
Boucheron 14, 18, 22, 23, 24, 25, 35, 52, *74, 96, 98, 144*
Boucheron Frédéric 14
Bouzarjomehri Sorab 54
Braeuer Juergen 56
Brandt Paul 23, 25
Braque Georges *169*
Breil 57, *228*
Bridgman Percy 39
Bronger Sigurd 56
Brozzi Aldo 27
Bruni Pasquale 57
Brynner Irena 43
Buccellati Mario 18, 35, 36, 42, 52, 57, *126–127*
Bucci Douglas 54
Bucherer 35
Budanov Sergej 42
Bulgari 35, 36, 40, 42, 43, 51, 57, *128–129, 156–159, 227*
Bury Claus 56, *184*
Bury Pol 46, *171*
Bykov Gennady 54
Bykova Natalya 54

C

Cacchione Ciro 52
Calder Alexander 36, 43, 46, 48, *166–167*
Calderara Maria 57
Calderoni 18, 27
Caldwell J.E.&Co. *131*
Cammarata Fabio 57, *217*
Campana Fernando and Humberto 57
Cannilla Franco 48
Capdevila Manuel 57
Capogrossi Giuseppe 48, *177*

Cardin Pierre 38, 44, 45
Carità Gianni 57
Cartier 18, 21, 22, 23, 24, 25, 27, 31, 32, 35, 37, 39, 41, 42, 46, 51, 54, *93–97, 99–107, 145, 153*
Cartier Jacques 25
Cartier Louis 23
Castañon Jorge 57
Cavalli Roberto 57
Cecchetto Giorgio 58
Ceraioli Giorgio 18
Ceroli Mario 48
César *173*
Chadel Jules 24
Chanel 20, 21, 22, 31, 32, 36, 38, 41, 54, *150, 162–163*
Chanel Coco 20, 30
Chang Peter 55, *188*
Chantecler 57
Chareau Pierre 26
Charlton Yard & Black 27
Chaumet 23, 52
Chavent Françoise and Claude 54
Chiappe 27
Chimento 57
Chistyakova Taisia 42
Chloè *219*
Chopard 52, 56
Church Sharon 54
Claflin Donald *156*
Clément Jean 37
Cocteau Jean 36, 41
Codevilla Mario 36
Cohen Julius 33, 40, 42
Coin Roberto 57, *229*
Colonna Edward 12, *77*
Consagra Pietro 48
Cooper John Paul 15, 16, *87*
Cooperman Marilyn 54
Coosemans Henry 28
Coppola Bruno 40
Coppola Lynda 40
Coro 32
Corvaja Giovanni 57, *214*
Counard Cappy 54
Cournault Étienne 34
Crivelli 57
Croninger Cara 48
Cross Susan 55
Cusi 18, 27, 36, 42
Cuyàs Puig Ramon 57
Czeschka Carl Otto 17

D

D'Avanzo Lucia 58
Dalí Salvador 36, 43, *169*
Dalisi Riccardo 53, 58, *211*
Damiani 52, 57
Danese 49
Dangelo Sergio 43
de Bernardi Italo 28
De Cal Francesco 43
de Castellane Victoire 54, *222*
De Decker Hilde 55
de Givenchy James 54
de Grisogono 57
de Large Edward 55
De Lucchi Michele 53, *204*
de Maria Milli 57
De Patta Margaret 36, 43, *178*
de Poli Paolo 43
de Rivera José 36
De Rosa 32
de Saint Phalle Niki 37
De Vecchi Gabriele 49, 58, *175, 213*
Debut Jules 14
del Bono Isabella 57
Delaunay Sonia *172*
Després Jean 33, 34, 36, *116–117*
Desrosiers Charles 14
Devlin Stuart 47
di Giacinto Sandra 57
Dinesen Agnete 56
Dior 53, 54, *163, 222*
Dior Christian 38
Ditzel Nanna 48, *181*
Dobler George 56
Dodo *228*
Donald John 47
Donna Karan 48
Doucet 23
Dova Gianni 43
Droog Design 55
Dubois Paul 14
Dufrêne Maurice 10, 13
Dunand Jean 22
Dunay Henry 54
Dunlop Sybil 26, *123*
Dupré Elisabetta 57
Dusausoy 23

E

Eichenberg Iris 55, 56
Eisenberg 32
Eisenman Peter 52, *204*
Enterline Sandra 54

Ernst Max 37, 43, *171*
ESG Jewels 56
Eshel-Gershuni Bianca 53, 54
Exner Helga & Bent 56

F

Fabergé Peter Carl 15, 18, 54, *89*
Fahrner Theodor 17, *80, 82–83, 123*
Falize 14
Falk Heinrich 17
Faraone 36, 42
Farnham Paulding 14, 27
Fasano 42
Fath Jacques 38
Fecarotta 27
Ferragamo Salvatore 57
Ferraz Dulce 57
Ferrè Gianfranco *220*
Fertey Louis 25
Feuillatre Maison 13
Fiessler Louis 17
Filipe Cristina 57
Fisch Arline 54
Flato Paul 31, 32, 33, 35, *147–149*
Flöckinger Gerda 47
Follot Paul 10, 13
Font Ana 57
Fontana Lucio 37, 43, *175*
Ford Steven & David Forlano 54
Fortuny y Madrazo Mariano 10, 12
Fouquet Alphonse 14
Fouquet Georges 10, 11, 14, 23, 25, 26, 33, *60–64, 98, 112, 115*
Fouquet Jean 33, *112–115*
Franchi Fausto Maria 58
Franzin Maria Rosa 58, *192*
Frascarolo Rino 43
Freda David 54
Frères Piel 26
Freund Elsa *178*
Fumanti *177*

G

Gafter Ella 54
Gaillard Lucien 13, 14, *68*
Gallé Émile 10, 12
Gandini Manuela 57
Garavelli 57
Garrard 18, 35, 52, 55
Gehry Frank O. *228*
GEM Montebello 47, 48
Gennazzi Colombo 28
Giacometti Alberto 37
Gillio Giuseppe 18
Goncharov Vladimir 54
Good Michael 54
Gossner Ingrid 56
Grasset Eugène 13
Griegst Arje 40
Grima Andrew 47, *199*
Gripoix Maison 31, 40, *162–163*
Gubelin 35
Gucci 53, 57, *222*
Guerrini Lorenzo 43
Guillaume Emmanuel & Sophie 56
Guillet Léon 31
Guttuso Renato 48

H

Hadgkiss 26
Hafner Stefan 57

Harper William 54
Hart Margit 56
Haskell Miriam 32, *160–161*
Hattie Carnegie 32
Heikkilä Juhani 56
Helg Franca 52, *201*
Hemmerle Stefan 56
Henkel & Grosse 31, *122*
Henry Hélène 26
Herbst René 26
Hermes 20
Hermsen Herman 56
Heron Susan 55
Hess Frank *160–161*
Heyman Oscar 33
Hipolito Leonor 57
Hiramatsu Yasuki 48
Hirtz Lucien 14, 25, *74, 98*
Ho Ron 54
Hobé and Boucher 32
Hocq Robert 46
Hoffmann Josef 16, 17, 26, *77–78*
Hollern Matthew 54
Horta Victor 10, 14
Hoving Walter 41
Hughes Graham 47
Hultberg AnnChristine 56
Hunt George Edward 26
Husted-Andersen Adda 36
Hvorslev Theresia 56

I

Illario 36
Iribe 31
Isozaki Arata 52
Itoh Kazuhiro 48

J

Jacoangeli Gaetano 18
Jacqueau Charles 24
Jamieson Nual 55
Janesich 21, 22, 27, 36, *124*
JAR Joel Arthur Rosenthal 54, *225*
Jean Nathalie 58
Jensen Georg 15, 26, 27, 37, 40, 48, 56, *137, 181*
Jocz Daniel 54
Joseff Eugene 32
Jünger Hermann 56

K

Kaminski Vered 53
Katz Martin 54
Kenneth Jay Lane 39
Kerman Daniella 54
Kerr William 15
Khramtsov Vladislav 42, 54
King Jessie Marion 16, *84*
Kleemann Georg 17
Klein Calvin 51, 53
Knobel Esther 53
Knox Archibald 15, *85*
Koch Robert 17
Kolar Ute 58
Kramer Sam *178*
Kranitzky Robin 54
Künzli Otto 56, *185*
Kuznetsov Felix 54
Kuznetsova Olga 54

L

Lacaze Renè *151*
Lacloche 23, 35, *121*
Lagerfeld Karl *219*
Lalique René 10, 11, 12, 13, 15, 16, 22, 23, *63, 69–75*
Lambert Théodore 10
Lane Neil 54
Langenbacher & Wankmiller 52
Lanvin 46, *165*
Larsen Helge 56
Laudani Marta *206*
Laurewick 26
Lechtzin Stanley 54
Levin Ed *178*
Lewers Darani 56
Lewis Keith 54
Leysen 26
Liberty & Co. 15,17, *84–85*
Liberty Arthur Lasenby 15
Lichtenstein Roy 37, 48
Linssen Nel 55
Linzeler& Marchak 23
Lipchitz Jacques 36
Lisca Polenghi Alba 58, *213*
Lobel Paul 36
Loew Susanna 56
Lossier 15
Lucchetta Stefania 57
Lurçat Jean 47, *169*

M

Macchiarini Peter 43, *179*
MacDonald Frances 16
MacDonald Margaret 16
Mackintosh Charles Rennie 16
MacNair James Herbert 16, *86*
MacNeil Linda 54
MAG_San Francisco Metal Arts Guild 43
Maierhofer Fritz 56, 57
Majorelle Louis 10
Mallet Stevens Robert 26
Man Ray 37, 43, 48
Mangiarotti Angelo *206*
Marcangelo Rita 57
Marchetti Stefano 58, *193*
Marchionni Margherita 57
Marcus & Co 15, 27, 33, 42, *146*
Marì Enzo 44, 49, 58
Marinot Maurice 21
Marotta Gino 48, *177*
Martin Catherine 55
Martinazzi Bruno 43, 44, *190*
Marx Falko 56
Masenza Mario 36, 48
Masenza-Fumanti 48
Masriera y Carreras Luis 15, 26
Matos Margarida 57
Matranga 27
Mattia Cielo 57
Mattioli 57, *229*
Mauboussin 23, 24, 33, 34, 35, *109, 142, 154*
Mauboussin Georges 24
Mawdsley Richard 54
Mayodon Jean-Claude 35
Mazer 32
Melchiorre & C. 18, 27, *88*
Melillo Giacinto 17
Melotti Fausto 48, *174*

Mendini Alessandro 52
Mercade Jaime 26
Metcalf Bruce 54
Mikimoto 22, 26, 57
Miluna 57
Minola Ada 43
Miranda Vincenzo 17
Missaglia 36
Mitchell Clarissa 55
Moderne Maison
Moennich Mathias 56
Mohl-Hansen Christian 26
Monet 32
Montague Fordham 15, 16
Montebello Giancarlo 48, 58, *214, 215*
Monzini Rossana 43
Morabito 17
Morellato 57
Morris Robert Lee 48
Morris Roger 55, *189*
Morris William 11, 12, 15, 16
Moser Koloman 16, 17, 26
Mucchi Genni 43
Mucha Alphonse 10, 11, 14, 15, *61, 63*
Muerrle Norbert 56
Munari Bruno 49, 52, *205, 207*
Munari Cleto 52, *202–204*
Murphy Henry George 26, *123*
Musy 18, 27, 36

N

Nanis 57
Neiman Marcus 40
Newson Marc *206*
Nielsen Evald 26
Nielsen Harald 26
Niessing 56
Nomination 57
Nossiter Dorrie 26, *137*
Noten Ted 55

O

Öfner Hans 26
Ohlsson Ohl 56
Olbrich Joseph Maria 12
Omega 47
Oppenheim Meret *202*

P

Paas-Alexandrova Jutta 54
Paganin Barbara 58, *214*
Pagano Sharra 57, *221*
Palden Willy 56
Pasquale Renzo 58
Patek Philippe 47
Patou Jean 25
Pavan Francesco 49, 50, *190*
Peche Dagobert 17
Pellini Donatella 57, *222*
Pennino 32
Percheron Marcel 34
Peretti Elsa 47, *195–197, 199*
Perrin Alain Dominique 46
Pesce Gaetano *210*
Peters Ruudt 55, *185*
Petochi 42
Peverelli Cesare 43
Philippe Alfred 32
Piaget 54
Picasso Pablo 37, 43

Picasso Paloma *224–225*
Pimentel Serpa Alexandra 57
Pinton Mario 43, 44, 49, *190*
Poiret Paul 10, 12, 20, 23, 31
Pomellato 57, *227*
Pomodoro Arnaldo 43, *176–177*
Pomodoro Giò 43, *177*
Pomodoro Teresa 48
Ponte Vecchio 57
Popov Dmitri 54
Portoghesi Paolo 50, 52, 53, *204*
Pousette-Dart Richard 36
Povolotskaya Vera 42
Prada 53
Prouvé Victor 13
Prutscher Otto 26
Puiforcat Jean 26

R
Rabanne Paco 44, 45, *164*
Ramshaw Wendy 47, 55
Rateau Jean-Jacques 21
Ravasco Alfredo 27, 28, 35, 36, *125*
Ravasco Giacomo 27
Reiling Reinhold 48
Reister Karl-Heinz 58, *212*
Renk Merry 43
Restelli Mario 28
Rezende Susana 57
Riccoboni Carla 57, *212*
Richemont Group 54
Rickert Franz 56
Rivière James 57, *210*
Robbert Eric 56
Rodríguez Antonio 57
Roethig Marion 56
Rohde Johan 26
Romanelli Marco *206*
Rosato 57
Roth Dieter 52
Rothmann Gerd 23, 56
Rothmüller Karl 17
Rowe Michael 55
Ruhlmann Jacques-Émile 21, 23
Ruser William 33
Ryan Jacqueline 57, *216*

S
Saint Laurent Yves 39, 45
Salminen Mirjam 56
San Lorenzo 52, 57, *200, 208–209*
Sandheim Amy 26
Sandoz Gérard 23, 25, 33
Sandström Margaret 56
Saronni Edoardo 28
Scanavino Emilio 43
Scarpa Afra 52
Scarpa Tobia 52
Scavia 57
Scemama Roger 39
Schaap & Citroën 26
Schaper Hugo 17
Scheidt Georg Anton *76*
Schiaparelli Elsa 30, 31, 32, 36, 39, 41
Schick Marjorie 54
Schippel Dorothea 56
Schlumberger Jean 32, 36, 41, *135, 154–155, 194*
Schmedes Anna 16
Schmuttermeier Elisabeth 17

Schullin 57
Seaman Schepps 32, 52, *149*
Selivanov Andrei 54
Serafini Enrico 43
Settepassi 36,42
Shedov Ivan 54
Sheltman 26
Sherman Sondra 54
Shirk Hellen 54
Short Jane 55
Sigillo 58
Silva Catarina 57
Silva Diana 57
Skubic Peter 46, *189*
Slutzky Naum 21
Smit Robert 47, *187*
Smith Art *180*
Snischek Max 16
Sonnabend Joan 48
Sordelli Alessandro 36
Sorresiig Poul 56
Soto Jesús Raphael 49
Sottsass Ettore 43, 44, 45, 52, 53, *203–204*
Sousa Manuela 57
Speckner Bettina 56
Spensen Frances 43
Stagni Maurizio 57, *217*
Starr & Frost 27
Steig Henry *181*
Sterlé Pierre 41, 42
Stern 52, 57
Stern-Schocken Deganit 53
Svensson Tore 56
Swarovski 31, 39, 45

T
Tanguy Yves *167*
Templier Raymond 23, 26, 33, 34, 36, *112, 118–119*
Tesarik Eva 56
Téterger Maison 13
Thesmar André Fernand 11
Thomas David 47
Tiffany Louis Comfort 12,27
Tiffany & Co. 14, 18, 23, 27, 32, 33, 35, 41, 42, 47, 52, 54, *90–92, 131, 132–135, 155–156, 194–197, 201, 224–225, 228*
Tigerman Stanley 52
Tolvanen Terhi 56
Tone Maria 42, 43
Tornquist Rossella 57, *218*
Torun Bülow-Hübe Viviana 40, *181*
Toussaint Jeanne 22, 24, 25, 37, 39
Trabert & Hoffer 32, 35
Tramontano Francesco 57
Traquair Phoebe Anna 16
Trifari 32, 39, 45

U
UAM Union d'Artistes Moderne 31, 34
Udall & Ballou 22, 27, 33
Uderzo Barbara 57
Uncini Giuseppe 48
Ungaro Emanuel 45
Unger Brothers 15
Uno A Erre 57

V
Van Cleef & Arpels 18, 21, 23, 24, 31, 32, 35, 39, 40, 41, 42, 52, 54, *98, 110–111, 138–141, 143, 151–152*
Van Cleef Alfred 24
Van de Velde Henry 10, 14, 17, *82*
van Leersum Emmy 46, 47, *183*
van Strydonck Leopold 14
Vautrin Line *170*
Verdegaal Truike 55
Verdura Fulco Santostefano di 31, 40, 41, 42, *150*
Versace 57
Vever Paul and Henry 11, 13, 23, 24, 25, *65–67*
Vhernier 57, *226*
Vigeland Tone 48, 49, 56, *188*
Vigna Giorgio 57, *214*
Vignelli Lella 52, *208–209*
Vignelli Massimo 52, *208–209*
Villa 18, 36, 57, *130*
Vionnet Madeleine 31
Vischer Robert 10
Visconti 57
Visintin Graziano 58, *192*
Vita Alberta 58
Viterbo Dario 27

W
Walling Christopher 54
Wallström Mona 56
Ward Ester 55
Warndorfer Fritz 16
Watkin David 47, 55, *186*
Webb David 42, *198*
Weckström Björn 56
Weingaertner Petra 56
Werner Louis 17
Westwood Vivienne 55, *223*
Wiener Werkstätte 16, 21, 26, *77–78*
Wilson Henry 15, 26, *86*
Winckler Susanne Arusha 56
Winston Bob 43
Winston Harry 33, 41, 52, 54, *108*
Wolfers Philippe 14, 26, 35, *79–81*
Worth Jean-Philippe 10
Wright 26

Y
Yard Raymond 42, 54
Yurman David 54

Z
Zanella Annamaria 58, *193*
Zenkova Zinaida 42
Zerrenner 17
Zilker Zandra 54
Zorzi Alberto 58, *192*
Zwollo 26

Photographic Credits

© Arnaldo Pomodoro, Milano: pp. 176, 177 (bottom centre)
© Asenbaum Photo Archive: pp. 77 (bottom right), 78
Archivio De Vecchi, Milano: p. 213 (right)
Gijs Bakker Archive, Amsterdam: pp. 182, 183 (bottom right), 189 (top right)
Reister Archive: p. 212 (right)
Bulgari Vintage Collection: pp. 128, 129,156 (bottom), 157, 158, 159
© Calouste Gulbenkian Foundation. Photo Carlos Azevedo: pp. 63 (right), 69 (right), 70, 72, 73, 75.
© Collection Centre Pompidou, Dist. RMN / Georges Meguerditchian, distr. Alinari, Firenze: p. 166
© Boucheron Collection: pp. 74 (right), 98 (left), 144
© Cartier Collection: pp. 93, 94, 95, 96 (bottom left), 97, 99, 100, 101, 102, 103, 104, 105, 106, 107, 145, 152, 153
Cheltenham Art Gallery and Museum, Cheltenham, Gloucestershire: p. 85 (bottom right)
Civiche Raccolte d'Arte Applicata del Castello Sforzesco, Milano: p. 125 (bottom left)
Collezione Damiani: p. 227 (top right)
Dior Collection: p. 222 (top left)
Collezione Gucci: p. 222 (top right)
Henkel & Grosse Collection, Pforzheim: p. 122 (right)
Maison Goossens Collection, Paris: p. 163
Collezione Mario Buccellati: pp. 126, 127
Collezione Orodautore, Arezzo: pp. 190 (bottom), 192 (top left), 223
Collezione Pomellato: p. 227 (bottom and centre)
Tiffany Collection: pp. 131 (bottom), 132 (top), 133 (left), 134, 135, 155, 156 (top), 194, 195, 196-197, 199, 224, 225 (top right), 228 (bottom left)
Verdura Collection, New York: pp. 150 (top right and bottom)
Vhernier Collection: p. 226

Fondation The Link of Times: p. 89
Fondazione Ferré, Milano: p. 220
Mucha Trust Foundation, London: pp. 61 (left)
Photo courtesy Sotheby's, Geneva: p. 109 (top left)
Photo Dea Gasparac: p. 214 (bottom right)
Photo Tom Haartsen: p. 189 (top left)
Fundació Gala-Salvador Dalí: p. 169 (top)
Image copyright The Metropolitan Museum of Art/Art Resource/Scala, Firenze: p. 71
Les Arts décoratifs, Paris. Photo Georges Fessy, All right reserved. © ADAGP, Paris 2010: pp. 65, 66, 67
Les Arts décoratifs, Paris. Photo Jean Tholance, All right reserved. © ADAGP, Paris 2010: pp. 68 (left), 98 (centre left and bottom right), 115 (top left), 116 (bottom), 154 (centre and bottom right), 169 (bottom), 170
Les Arts décoratifs, Paris. Photo Laurent Sully Jaulmes, All right reserved. © ADAGP, Paris 2010: pp. 68 (right), 76 (right), 98 (top left), 98 (bottom right),115 (centre and bottom right)
© Bruno Munari by appointement Maurizio Corraini srl.: pp. 205 (left), 207
Museo del Risorgimento, collezione De Marchi, Milano: p. 125 (bottom left)
National Design Museum, Smithsonian Institution: p. 77 (top left)
Petit Palais, Musée des Beaux-Arts de la Ville de Paris: pp. 62, 64
© Giò Pomodoro, Milano: p. 177 (top and bottom right)
© Primavera Gallery, New York: pp. 113 (bottom and top right), 116 (top right), 117, 118, 119 (bottom left), 123 (top left), 142 (top right), 150, 162
© Roger Viollet: 119 (top)
Royal Museum of Scotland Collection: p. 86 (top right)
© Ettore Sottsass jr.: pp. 203, 204 (top left)
Stedelijk Museum, Françoise van den Bosch Collection, Amsterdam. p. 183 (top right)

Tadema Gallery, London: pp. 77 (right), 82 (top left), 86 (left), 87, 123 (right), 137 (top centre)
20TH CENTURY FOX / THE KOBAL COLLECTION: p. 38
The Montreal Museum of Fine Arts/Giles Rivest: pp. 167 (centre), 168 (right), 178 (top and bottom left), 180, 181 (top left and bottom right)
The Montreal Museum of Fine Arts/Richard P. Goodboy: pp. 178 (bottom right), 179
The Montreal Museum of Fine Arts/Christine Guest: pp. 167 (right), 168 (left)
The Museum of Fine Arts, Houston: p. 189 (bottom left)
Toledo Museum of Art, Toledo: p. 115 (top right)
Van Cleef & Arpels' private collection: cover, pp. 98 (top right), 110, 111 (top left), 138 (bottom), 139, 140, 141, 143, 151 (top), 151 (right)
Walters Art Gallery, Baltimore: p. 90 (bottom right)